SAP PRESS Books: Always on hand

Print or e-book, Kindle or iPad, workplace or airplane: Choose where and how to read your SAP PRESS books! You can now get all our titles as e-books, too:

- By download and online access
- For all popular devices
- And, of course, DRM-free

Convinced? Then go to **www.sap-press.com** and get your e-book today.

Accelerated Financial Closing with SAP®

SAP PRESS

SAP PRESS is a joint initiative of SAP and Galileo Press. The know-how offered by SAP specialists combined with the expertise of the Galileo Press publishing house offers the reader expert books in the field. SAP PRESS features first-hand information and expert advice, and provides useful skills for professional decision-making.

SAP PRESS offers a variety of books on technical and business-related topics for the SAP user. For further information, please visit our website: *www.sap-press.com*.

Peter Jones
Implementing SAP Business Planning and Consolidation
2013, 650 pp., hardcover
ISBN 978-59229-422-0

Paul Ovigele
100 Things You Should Know About Financial Accounting with SAP
2011, 343 pp., hardcover
ISBN 978-59229-364-3

Narayanan Veeriah
Configuring Financial Accounting in SAP
2012, 792 pp., hardcover
ISBN 978-1-59229-377-3

Aylin Korkmaz
Financial Reporting with SAP (2nd Edition)
2012, 745 pp., hardcover
ISBN 978-59229-391-9

James Fisher, Elizabeth Milne, and Birgit Starmanns

Accelerated Financial Closing with SAP®

Galileo Press

Bonn • Boston

Galileo Press is named after the Italian physicist, mathematician, and philosopher Galileo Galilei (1564—1642). He is known as one of the founders of modern science and an advocate of our contemporary, heliocentric worldview. His words *Eppur si muove* (And yet it moves) have become legendary. The Galileo Press logo depicts Jupiter orbited by the four Galilean moons, which were discovered by Galileo in 1610.

Editor Katy Spencer
Copyeditor Julie McNamee
Cover Design Graham Geary
Photo Credit iStockphoto.com/14992091/© stevedangers
Layout Design Vera Brauner
Production Graham Geary
Typesetting SatzPro, Krefeld (Germany)
Printed and bound in the United States of America, on paper from sustainable sources

ISBN 978-1-59229-446-6

1st edition 2014

Library of Congress Cataloging-in-Publication Data
Starmanns, Birgit.
Accelerated financial closing with SAP / Birgit Starmanns [and three others]. -- 1st edition.
pages cm
Includes bibliographical references.
ISBN-13: 978-1-59229-446-6
ISBN-10: 1-59229-446-4
1. SAP ERP. 2. Closing (Accounting)--Data processing. 3. Accounting--Computer programs.
4. Financial statements--Computer programs.
I. Title.
HF5681.C45.S73 2013
657--dc23
2012044608

Contents at a Glance

Dear Reader,

It seems like everything in today's modern world is accelerating. In some instances, this acceleration can be an out-of-control maneuver that leaves you reeling, but with the proper guidance and the right person behind the wheel, accelerating your business processes can be exhilarating, record-breaking, and the path to innovation.

I knew a few months into our manuscript development that we had found just the right author team to take the wheel. James Fisher, Elizabeth Milne, and Birgit Starmanns offer a unique blend of true experience and objectivity; they have a sense of what information people really need to know and the voice to effectively share it.

Accelerated Financial Closing with SAP spans SAP's portfolio of finance and analytics solutions, including applications from enterprise performance management, business intelligence, and governance, risk, and compliance portfolios. To initially conceive of such a topic in a way that the final product is both functional and accessible is a challenge. I think you will agree that the authors have delivered on such an ambitious title and approach.

Of course, we at SAP PRESS are always interested in your opinion. What do you think about *Accelerated Financial Closing with SAP*? How could it be improved? Since your comments and suggestions are the most useful tools to help us make our books the best they can be, we encourage you to visit our website at *www.sap-press.com* and share your feedback.

Thank you for purchasing a book from SAP PRESS!

Katy Spencer
Editor, SAP PRESS

Galileo Press
Boston, MA

katy.spencer@galileo-press.com
www.sap-press.com

Contents

Foreword

If you are reading this foreword it probably means you are already involved in the world of corporate reporting and financial accounting in some way. Perhaps, like us, you are employed in a corporate finance function or providing advice and implementation services in a consulting organization; perhaps you belong to the audit profession or are employed in an IT role delivering solutions for accounting, consolidation, and disclosure; or possibly you are still studying before entering the profession. It is a role in which some things, such as the responsibility to ensure timely and accurate reporting that fully complies with external regulations, will always be constant. But even during the time we have been in our roles, we have seen significant changes such as the introduction of Extensible Business Reporting Language (XBRL); the steady, but by no means certain, worldwide move toward International Financial Reporting Standards (IFRS); the increasing complexity of business transactions and the respective reporting rules; and the increasing demand from investors and other stakeholders for greater transparency and more information about the future, such as that proposed by the International Integrated Reporting Council (IIRC).

Although many of these changes that are designed to improve reporting by providing greater insight on corporate performance have yet to be mandated, the management board of SAP recognized some time ago that as one of Germany's largest listed companies and the world's leading provider of business software, we should adopt best practices in corporate reporting at the earliest opportunity. This led us to adopt XBRL reporting although we are currently not faced with a respective legal requirement. Only recently, we were one of the first companies to not only add but integrate nonfinancial information in our 2012 annual report in order to help readers better assess the quality and sustainability of our financial results. Being part of such innovative reporting is demanding but also particularly rewarding. However, freeing up time within our corporate accounting team to work on value-adding activities—such as integrated reporting, better visualization, and improving the quality of our narrative—means that, like most other areas of finance, we constantly need to improve our efficiency and productivity.

Last year, we made significant headway when we shortened our quarterly reporting by one full week, thus setting a benchmark compared to other German companies. Such step-changes in accelerating the speed of closing without sacrificing accuracy or reliability are all down to the software solutions that have helped us automate much of the manual effort involved in preparing reports so our team can now focus more on value-adding activities. We are in the fortunate position of being able to work with colleagues in the various solution development teams responsible for delivering the SAP Enterprise Performance Management suite, many of whom have contributed directly or indirectly to this book. This has given us privileged opportunities to meet with the corporate accounting staff of other leading companies to help define functionality, to test early versions of the software, and to share our successes on reference calls with prospective customers and by presenting at conferences.

Like others, we are constantly alert as to how innovative functionality delivered in the most recent versions of the software and the new generation of technologies will help us meet with anticipated changes in regulatory reporting and improve efficiency and effectiveness in the future. Already, the availability of intuitive and easy-to-use analytics has allowed us to provide stakeholders with customizable, slice-and-dice, reporting online, and it will not be long before using mobile devices for alerting and approvals will shorten a number of key processes in reporting and disclosure. But perhaps the most significant technology that looks set to benefit corporate reporting is in-memory computing that will slash the time taken to produce or update a financial consolidation from minutes and hours down to nano-seconds. There is great excitement within our corporate reporting team as they look forward to our first period-end close using our own high-performance, in-memory calculation engine—SAP HANA—and we look forward to being able to report transformational improvements in efficiency and productivity later this year.

So while we can be sure that corporate reporting will become ever more demanding with the business transactions to be accounted for and the reporting rules becoming more complex, the local and national regulators asking for additional information, and the analysts and investors seeking deeper insight into corporate performance, we can rest assured that software providers, such as SAP, will always be there to help us meet and rise above whatever challenges come our way.

In writing *Accelerated Financial Closing with SAP*, our colleagues and subject matter experts have produced a book that covers each step in considerable detail all the way from the subledger and General Ledger closes, through intercompany reconciliation, consolidation, disclosure, and filing. At each stage, they discuss the process and access controls that need to be in place to ensure good governance and compliance and illustrate how automation brings transformational benefits with real-life examples provided by SAP valued clients such as Altron, HMY, and Sandvik. Having worked as part of corporate finance teams, inside consulting organizations, and most recently for SAP, the authors have a wealth of practical experience that they share by providing advice on how to develop an action plan for improving your financial reporting as well as and how best to implement secure tangible benefits for your organization. The book concludes with a discussion of some of the changes in corporate reporting anticipated in the future and discusses how companies can best prepare for them today.

Because this book covers both the accounting and reporting processes and the technology needed to automate them, we are more than confident that it will be a valuable resource to those already working in corporate reporting as well as those anticipating entering the profession. Our only regret is that it was not available earlier in our careers!

Christoph Hütten
Senior Vice President and Chief Accounting Officer
SAP AG (Germany)

Sonja Simon
Head of Group Accounting and Reporting
SAP AG (Germany)

Preface

Accelerated Financial Closing with SAP spans SAP's portfolio of finance and analytics solutions, including applications from its market-leading enterprise performance management, business intelligence, and governance risk and compliance portfolios. It aims to explain how these solutions can be deployed alongside existing SAP ERP Financials implementations and break down traditional barriers to a fast, high-quality financial close process. This title provides a comprehensive guide for finance and controlling professionals seeking to understand how their existing and future investments in SAP solutions can be leveraged to help their organizations run a best-in-class finance close process.

Target Audience

This book intends to address two key audiences in today's enterprise. First, finance executives will benefit from an up-to-date overview of the complete end-to-end financial close process. Leveraging industry best practices and real case study examples, we will do the following:

- Provide insight into the business drivers for and the benefits of a fast, high-quality financial close process.
- Give an overview of the technology landscape that is now available to support it.
- Examine the impact of the latest changes to regulatory reporting and the performance management process.
- Demonstrate how industry peers have improved their financial close processes, reduced risks, and enabled finance to become a strategic partner to the business.

Second, we will address the needs of business process owners and program directors charged with running and optimizing the financial close process within their organization. For this reader, this book will do the following:

- Set out a clear action plan for how corporate finance teams can approach the challenge of improving the financial close process.
- Demonstrate how a new generation of solutions from SAP can systematically break down barriers to a fast, efficient financial close process.
- Explain how by converging the previously disparate disciplines of business intelligence; governance, risk, and compliance; and enterprise performance management on a solid foundation of SAP ERP, finance teams can seek to improve service quality and reduce costs.

The chapters in this book break out the key components of the financial close and discuss how finance solutions from SAP can be leveraged alongside process best practices to achieve immediate yet sustainable improvements to the financial close.

Chapter Overview

The chapters in this book are designed to systematically help you with actionable steps to improve the financial close process in your organization. The first chapters provide an overview of the key concepts surrounding a fast, accurate close process, including an understanding of the drivers for an improved process and the most commonly cited barriers to it. We examine the ways in which you can build a business case for future investment and outline a simple four-step action plan that can be used to design a fast close initiative from the first initial benchmarking processes through to ongoing improvements.

The subsequent chapters then dissect the most important parts of the financial close process and examine in details how the process should function as a practice and how technology from SAP can be used to help improve the process. Real-life examples help to illustrate how SAP customers are already benefiting from implementations of these technologies.

The book closes with a look to the future, highlighting key developments finance professionals need to be aware to drive long-term sustainable value from the financial close process and how this positions finance professionals to better partner with the business, driving not just sound stewardship but entrepreneurship, positioning finance as a true strategic partner to the business.

Summary

Ultimately, this book is designed as a practical guide that enables finance and controlling professionals to optimize their financial close process using SAP solutions. Today this portfolio is broader and more extensive than it has ever been and by deploying an end-to-end solution for your financial close, not only will you achieve a faster more accurate close, but you will provide the basis for broader finance transformation whereby the cost of finance is reduced and the finance function is positioned as a driver of strategic change across the organization.

Acknowledgments

Just as the financial close is not a one-person show within an organization, this book would not have been possible without the help of a sizable team, both internal and external to SAP.

We would first like to thank our customers, who have put their trust into our solutions and have collaborated with us to share their success stories. We value a consistent dialogue with our customers as part of their implementations, and their expectations and feedback allow us to continuously improve our solutions. Thank you also to Richard Barrett and Christine Boyazi for compiling the customer stories. In addition, Christoph Hütten and Sonja Simon from SAP are not only our customers for selected close solutions, but they also speak on our behalf often and kindly authored our Foreword.

The SAP ecosystem and our partners are also critical to our success, and we want to thank all of those partners who help support SAP with our work around the financial close including Accenture, Aster Group, Blackline, Capgemini, cundus, Column5, Deloitte, Driver6, Ernst & Young, Greenlight Technologies, IBM Global Business Services, KPMG, Macrospect, OpenText, Optimal Solutions, Performance Analytics, PricewaterhouseCoopers, Protiviti, Redwood, SandPoint Consulting, Strafford, and TruQua.

We want to thank our colleagues in solution and product marketing, and solution and product management, who were supportive, made suggestions, helped review our manuscripts, and kept us honest. Thank you to Marie Alami, Kirk Anderson, Pras Chatterjee, Franz Deitering, Sue Drouin, Helen Dwight, Arif Esa, Mario Farag, Malcolm Faulkner, Mirko Fellner, Bernhard Fischer, Damien Fribourg, Christian Geiseler, Chris Grundy, Carsten Hilker, Craig Himmelberger, Erin Hughes, Thorsten Jopp, Sean Johnson, Stefan Karl, Aundrea Lacy, Michael Lortz, Pia Luebeck, Bruce McCuaig, Steve McHugh, Christian Mnich, Karuna Mukherjea, Martin Naraschewski, Stephane Neufcourt, Irma Notorahardjo, Joseph Pacor, Serena Perfetto, Jerome Pugnet, Katharina Reichert, Jason Reid, David Roberts, Bruce Romney, Janet Salmon, and David Williams. We would also be remiss if we did not thank our management for supporting us on this endeavor, including Marty Etzel, Aiaz Kazi, Ingrid van den Hoogen, Denise Broady, and Kai Finck.

We would also like to add personal thanks to friends and colleagues who have helped us get to where we are today and whose support for our careers made this book possible, including Charles Muldoon, David JH Jones, Stephanie Buscemi, Sanjay Poonen, Anthony Reynolds, and Trevor Walker. Thank you also to our families and friends for their moral support and understanding when we locked ourselves away to complete the writing process.

And of course, this book would not have been possible without the collaboration and trust of the SAP PRESS team, including Jon Kent, Katy Spencer, and Julie McNamee, who patiently guided us through the process of writing our first book.

James Fisher
Vice President, Product Marketing, Analytics
SAP

Elizabeth Milne
Senior Director, Product Marketing, Accounting and Financial Close
SAP

Birgit Starmanns
Senior Director, Product Marketing, Finance Solutions
SAP

Improving quality and streamlining the financial close process remains a priority for many finance and controlling professionals. Increasing regulatory pressures and evolving technologies continue to present both challenges and opportunities. SAP's end-to-end portfolio of financial close solutions is designed to deliver best practices and enable finance transformation. This chapter helps you get started.

1 Introduction to the Financial Close

The earliest records of accounting go back more than 7,000 years. Double-entry bookkeeping dates back to the fourteenth century. Today, the landscape for accounting and the financial close continues to evolve. *Financial excellence* is achieved when resources, people, and technology are combined to optimize and streamline financial processes, decrease operating costs, manage working capital and cash flow, and maximize profitability. A streamlined, efficient, high-quality financial close process is therefore a key priority for CFOs. The process spans all three of the major dimensions of the CFO role: the need to effectively manage risk and compliance; the need to help outperform stakeholder's financial objectives and create sustainable value; and the need to streamline financial operations and reduce cost.

In its simplest form, the term *financial close* describes the process by which a corporation completes its accounting cycles and produces financial statements for internal management and external legal or statutory reporting. The requirement to close books quickly, with quality and in full compliance with global regulatory standards, is key to the ultimate value and success of this process and offers a host of complexities than can often cloud what is in essence a well-established business process.

In the late 1990s, companies became more efficient at closing their books and reporting financial information, but the emergence of compliance regulations such as the Sarbanes-Oxley Act and the introduction of International Financial Reporting Standards (IFRS) placed additional reporting demands on organizations. The result was that once improved financial reporting processes for many reverted to a time-consuming and labor-intensive effort to ensure both the quality and timeliness of financial data. Once again, companies began to invest in transformational initiatives for the finance function, often seeking to leverage technology to enable this change.

Today's changing economic conditions, the resulting demands from internal and external stakeholders, the changing nature of financial reporting, the importance of sustainability, and the growth in new regulatory requirements for the publication of financial and business data in the form of *eXtensible Business Reporting Language (XBRL)* means that the focus on achieving and maintaining an efficient, high-quality financial close process remains critically important.

In fact, research sponsored by SAP and conducted by industry analyst firm Ventana Research in early 2012 shows that compared to 2007, companies are actually taking longer to close their books. Of the companies surveyed, 38% can now close their quarterly or half year in less than six working days, down from 47% in 2007.

Closing fast enables quicker access to financial information, which gives management the foundation for timely and better informed planning and decision making because rather than chasing numbers, financial and business analysts have the data at their fingertips and can better respond to ad hoc requests. However, it's not just about speed; efficiency, service, and quality are also key drivers for change. Perhaps more importantly, the accelerated financial close demands a high-quality close, where processes are monitored to ensure a foundation of trusted information for decision making and regulatory reporting. One is not possible without the other, so in this book, when we use the phrase "accelerated financial close," we are actually talking about the combination of speed, efficiency, and quality.

1.1 The Business Case for a Fast High-Quality Close

Companies seek an accelerated financial close for several reasons. The business case for a fast-close initiative is often driven by a combination of benefits for the enterprise as a whole, the benefits for the internal and external stakeholders who manage the process or use the information it produces, or by a need to comply with external financial reporting regulations.

1.1.1 Internal and External Stakeholders

Stakeholders represent the various touch points in an organization where the fast high-quality close has a direct impact. Typically, stakeholders include a combination of people who produce financial information and manage aspects of the financial reporting supply chain, who help assure it, and all those who consume it. They are both internal and external and include executive management, corporate, departmental and business unit, subsidiary accounting and controlling teams, and business analysts on one hand, and auditors, investors, market analysts, and increasingly prospective customers on the other.

Communicate to Stakeholders at the Right Time

"The ability to prepare trusted financial statements in a timely manner is not only a reflection on the strength of a company's financial reporting and control systems but also ensures finance professionals can communicate the right information to key stakeholders at the right time."
—Director of Accounting, Major UK PLC

1.1.2 Regulatory Drivers for the Accelerated Financial Close

Not surprisingly, the single biggest impact on close cycles in recent years has been the result of a dramatically changing regulatory landscape. Since the well-publicized corporate scandals of 2001 and 2002, and more recently the impact of the credit crisis in late 2008, businesses have faced an ever-changing regulatory landscape, elements of which remain uncertain to this day and in which the only certain thing is the prospect of yet more change to come.

Regulation has impacted the financial close process by both increasing the burden on financial reporting processes and making it more difficult to report with the speed previously enjoyed. At the same time, the same regulations actually set out requirements by which an organization needs to report more quickly.

Requirements and changes in the form of IFRS, EU Accounts Modernization Directive, and the Sarbanes-Oxley Act (SOX) added complexity to the regulatory environment. The United States perhaps bore the brunt of the regulatory burden where SOX created an additional financial reporting hurdle for all those companies that are required to meet the demands of the Securities and Exchange Commission (SEC).

On one hand, there was a drive for faster reporting. For example, Section 409 of SOX requires public companies to disclose any material event that results in a change to the financial condition or operations of the issuer. Under the rules, the issuer has four days from the trigger of the material event to report on the event. This requires financial and operational systems and processes that bring material events to the attention of management more quickly than before.

To add to this are the rules associated with 10K/10Q filing deadlines. These were accelerated in September 2005 following an amendment to the SEC Act of 1934. Public companies with a public float of more than US$700 million are now subject to a 60-day deadline for form 10K and a 40-day deadline for 10Q. Similar deadlines exist in Europe.

On the other hand, this drive for faster reporting conflicts with our drive for greater accuracy. Section 302 of SOX requires the formal management certification of the accuracy of financial statements; this covers both omissions and misleading or untrue statements. As a result, those required to put their name to these statements now want to take steps to ensure their accuracy, with the net effect of increasing the time it takes to produce financial statements.

In addition, Section 404 of SOX has been one of the factors that many believe is leading to an increase in the time companies are taking to close and obtain audit sign-off. Section 404 requires each annual report of a public company to include a report by management on the company's internal control over financial reporting. It also requires the company's auditor to attest to and report on management's assessment of the effectiveness of the company's internal control over financial reporting—again leading to further delays in the reporting processes.

Other changes are underway as well. We continue to see the ongoing and increasingly global adoption of IFRS and more and more regulators and agencies from around the world are requiring the submission of electronic financial data to their systems via XBRL. There is particular uncertainty in the United States around the conversion or convergence of US-GAAP and IFRS, which only adds to challenges many are facing.

This pace of change in the regulatory landscape will also continue to evolve well into the future, not just in terms of increasing adoption of standards such as IFRS and XBRL but also through the introduction of new standards and reporting requirements either on a legal or a voluntary basis.

At the time of writing this book, a particularly interesting example of such a development is the proposal currently being formulated and piloted with more than 70 global organizations, including SAP for *integrated reporting*. This new approach to reporting extends the external reporting framework well beyond historical financials to span all dimensions of the enterprise, including but not limited to sustainability-related metrics. The International Integrated Reporting Committee (IIRC; *www.iirc.com*) is currently going through a Consultation process having published its draft framework in April 2013.

Such changes will continue to burden financial reporting teams and drive a need for internal processes that are capable of adapting and incorporating such changes in a cost-effective and non-disruptive way.

1.1.3 Benefits of the Accelerated Financial Close

Organizations can realize numerous benefits by investing to speed financial close cycles for both internal management reporting and external legal, or statutory, reporting. Overall, closing remains a priority for the majority of companies with 82% of respondents to the 2012 Ventana Research study indicating that it was either important or very important to shorten the financial close process, which is consistent with an earlier study that Ventana conducted in 2007.

The benefits of a fast close have multiple touch points both internally and externally. We have identified some of the most well-researched benefits and subsequently the most common contributing elements of a business case for a fast-close project:

- Faster access to financial information
- More time for value-added analysis
- Work-life balance
- Improved control systems and quality
- Greater time savings and cost savings during the close process
- Better investor relations

In reviewing these benefits, perhaps the first point to note is that good corporate governance is inseparable from the benefits of a fast and efficient close. It's impossible to achieve one without the other, and when building a business case, an organization should not be looking at a benefit trade-off between quality and speed.

Faster Access to Financial Information

By reducing the close time, businesses benefit from much faster access to information relating to the performance of their business. As part of an integrated and coherent performance management process, this allows management to focus attention quickly on problem areas and make faster business decisions to improve future performance.

More Time for Value-Added Analysis

By streamlining close processes and reducing the number of staff days required, you free significant time for accounting staff. This can be used to add more depth and value to the written reports produced at the end of the quarter and year and also allows more time for ad hoc financial analysis during the monthly cycle, which improves the quality of decision making.

Removing Manual Drudgery

"It's the ability to remove the manual drudgery, kill that, and give time back to the accountants to allow them to do their job. That was the main driver of the business case for me and from me to my management."
— Former FTSE 100 Company Financial Controller

Work-Life Balance

It's also important not to overlook how the fast close creates a more manageable work-life balance for staff in the accounting department. Quite often, the length of a close cycle is only the tip of the iceberg when it comes to the effort involved, and it's not uncommon for staff to work significantly longer hours during the close. Chapter 8 discusses intercompany reconciliation in more detail.

Improved Control Systems and Quality

A financial-close initiative should establish a number of best practices for financial reporting, including automation, workflow management, and data-entry validation. One of the keys to a fast close is "right-first-time" reporting, which not only increases quality earlier in reporting processes, but the additional time spent on analyzing the data also leads to better quality reporting that delivers greater value. Because the fast close is about streamlining and industrializing the close process, internal control systems are inherently improved, which, in turn, improves the audit sign-off process.

Greater Time and Cost Savings during the Close Process

The cost impact of a fast close is substantial. A streamlined close process offers time savings in terms of manual intervention, error reconciliation, variance analysis, and data processing and collection across a variety of close processes. These time savings can then be quantified into numbers of staff days, which, in turn, can result in reduced head count, fewer temporary staff working on low-value activities, and reduced recruitment costs. These savings, however, are not limited to possible financial rewards. When applied to value-added activities, freed time increases revenues and lowers costs. Particularly relevant is the application to Section 404 of SOX, where fast-close initiatives not only aid compliance but also assist in driving down the high costs associated with Section 404 compliance by establishing sustainable and repeatable processes to reduce audit fees.

Better Investor Relations

The ability to publish statutory results ahead of shorter regulatory deadlines is, in itself, only part of the benefit for companies that close fast. Publishing faster than industry peers and more closely monitoring business performance are associated directly with the management capability of a company and, in turn, the company's image. It not only implies a level of expertise but also allows for speedier communication at a greater level of detail to investors and analysts, giving them greater comfort. Additional transparency enables greater access to capital for those reporting earlier. It means the reporting of material events can be performed in a timelier manner, which can have a positive impact on stock value. Additional analysis, including the use of narrative and commentary, also has a big impact on how a company is perceived. The importance of maintaining good financial close processes is also reinforced by many of the traditional financial services rating agencies that have introduced specific financial governance products. These products, like credit ratings, serve to measure and report the financial health of a company, particularly those that are publicly traded. Governance Metrics International, Standard and Poor's, Moody's, and Fitch Ratings record a range of measures spanning audit integrity to the quality of financial disclosures and controls. These metrics are critical because they have a direct impact on the cost of capital, which in itself presents a compelling reason to invest in reducing the time it takes to close and report.

1.2 Components of the Financial Close

Not unsurprisingly, there are varying views on which capabilities should form part of an overall financial close solution. Certainly, the most common views as defined by financial close solution providers tend to focus on one specific area covered by a product they have developed. Others, including leading IT industry analysts, have also attempted to define the process steps, which has led to the emergence of a relatively new category of financial close solutions and processes: *financial governance* processes and applications.

Gartner's Definition of Financial Governance Capabilities

Gartner states that the financial governance capabilities are: "Financial consolidation, financial statement generation, intercompany transaction management, reconciliation management, financial controls and compliance, financial close management, access and segregation of duties controls, financial risk management, financial analytics."
—Gartner, Inc. "Gartner Q&A: Current Issues in Financial Governance", April 2011.

The most established of these definitions was delivered by Gartner Inc. and was most recently updated in April 2011. However, while this definition provides a good overview of the component parts of financial governance, the category itself fails to fully represent the entire end-to-end process. In particular, it does not cover a number of closing steps within the *General Ledger*, associated subledgers, as well as the critically important requirements surrounding data and master data management.

As a result, SAP's view on the components of the financial close, while entirely inclusive of the elements set out by Gartner, is differentiated and unique in the way it seeks to encompass and support the close process along the entirety of the financial reporting supply chain—from source transaction through to digital disclosure. The resulting solution therefore spans SAP's portfolio of finance solutions, including SAP ERP Financials; Enterprise Performance Management (EPM);

SAP Governance, Risk and Compliance (GRC); and SAP BusinessObjects Business Intelligence (BI), as shown in Figure 1.1.

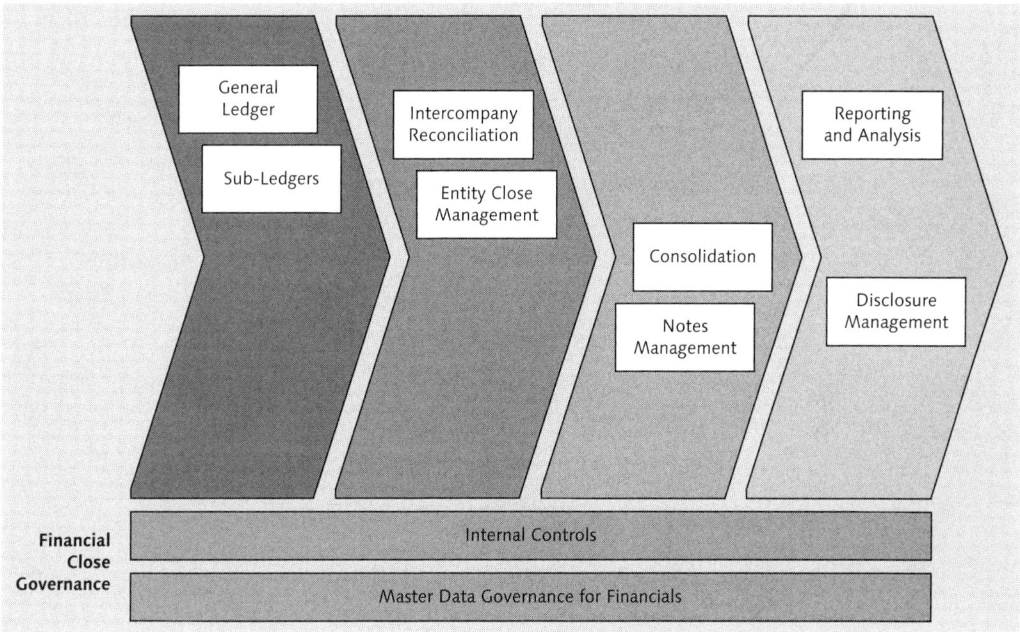

Figure 1.1 SAP's Definition of the Components of the Financial Close Process

Subsequent chapters in this book will examine the most critical components of the close process at a detailed level by articulating how SAP solutions can enable an accelerated high-quality close in your organization.

1.3 How Fast Is Fast?

When measuring the speed of a financial close, it's important, as Section 1.2 indicates, to understand that there are numerous ways in which the close process can be defined and ultimately be measured. It's critical to ensure you are comparing apples with apples in terms of the way days are counted and which part of the process you are counting.

First, it's important to understand if you are counting in elapsed days that include weekends, or working (or business) days. Second, you need to understand exactly what is meant by "the close." The definition will of course differ depending on whether you are looking at a legal or management close process, but some refer to the entire process—from period end, through to published financial statements—while others describe the close as simply the number of days between the period end and the point by which financial information is delivered to the group. It's important to determine how you will measure your process and communicate this definition consistently.

The simplest and most publicly accessible way to establish a fast-close benchmark is to look at the published legal year-end reporting periods, including the time taken to announce results and the time to obtain audit sign-off. BPM International, a network of consulting firms specializing in financial close and performance management consulting, completed its last study of more than 1,000 global companies in 2011 and found extremely diverse results, with the fastest company to report being Cisco Systems, which announced results in just 11 days after the end of the year. As you would expect, BPM International (*www.bpm-international.com*), a network of consulting firms specializing in financial close and performance management consulting, completes an annual study of the financial close processes at more than 1,000 global companies and its 2013 findings show that the fastest company to report was Wells Fargo, which announced results in just 11 days after the end of the year. As you would expect, there are significant differences between the best and worst performers, as well as significant geographic variations, with the best performers in the United States typically closing faster than those in Europe. The fastest performers in Europe were Novartis, Unilever, and SAP all reporting in 23 elapsed days, equivalent to 56th fastest globally.

As indicated earlier in this chapter, the study conducted by Ventana Research in early 2012 shows that compared to 2007, companies are actually taking longer to close their books. Only 38% of companies surveyed can now close their quarterly or half year in less than six business days, down from 47% in 2007 (see Figure 1.2). In terms of the monthly close process, the picture is not much better with only half of those surveyed closing their books in less than six business days of the month end, down from 70% on the 2007 numbers (see Figure 1.3).

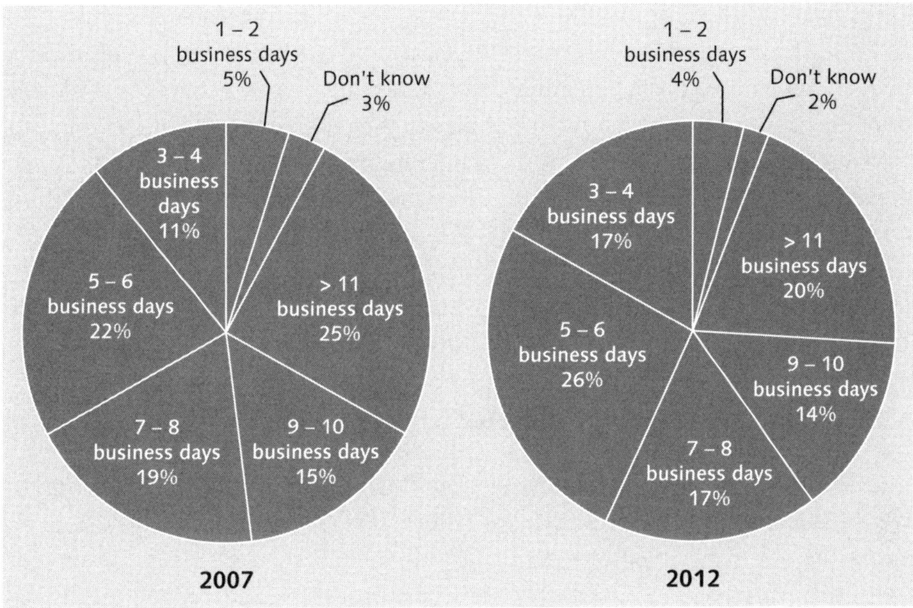

Figure 1.2 Number of Business Days to Close Quarterly or Half Year

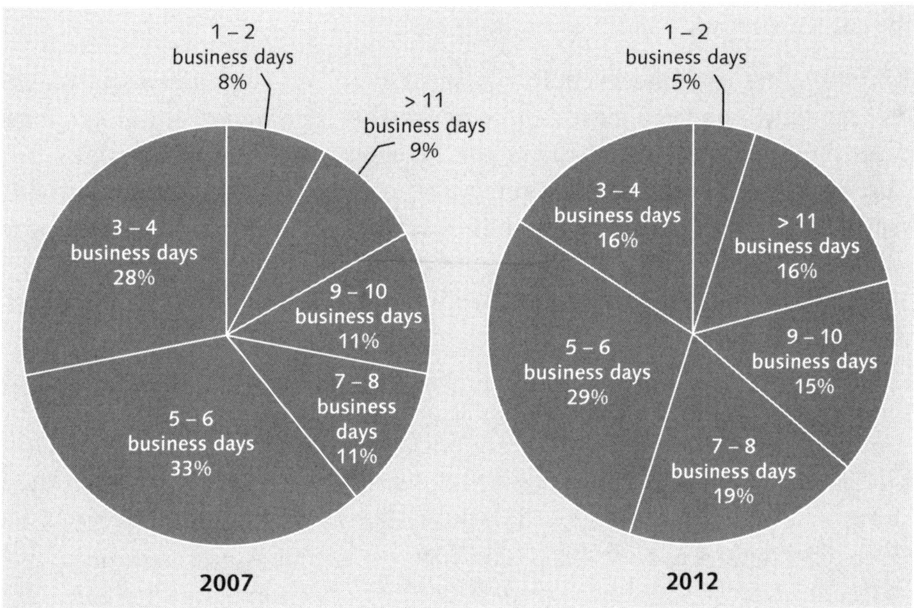

Figure 1.3 Number of Business Days to Close Monthly

There is no 100% right or wrong answer as to how fast a company should close and report. To determine how quickly you should close and report, you need to understand where you sit compared to your peers, either by geography, industry, or organizational size, and how this relates to the relative complexity of your performance management and financial reporting process. Determining this benchmark should be the first stage of any close project because it helps you establish a *SMART* (specific, measurable, achievable, relevant, and time-bound) objective on which you build a project plan to shorten your reporting time. We will return to this SMART concept in Chapter 2.

1.4 Barriers to a Fast, High-Quality Close Process

Considering the growing complexity of the financial close process and the multiple touch points and opportunities for failure, it's not unsurprising that there is a vast array of prospective barriers to a fast, high-quality close process. The majority of these barriers are related directly to the processes, people, and technology that can be found at both the head-office and reporting-unit level and affect multiple teams and processes. In addition, numerous "environmental" issues add to the challenges many organizations are facing.

By identifying and understanding these barriers, you can outline a strategy through which you can remove them systematically from your close process. Some of the most frequently cited barriers—based on our experience of supporting fast-close initiatives in the corporate centers of today's global enterprises—are presented in Figure 1.4. Each of the identified barriers has been grouped according to type—compliance, people, process, and technology—which immediately provides an indication as to how you may start to think about addressing these barriers. Although we are confident that this list is representative, it's important to note that it's not an exhaustive list, so your own organization may not identify with all of these and there may be barriers to your own financial close that are not listed. A first step in any close project is therefore identifying which apply to your close process and which do not, a topic we will return to in Chapter 2. We have taken the most common barriers and have explained these further in Section 1.4.1 through Section 1.4.6. They include compliance-related pressures, data quality and collection errors, intercompany reconciliation, poor performance from consolidation applications, lack of process automation, and weak audit trails.

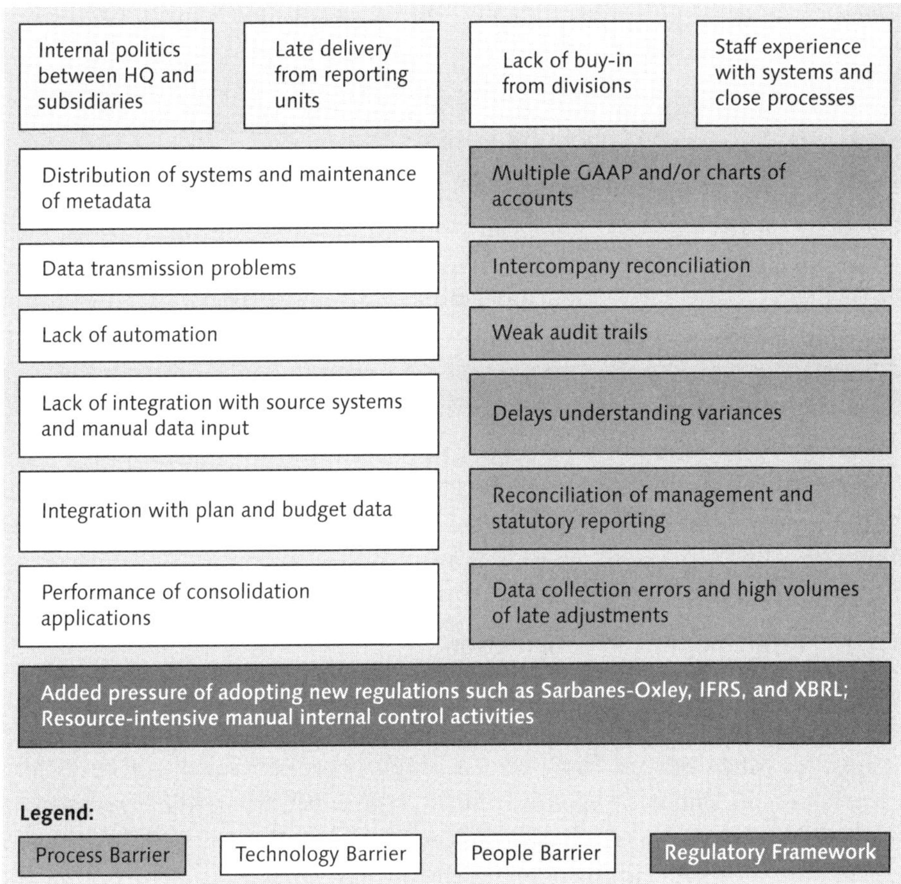

Figure 1.4 Typical Barriers to a Fast, Effective Financial Close Process

1.4.1 Compliance-Related Pressures

Although compliance-related issues are often seen as a hindrance to a fast close, compliance should itself not be seen as a direct barrier to a world-class financial close process. In many respects, compliance processes, particularly strong controls processes, should help streamline functions if implemented correctly and with the right degree of automation. However, the fact remains that compliance and an ever-changing regulatory landscape has and continues to make life more complicated. Many do in fact directly contribute the delays reported by the Ventana Research study as a direct result of a combination of both economic and compliance-related pressures, with 49% of respondents indicating this is the reason for their longer reporting cycles.

1.4.2 Data Quality/Collection Errors

The inability of many to achieve a "right first-time" close process is a critical barrier to the fast close and is a symptom of many broken or failing processes and systems. It's linked to manual data entry, late delivery from reporting units, a lack of validation and controls, poor integration with source systems, and a lack of integration across multiple close processes. Data needs to be collected often from different charts of accounts and multiple sources, including different ledger systems, HR systems, and spreadsheets. Once collected, the data must be normalized into a common chart of accounts so the real process of consolidation in accordance with often multiple accounting standards can begin. Often the data collected will be both financial and non-financial, and it will include supporting text and commentary.

1.4.3 Intercompany Reconciliation

The intercompany process all too often sits on the critical path for the close cycle causing significant delays while operating units resolve unmatched intercompany transactions and balances. Time spent at both the head office and local operations contributes to a significant number of man-days, which are needlessly wasted on this essential but cumbersome process. This has for many years been cited as one of the most common and frequently occurring barriers to a fast-close process.

1.4.4 Poor Performance from Consolidation Applications

The consolidation process is by its nature iterative and involves many rounds of consolidation, review, and adjustment before the process is finalized. The performance of consolidation applications is becoming highly important as organizations look to enhance the close process and save time in every area. In the first wave of fast-close projects, many companies moved from spreadsheet-based models to a best-of-breed closing application to gain some speed advantage; however, in doing so, these companies became hampered by ingrained performance issues. Many are now seeing this as a bottleneck on the critical path, and as they optimize other elements of the close process, the delays caused by poor performance on numerous iterations of the consolidation mount and become more measurable. Chapter 9 discusses consolidation in more detail.

1.4.5 Lack of Process Automation

The close process comprises multiple elements, many of which can be automated to both directly speed the close process and indirectly achieve a faster close by reducing errors or freeing time. Examples of key processes that can be automated include intercompany matching and elimination, internal controls testing, consolidation entries, currency conversion, business rules, ownership and control calculations for minority interests, equity elimination, cash flow, and GAAP conversions. However, the so-called "last mile of finance" has probably become the area where the most scrutiny is now being placed in terms of both increased automation and increased collaboration across the finance organization. Over recent years, new reporting requirements resulting in a need for more detailed disclosures and new filing requirements in the form of XBRL have increased complexity and as a result slowed this part of the close process considerably.

1.4.6 Weak Audit Trails

Not only an issue during the close process where central finance teams may seek to investigate and verify figures, the lack of strong audit trails also have a key impact on the post-close audit sign-off in compliance with SOX 404 and the costs associated with it. According to Ventana Research, 40% of respondents indicated more complex approval and sign-off processes were the cause of the delays they were seeing in their close process as Figure 1.5 indicates. A detailed and automated audit trail from source to disclosure (including the last mile of finance) can be a key tool especially when a close process, as so many do, features lots of late data changes and journal entries. However, even when some systems do feature rudimentary audit features, it is often at the expense of application performance, one further impact that has become a close barrier in its own right.

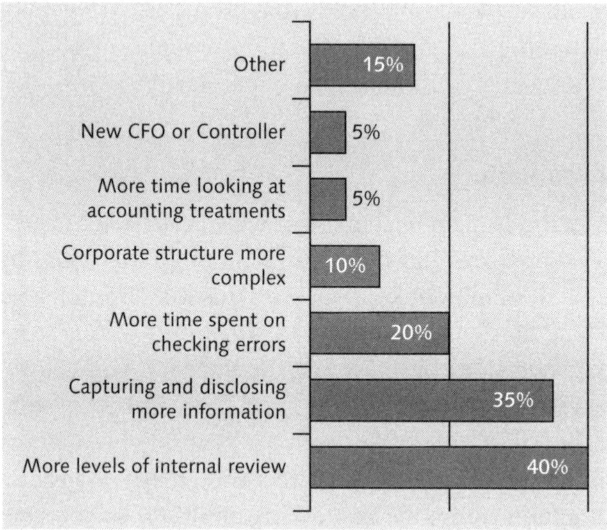

Figure 1.5 Causes of Delay in the Financial Close Process

1.5 Summary

Establishing a common framework for the financial close across your team is critical in any close project. This first chapter has set out to do that in the context of this book so that the reader has a common understanding of the way in which SAP views the close process. Understanding the business case drivers, how quickly people report today, and the most common challenges in the financial close process is therefore critical as we move on to the next chapter in this book, where we will look at how this understanding can be applied to construct a project action plan for your own financial close initiative.

For all transformational projects, it's critically important that you define a project plan that helps you set out your objectives, demonstrate success, manage change, and ultimately drive a long-term business outcome. This chapter examines the need for such an approach and proposes a structure readers can implement as part of their own fast-close project.

2 Creating an Action Plan for Improving Your Financial Close

Understanding the drivers and barriers for a faster close process is important, but before you can start your project, you need to plan for it effectively. A financial close project, like any other corporate initiative, requires a structured approach with a methodology that's supported by people, process, and technology; is manageable; and has clear but realistic objectives. A full financial close project can and, in most cases, must extend beyond corporate-centric processes and functions and therefore involve a broad community that adds complexity to the process.

That being said, the project doesn't necessarily have to result in a major change program and—provided you structure your approach, deliver the appropriate and sponsored resources, and manage the project—it's possible to make significant gains relatively easily.

As a result and based on our experiences working with our partners and customers, we advise that you create an action plan for your project that breaks down the transformation process into meaningful but manageable steps. There are a number of ways to create and build such a plan, and many consultancies and indeed SAP partners will be able to offer their own approach. Typically, however, they all focus around four principal steps. For the purposes of this book, we have created our own action plan, which represents these market best practices and spans the following four steps. We will go on to explain each of these in more detail in this chapter.

1. Establish vision, benchmarking, and sponsorship.
2. Implement quick wins.
3. Identify and deliver big wins.
4. Establish a framework for continuous improvements.

The aim is very simple: to create a project plan that can be delivered based on your existing or budgeted resources and that guides you through the process to set out your objectives, demonstrate success, manage change, and ultimately drive to a long-term business outcome.

2.1 Vision, Benchmarking, and Sponsorship

It is often said that poor project planning is one of the primary causes of project failure, so starting out on the right path from the beginning is critical. To be successful, the first stage of an effective project plan needs to establish a clear set of goals based on a detailed as-is review, which will help you define your vision and objectives for the close. This vision needs to articulate the benefits your project will bring to the organization and then acts as the basis on which you establish clear sponsorship from senior management.

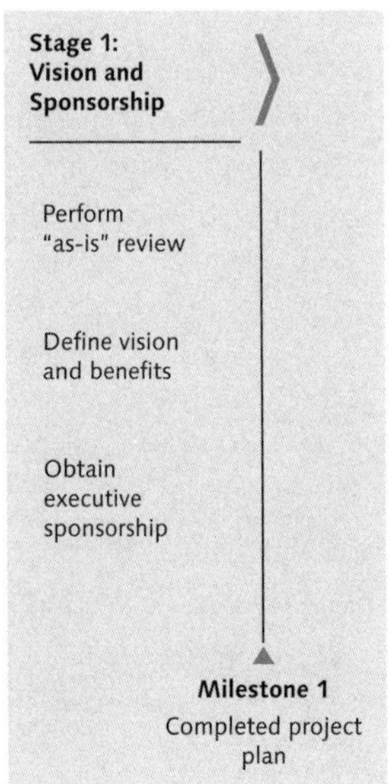

Figure 2.1 Stage 1: Vision and Sponsorship

Figure 2.1 demonstrates this stage, the core components, and how a complete project plan needs to be aligned around a continuum of change management. We will detail each of these core components in the subsequent sections of this book.

2.1.1 Perform "As-Is" Review

As discussed in Chapter 1, there is no 100% right or wrong answer as to how fast a company should close and report. As a result, you need to determine this based on a number of factors (typically industry, size, and geography), which are specific to your own organization. However, before you can define a target, you first need to conduct a review of your own processes and benchmark those with peers.

The review piece is critical, and you need to clearly map out your financial close process. It might be prudent to do this in the form of a project plan or process flow diagram where you determine who is involved, the flow of data and financial information through the process, the critical path, and key milestones. You should make careful notes of the resources, costs, and time frames involved at each stage of the process, as well as the IT systems that support it. It's unlikely that all of the information you will need will reside in one system.

You also need to understand where you sit compared to your peers—by geography, industry, or organizational size—and how this relates to the relative complexity of your performance management and financial reporting process. Benchmarking is something individuals do relatively easily by determining standard metrics (such as how long the close takes) and simply comparing to a defined peer group. Alternatively, most consulting organizations with established financial close practices will have more complex benchmarking processes that they can apply to your organization. By combining peer benchmarking at various stages of the financial close process with your detailed as-is review, you should create a solid foundation on which you can identify which of the typical barriers to a fast close (as discussed in Section 1.4) apply to your organization and in turn which of these you need to focus your efforts on. You can then start to define the next part of the process relating to how you want to improve and address these barriers.

2.1.2 Define Vision and Benefits

After you have reviewed your own processes, the next step is to define your vision, which primarily equates to a description of how you want your close process to run and in doing so set out the benefits you expect to deliver for the business based on those we discussed in Section 1.1.

Your targets should represent resources, timelines, and costs, and although taking a view across the entire process may be easier, you may find it more effective long term to break your targets down by subprocesses. For example, you may determine that you should receive financials into the group HQ by working day 3, and complete the corporate close by working day 5, as opposed to simply saying the entire process should take 8 days.

As we first discussed in Section 1.3, objectives should be "SMART" (specific, measurable, achievable, relevant, and time-bound) and ultimately should become the yardstick for your entire project by which you measure progress and success. For more information, Paul J. Meyer describes the characteristics of SMART objectives in *Attitude Is Everything* (The Meyer Resource Group, 2003).

Specific

When defining objectives its first important that you select a specific goal over and against a more general one. This means the goal is clear and unambiguous; without vagaries and platitudes. To make goals specific, they must tell an individual or team exactly what is expected, why is it important, who's involved, where is it going to happen, and which attributes are important. A specific goal will usually answer the five "W" questions:

- **What:** What do I want to accomplish?
- **Why:** Specific reasons, purposes, or benefits of accomplishing the goal.
- **Who:** Who is involved?
- **Where:** Identify a location.
- **Which:** Identify requirements and constraints.

Measurable

Its also critically important that you leverage concrete criteria for measuring progress toward the attainment of the goal. It goes without saying that if a goal is not measurable, it is not possible to know whether a team is making progress toward successful completion. Measuring progress is supposed to help a team stay on track, reach its target dates, and experience the exhilaration of achievement that spurs it on to the continued effort required to reach the ultimate goal. A measurable goal will usually answer questions such as the following:

- How much?
- How many?
- How will I know when it is accomplished?

Achievable

Setting objectives that teams cannot possibly meet is not motivational so although an goal may stretch a team in order to achieve it,it must be realistic and attainable. When you identify goals that are most important to you, you begin to figure out ways you can make them come true. You develop the attitudes, abilities, skills, and financial capacity to reach them. The theory states that an attainable goal may cause goal-setters to identify previously overlooked opportunities to bring themselves closer to the achievement of their goals. An attainable goal will usually answer these questions:

- How can the goal be accomplished?
- What resources do I need to accomplish it?

Relevant

Its also important that you choose goals that matter. In the context of a fast close project, a goal to "Ensure 75% of sales orders are delivered within 3 working days" may be specific, measurable, attainable, and time-bound, but it lacks relevance to project in hand. Many times, you will need support to accomplish a goal: resources, a champion voice, someone to knock down obstacles. Goals that are relevant to your boss, your team, and your organization will receive that needed support. Relevant goals (when met) drive the team, department, and organization forward. A goal that supports or is in alignment with other goals would be considered a relevant goal. A relevant goal can answer yes to these questions:

- Does this seem worthwhile?
- Is this the right time?

- Does this match our other efforts/needs?
- Are you the right person?

Time-bound

Finally the use of a specific time frame in goal setting is important as it gives a target date for which an individual and team and work towards. A commitment to a deadline helps a team focus its efforts on completion of the goal on or before the due date. This part of the SMART goal criteria is intended to prevent goals from being overtaken by the day-to-day crises that invariably arise in an organization. A time-bound goal is intended to establish a sense of urgency. A time-bound goal will usually answer these questions:

- When?
- What can I do six months from now?
- What can I do six weeks from now?
- What can I do today?

By defining SMART objectives as outlined, we can now have a definite idea of our vision for our financial close process and clearly articulate the benefits to our business of such an undertaking. The next step in our action plan is sponsorship.

2.1.3 Sponsorship

This is a critical part of the project, and while there is some evidence to suggest that a lack of sponsorship will hinder your chances of success, there is significantly more evidence to demonstrate that the most successful projects have extremely strong executive project sponsorship.

It's important at this point not to confuse project sponsorship and project management. The latter manages the project day to day and is responsible for delivery. The role of the executive sponsor is a role within the project management function. Usually a senior member of the project board and often the chair, the sponsor will typically be a senior executive who will be responsible to the business for the success of the project. Depending on your size of organization and the scope of the project, exactly who this is may, of course, vary.

The sponsor has a number of responsibilities for the project:

- Provides leadership on the organization culture
- Owns the overall business case
- Keeps the project aligned with the organization's strategy and direction
- Governs risk associated with the project
- Focuses on realizing benefits
- Identifies opportunities to optimize cost/benefits
- Drives sponsorship
- Provides feedback and lessons learned

The sponsor will therefore become a primary stakeholder for the project manager, and typically they will interact around things such as the decision-making framework, the business priorities and strategy, support for communication to the wider business, and a host of other associated governance activities. The executive sponsor needs a range of skill sets, including appreciation of corporate strategy, ability to prepare a business case, and profound knowledge of the organization's operations. The sponsor also needs to know his way around the organization and command respect within it. The project sponsor and project manager should form an effective partnership with each other. The project manager should orchestrate all players involved in delivering the project while the project sponsor coordinates all departments of the organization and associated stakeholders to ensure the full benefits from the business case. Again, the precise structure of the project team is somewhat dependent on your organization and scope of the project. Although the roles are distinct, it may be possible for one person to drive both roles in smaller projects.

Ultimately, however, in the case of the financial close, the more senior the sponsor the better. Although in most organizations the financial controller owns the overall close process, the most successful fast-close projects are typically sponsored by the CFO. Some level of reporting to the CEO on large transformation projects is also not uncommon.

Sponsorship from the outset of the project is critical, but it is possible to grow sponsorship over the duration of the project. This is critically important as we move into the more complex and challenging parts of the transformation. The starting point is to focus on a series of quick wins.

2.2 Quick Wins

The second stage in the action plan covers the implementation of your quick wins, and essentially this is where most people will feel the rubber hit the road and where you start to actually make changes to your financial reporting process that will result in tangible benefits in both the speed and quality of your financial close process. Figure 2.2 sets out this stage of the process and shows four of the most common quick wins to consider:

- Creating a close scorecard
- Peer-to-peer intercompany reconciliation
- Right-first-time close
- XBRL publishing

Before we explain these in more detail, it's critical to understand why quick wins are so important to your project. Ultimately, it is simply not possible to change the entire close process in one go, so quick wins serve to demonstrate that time savings are achievable, which in itself reinforces the level of executive sponsorship a project receives and puts people into a positive and determined frame of mind for delivering the bigger wins. The key is to understand that not all of the barriers to a close require huge amounts of effort to improve. In some cases, it is possible to very easy make significant gains. Keep in mind that the position of each win will vary based on the specifics of your organization.

The trick is to evaluate the options open to you and prioritize them according to the amount of time and effort needed to implement and the size of the impact on your close cycle. Those with the least required effort but maximum impact are the most attractive and should be your quick wins. Conversely, those that require a significant event but are also deemed to have a big impact are known as big wins (discussed further in Section 2.3). Naturally, anything that requires a big effort and that will have very little impact on the performance of your close process should be considered out of scope unless there is another compelling reason to address this, such as cost, for example. Figure 2.3 represents a simple way to compare and contrast the various efforts and can be used to help select which wins to focus on.

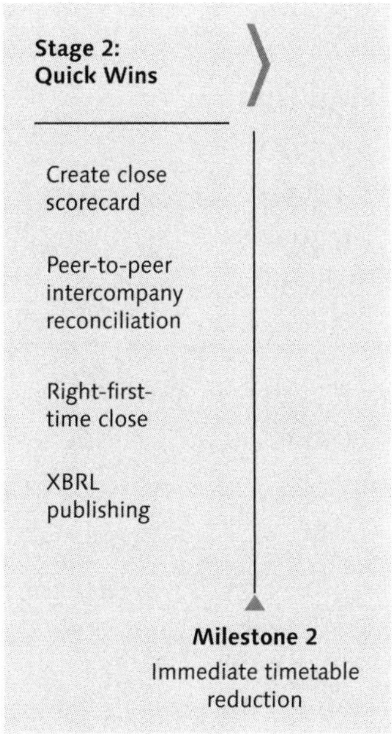

Figure 2.2 Stage 2: Quick Wins

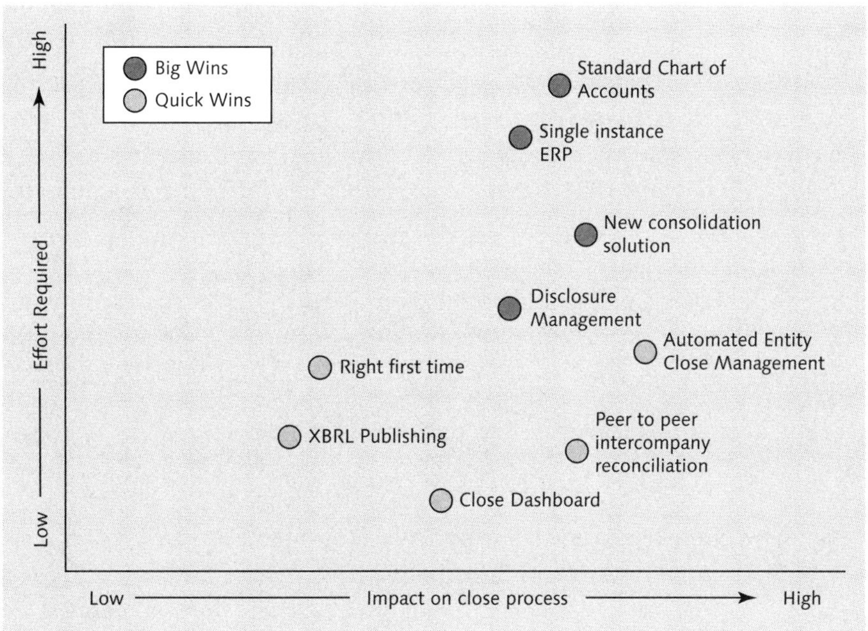

Figure 2.3 Comparing Quick Wins and Big Wins

While later chapters will look at a number of these quick and big wins in more detail, particularly showing how SAP solutions can support them, it's worth illustrating a few to fully explain how they work as quick wins and add value.

2.2.1 Creating a Close Scorecard

It is often said that what gets measured gets managed, and this holds very true for the financial close process. Although a reasonable proportion of the customers we work with measure and record different aspects of the close process, it's surprising how few, in fact, the vast majority, simply fail to report on this data and put it to good use. Those organizations that are typically best in class at the financial close, on the other hand, do make good use of the data.

They do this by creating a *close scorecard*, which serves to collect data and report on the effectiveness of different stages in the reporting process. The most common approach is to report on the time it takes for operating units to report financials to the central team. This information can then be used to show the best and worst performers in a group. Such a scorecard need not be complicated and in its simplest form can simply be a league table showing who is fastest or on time and who is lagging and slowing the process. Repeated monthly, this soon becomes a strong motivational tool as no one likes being held out as a poor performer.

It's of course possible to create more complex models as Figure 2.4 illustrates, but one of the most effective we have seen is still relatively simple provided your financial reporting systems are capable of recording and collecting the data. Essentially, central teams collect data on a number of dimensions spanning the time it takes for an entity to report, the number of errors associated with the submission, and the materiality of the entity to the overall group's financial position. Then, they can plot this on a bubble chart with speed and error representing the two axes and the size of the bubble representing materiality. As indicated, the example in Figure 2.4 is more complex and records many more details, including data points on individual subprocesses and owners of those processes. The depth of complexity is again up to the organization and the scope of the project, but clearly, any level of monitoring has a significant impact.

Although more complicated, such an approach allows for a further level of management and ultimately coaching. Clearly submitting on or ahead of deadlines is good, but if the process is full of errors, then it's a wasted effort. In addition, an entity that is highly material to the overall financial position of the business and is only a few hours late may actually be more important to fix than an immaterial entity that is a few days late.

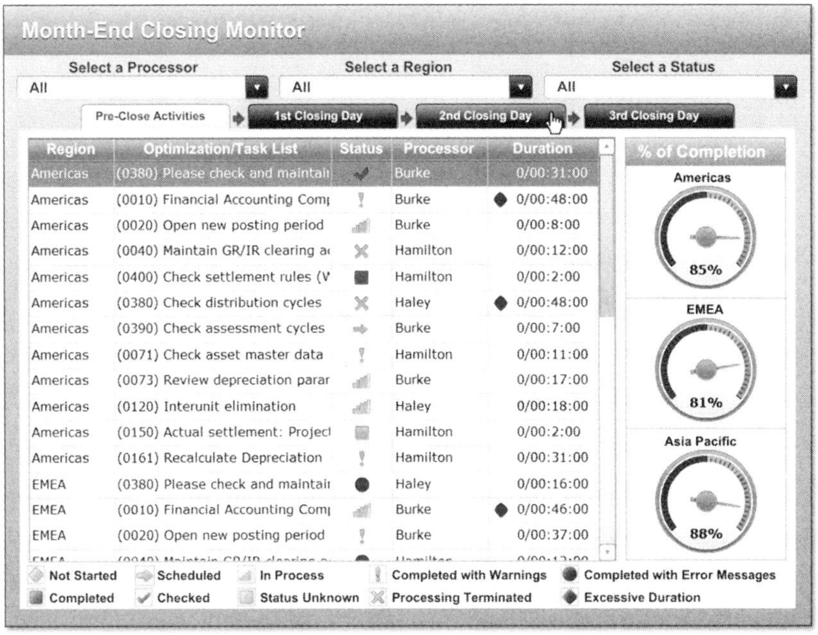

Figure 2.4 Example of a Close Dashboard Report

By looking at the different dimensions just described, a more effective management process can be implemented where best and worst performers are more easily identified and where the best practices of the best can be used to coach the worst. We have seen many organizations use this as part of a formal post-close review process after each close cycle is completed. Some even go as far as to use such benchmarking as part of the management by objectives (MBO) process for key controlling staff.

Chapter 6 of this book looks at various aspects of process governance and entity closing in more detail. This chapter will focus on how the SAP Financial Closing Cockpit can be used to help measure and manage the entity close process.

2.2.2 Peer-to-Peer Intercompany Reconciliation

Monitoring and managing the process as a whole will only get you so far, however, and sooner or later, you will have to address fundamental issues in your close process, including accounting practices. In all the time that we have worked in the financial close process, the area that has consistently been identified as a major cause of delay is intercompany reconciliation. As Section 1.4.3 highlights, the intercompany process all too often sits on the critical path for the close cycle causing significant delays while operating units resolve unmatched intercompany transactions and balances.

Time spent at both the head office and local operations contributes to a significant number of man-days, which are needlessly wasted on this essential but cumbersome process. To some extent, this is hardly surprising considering the complexity of the process. In the past, the technology to support the process was highly manual with email and faxes forming the basis of communication between the counter parties to ensure intercompany balances matched. Often errors were only discovered during the consolidation process when intercompany elimination reports were run.

Chapter 8 of this book looks at how today's web-based solutions, such as SAP Intercompany, can be implemented extremely quickly as a quick win to remove the intercompany process from the critical path. Significant gains can be made very quickly by implementing a peer-to-peer based communication process ensuring that intercompany balances and transactions (as shown in Figure 2.5) match prior to starting the consolidation process.

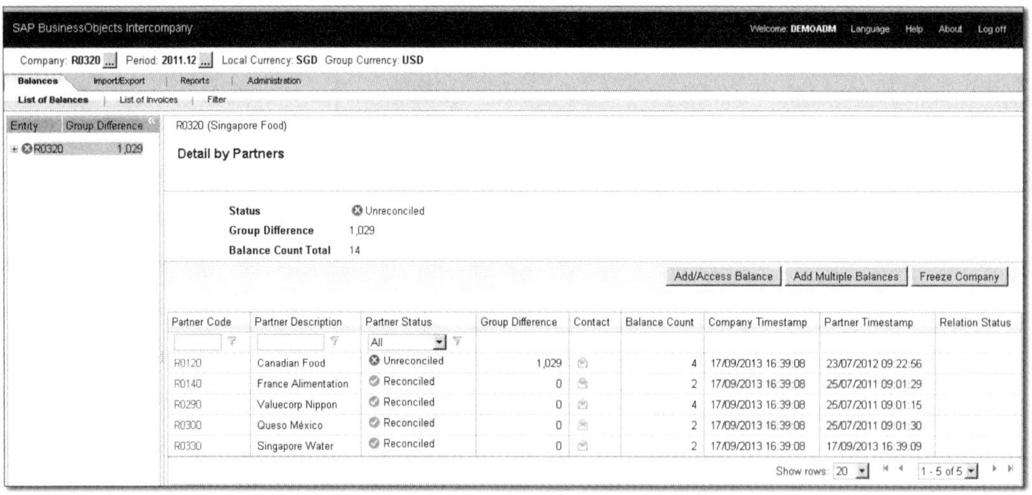

Figure 2.5 Peer-to-Peer Intercompany Reconciliation with SAP Intercompany

2.2.3 Right-First-Time Close

Errors in the financial close process are of course not just limited to errors in the intercompany process. There are numerous other points of failure. As Section 1.4.2 describes, the inability of many to achieve a "right-first-time" close process is a critical barrier to the fast close and is a symptom of many broken or failing processes and systems. It's linked to manual data entry, late delivery from reporting units, a lack of validation and controls, poor integration with source systems, and a lack of integration across multiple close processes.

As a result, taking simple steps to ensure the accuracy of data coming into the financial close process can have a huge impact, which is why it's identified as a quick win. Later chapters in this book will examine this in much more detail, but a combination of using a good data integration solution that draws data from source systems, validates it, and loads it automatically into reporting and consolidation environments is extremely powerful. Chapter 3 of this book examines how solutions such as SAP Financial Information Management can be quickly implemented to deliver these capabilities in such a way that finance teams can own and manage this process with the additional benefit from enhanced audit capabilities. Chapter 7 will go on to look at how more controls can be implemented to ensure additional levels of accuracy. For example, delays to the financial close process are caused not just by erroneous data (such as assets not equaling liabilities) but also by missing data or analysis. A common failure, for example, occurs when an entity forgets to include commentary explaining why a given number varies from a plan or budget number. The ability to check this at the point of submission and ensure that this information is provided before the process progresses too far significantly improves the speed and quality of the overall close process.

2.2.4 XBRL Publishing

Unlike the intercompany process, which has been around as part of the close process from the outset and is a well-known target for quick wins, the XBRL process is relatively new. However, just like the intercompany process, XBRL also presents an opportunity for a quick win. XBRL is one of the biggest changes to impact the world of financial reporting in the past 10 years, apart from perhaps the introduction of IFRS, and its use for filing financial and business information to key regulators, banks, and tax authorities is increasingly becoming standard practice.

Chapter 10 in this book looks in more detail at the role of XBRL in the so-called "last mile of finance," the stage in the process that takes place at the end of the financial close, as described in Section 1.2. Typically, this stage of the process takes a lot of time, effort, and money, and it is often the least automated part of the financial close.

Although we would typically regard the implementation of a broad reporting and disclosure solution as a big win given the breadth of the solution coverage, it is possible to streamline the XBRL filing process relatively easily. Implementing a solution such as SAP Disclosure Management just for XBRL filing can be achieved quickly and without the need for extensive outsourcing of the filing process, which is the common alternative.

As described earlier, these are just a few examples of typical quick wins. In your organization, these may be different; after all, what is easy for some may be challenging for others. As with the process of defining your financial close objectives, it's about reviewing your processes and identifying what works for your business. What is clear is that using quick wins to demonstrate success and drive additional sponsorship for bigger wins is often overlooked but always valuable.

2.3 Big Wins

As we described earlier, the third stage of the action plan is to identify and deliver big wins. This is based on the assumption that quick wins by themselves may not lead you to achieve all your targets or that more often than not, you're unable to implement quick wins given your current system's landscape. Big wins require greater resources and more time but often enable significant reductions in the time the close process takes. The subsequent chapters in this book look in much more detail at how financial close solutions from SAP can help you address and implement big wins in your organizations, but for now, here are some examples of big wins, as detailed in Figure 2.6:

- Establishing a standard chart of accounts
- Implementing a common single instance of SAP ERP
- Implementing a broad reporting and disclosure framework
- Addressing major issues in the corporate and local close processes

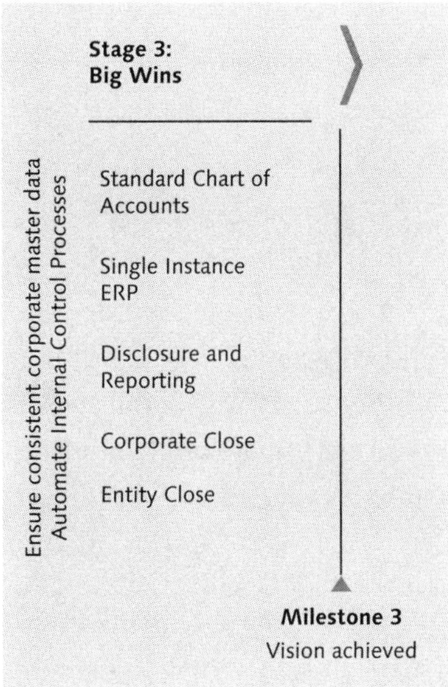

Figure 2.6 Stage 3: Big Wins

2.3.1 Standard Chart of Accounts

Establishing a standard chart of accounts across the entire enterprise is a huge undertaking. Although this can bring many benefits, including timetable reduction, it can affect every general ledger (GL) in every subsidiary, and for many looking to make incremental gains, it is often considered too challenging. As a result, any implementation of a standard chart of accounts is more often than not a broader initiative than a simple fast-close project. It should be considered carefully and often with the aid of third-party expertise.

2.3.2 Common Single Instance of SAP ERP

Like a standard chart of accounts, the implementation of a common single instance of SAP ERP may be a large project. From an SAP perspective, it's often seen as the holy grail; however, while there are huge benefits of such an approach, it is not in itself a barrier to a fast close in our experience. Accordingly, while we often see the implementation of SAP ERP solutions as part of a financial close project for those looking to make incremental gains, it too is often overlooked. It's more common that there is either a regional implementation of SAP ERP or a consolidation of multiple instances into fewer regional deployments. Chapter 4 in this book addresses GL and sub-GL close processes in more detail.

2.3.3 Reporting and Disclosure Framework

As introduced in Section 2.2.4, a broad solution that addresses the last mile of finance can have a significant impact on your financial close process. The XBRL component is actually the easiest part of this, which is why it is included as a quick win. However, even more significant gains and cost savings are possible by taking a broader view and developing a more established and controllable reporting and disclosure framework, which also has a significant impact on data quality. The basis for this big win is to move beyond manual, error-prone last mile of finance processes using Microsoft Word and Excel documents, separated from the secure and auditable financial reporting and consolidation systems and to move to implementing a full collaborative disclosure management system such as SAP Disclosure Management. As mentioned earlier, Chapter 10 in this book examines this in more detail.

2.3.4 Corporate and Entity Close

The final area of big wins relates to a broad range of solutions to common barriers to a fast close within the corporate and local close processes. These are classified as big wins because they often require the implementation of new consolidation software to be the foundation on which they are implemented. Existing applications are often unable to deliver suitable quick wins or to provide a sustainable infrastructure for the fast close in your organization.

For example, implementing new systems that facilitate the harmonizing of packs and processes across reporting cycles can have significant benefits. Standardizing on the same data flow each month helps to avoid discrepancies and reduces timetables because the increased volumes this standardization typically produces forces subsidiaries into automating processes and standardizing their own systems. The end result is often better data quality and shorter timetables. Implementing a new framework will allow you to support this if your current systems are not able to.

Similarly, where manual data entry processes exist, replacing them with direct integration between source SAP ERP or GL applications and EPM applications reduces errors. The same is true when establishing a control environment identifying the most effective and efficient controls for the financial close processes and then streamlining and automating them to minimize the compliance burden. The development of a framework to monitor and control the entire close process from local close activities in an SAP ERP application through to final statement production in consolidation applications offers significant opportunities to improve quality and reduce the time the close takes. Subsequent chapters in this book address these points further and demonstrate how technology can help deliver these best practices.

2.4 Continuous Improvements

After you have completed the implementation of quick wins and big wins, it is assumed that you have met your objectives. If that is not the case, then as a project team, you need to decide if you have achieved enough or if additional steps, still under the guise of quick wins and big wins, need to be implemented. Even if you have met your goals and celebrated that success, your journey is not over. In many respects, it's the start of a whole new one as one of the best pieces of advice we share with our customers is that a fast-close initiative should not be regarded as a one-time project. Yes, you need to establish a project and run this with SMART objectives over a given period of time, but the final stage of the project should look to establish, as part of your ongoing financial close process, a framework for continuous improvement.

This is critically important because as Chapter 12 in this book demonstrates, the only certainty we have in the world of financial reporting and regulation is that there will be more change to come. These changes could easily—as we have seen in the past with say the introduction of IFRS in Europe and the adoption of XBRL reporting in the United States—have a profound impact on the process and system landscapes that you ultimately design in your fast-close project.

The example of IFRS in Europe is particularly interesting. In the preceding years, many organizations had invested in fast-close initiatives and had made promising gains in terms of speed, quality, and the costs of their financial close processes. When it came to implementing IFRS, many applied the accounting changes and in doing so added more resources to the overall process. At the same time, the requirements compelled organizations to collect and report on more information, and many did this by reverting to manual data collection processes often involving spreadsheets, which their earlier financial close project had sought to eradicate. These manual processes took longer, were less auditable, and therefore extended the close process.

Being able to plan and predict such changes is of course challenging, but two key lessons emerge. First is that many who reverted to manual processes did so simply because they had not implemented flexible solutions, and therefore the collection of the additional data was challenging. As later chapters in this book will demonstrate, financial close solutions such as SAP Business Planning and Consolidation are designed to be owned and managed by finance, giving them the flexibility to change and evolve processes as requirements dictate. The second is more cultural in the sense that people simply lost sight of the investment and gains they had previously made and threw everything, including the proverbial kitchen sink, at the problem without looking at it in the context of the overall close process.

Best practice would dictate that when looking to accommodate such a change, you plan to do so in such a way that you further optimize the close. This requires more flexibility and up-front planning, but it is possible. This is why the best in class will typical look for post-close reviews after each close. They review the best in class practices and use this knowledge to coach the weaker performers. They use the review to spot potential issues early and adjust processes so it does not impact the critical path. In doing so, many businesses not only maintain the close times they had previously established, even in light of changing requirements, but further optimized them.

As Figure 2.7 illustrates, the final stage of a close project can, if the motivation is there, be applied to other areas of the business, such as planning, budgeting, and forecasting. Planning and budgeting is an area that—like the financial close—is often criticized for taking too long, costing too much, and often resulting in conflicting results. Many of the lessons from a financial close project, particularly in terms of the application of a similar action plan, can be used to shorten planning and budgeting cycles. It is also possible to create immediate benefits directly out of the steps you take to streamline your financial close.

One such approach relates to the use of integrated planning and consolidation systems. Not only do solutions such as SAP Business Planning and Consolidation offer benefits during the close because actual and plan data exists in the same environment, but the reporting processes, collaboration tools, and validations, which should all form part of a best practice close process, can be used to address common issues in the planning cycle as well. As part of a post-financial close project review process, we encourage you to think of how the lessons you learned within your own organization can be applied in other areas of the business.

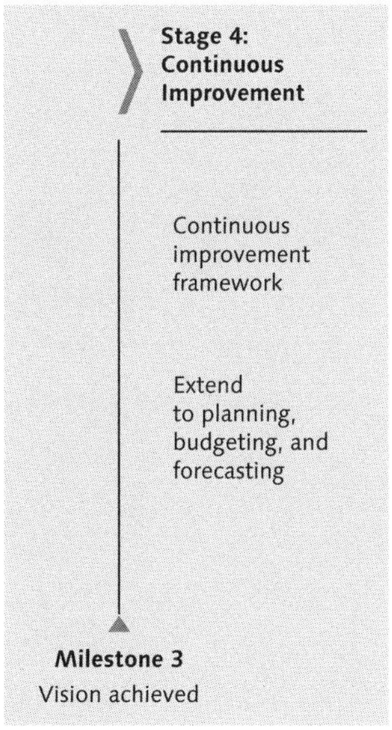

Figure 2.7 Stage 4: Continuous Improvement

2.5 Summary

The four-step action plan we have outlined (see Figure 2.8) is just one example of a number of ways in which a project team can structure a financial close project. There are numerous examples of actions plans out in the market as well. Accordingly, you should select an approach that works for your organization because like much of this, there is no single right or wrong answer. However, the critical message is that the plan needs a structure and needs to be a managed project that starts with benchmarking and sponsorship, maps clear steps and actions to deliver against a target and objective, and prepares a culture of ongoing focus and improvement.

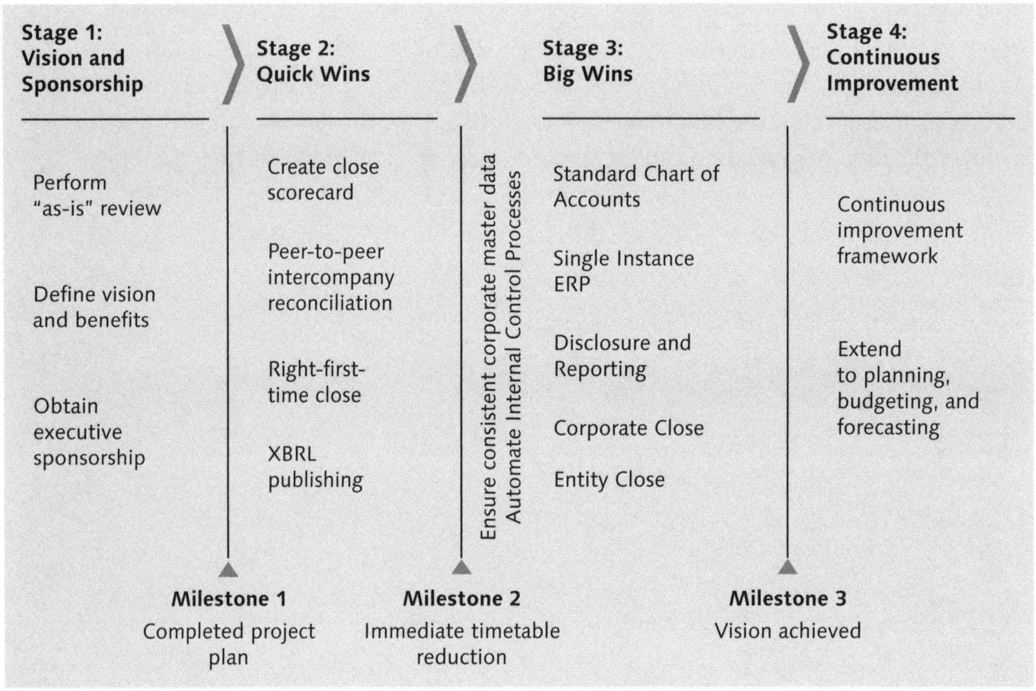

Figure 2.8 Complete Fast-Close Action Plan

As we move through the subsequent chapters in the book, we will look in more detail at the functional processes within the close, including how process, people, and technology changes can address the barriers to a close as outlined in Chapter 1. In particular, we will explain exactly how technology solutions and deliver best practices to address quick wins, such as intercompany reconciliation and close process monitoring, all the way through to the implementation of bigger wins that leverage new consolidation and reporting infrastructures.

"Garbage in, garbage out" is a saying heard often during software implementations. It is meant to convey the fact that no matter how sophisticated a software system is, if you don't load the right data in, you won't get the right data out. In this chapter, we will look at how an enterprise can manage their data.

3 Information Management

Organizations collect data from various sources, make calculations, and then report results. For the purpose of the financial close, the "stuff" in Figure 3.1 and throughout this scenario is financial information.

Figure 3.1 Software in its Purest Form

This chapter discusses how organizations get information "in" and the challenges with managing that data. The "who" within an organization varies depending on how the organization is set up. Most organizations have an IT department and a finance department. Many organizations also have a hybrid department responsible just for the finance systems. More and more as financial software is developed, it is designed to be owned and operated by the business user, not the IT user. The initial implementation involves both IT and finance, but the ongoing maintainance is owned by the finance department. This provides the finance department more autonomy to create the reports and processes to meet their needs without the dependency on IT.

Traditionally, the data required during the financial close resides in multiple heterogeneous source systems and general ledgers distributed throughout the enterprise. The financial close process usually involves combining information from multiple systems. These systems include general ledger systems and subledger systems (such as sales or human resource data). Some organizations have multiple instances of their general ledger system and not always from the same provider. Often when a company has acquisitions, it will acquire legacy technology. As such, information needs to be moved and combined for consolidated financial reporting.

Because the data exists in different formats and systems, finance must depend on IT to aggregate and standardize the data required—a difficult, costly, and time-consuming process that can lead to outdated reporting and analysis. Accessing, mapping, verifying, and loading financial information can present a serious logistical challenge, often requiring manual reentry of data or the use of intermediate text files. These processes are not only labor intensive but can also lead to poor data quality and inaccurate results. And this, in turn, can cause the finance department and its internal customers, such as line-of-business executives, to distrust the information they receive from IT. These challenges are compounded by the fact that CFOs and their teams are under increasing pressure to do the following:

- Deliver accurate, up-to-date information to support the financial closing process—either traditional or "fast close"—and generate reliable reports and analyses.
- Integrate data across multiple applications.
- Cost-effectively meet compliance requirements and deadlines.
- Support internal customers who need data to drive their own business processes and improve planning and decision making.

Organizations require a reliable, transparent, and repeatable financial information management process to maximize productivity, achieve transparency, minimize the cost of compliance, and increase overall confidence in their profitability analysis, business plans, and financial results.

Moving data from one system to another creates many challenges. If not maintained or implemented properly, errors can occur that hinder the financial close and threaten the reliability of reports and data governance. Figure 3.2 outlines many of the challenges faced by the CFO and, in turn, the finance department.

As the role of the CFO evolves to be more strategic, there's an ever-growing need for reliable, transparent, and repeatable quality management for enterprise data involved in everything from master data, performance management reporting, and compliance to strategic business decision making. But managing financial information has proven to be challenging for the majority of organizations.

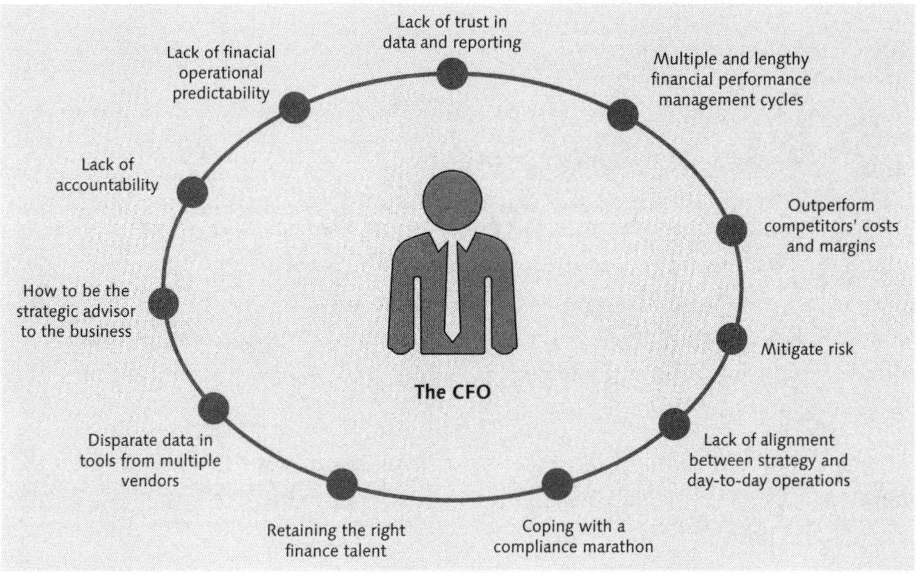

Figure 3.2 The CFO's Challenges

3.1 Defining Data and Information

For the financial close, "information" includes financial data that needs to be collected to create financial reports. The word "data" is extremely broad. Let's break it down into two parts: Master data and transactional data.

- **Master data**
  Master data is the essential data that describes your business and the business entities that your company uses, sells to, or interacts with, such as customers, employees, suppliers and partners, products and services, materials, locations, General Ledger (GL) accounts, and profit centers. Later in this chapter in Section 3.2, we will discuss the SAP Master Data Governance solution.
- **Transactional data**
  Transactional data records the transactions of a business. General ledger and subledger systems record information related to sales, accounts payables, accounts receivables, billing, and so on. Section 3.3 will discuss how SAP BusinessObjects Financial Information Management helps you streamline this process.

Now that we have looked at the diferent types of master data, let's review the intricacies of master data management.

3.2 Master Data Management

In your enterprise, performing accurate reconciliations and group closes in a timely manner is important. You must efficiently support enterprise-wide compliance with such regulatory standards and legal requirements as International Financial Reporting Standards (IFRS), the Sarbanes-Oxley Act, and various Generally Accepted Accounting Principles (GAAP). Your reports to stakeholders must be precise and timely.

To meet your individual requirements , the quality of your financial master data must be high, but to improve its quality, you must involve your stakeholders early in the process of reviewing master data. These goals are within reach when you establish a single source of truth for financial master data. The only question you have to worry about is: how? If your approach to financial master data management is manual or homegrown—perhaps simply a spreadsheet—maintaining consistent data across the enterprise and governing that data is going to be a problem. You more than likely experience serious impediments to good governance, although your staff works hard to create and maintain financial master data manually across several software landscapes and a variety of applications. You have no clear audit trail. Nor do you have a clearly structured change-approval process for your financial master data. What's more, spreadsheet-based and homegrown solutions usually have no process for managing time-dependent versions of the master data. Without an integrated approach to enterprise-wide data maintenance and governance, the return for your efforts will likely be the following:

- Inconsistent financial master data
- Manual reconciliation of data in preparation for month-end, quarterly, and year-end closings
- Uncertainty about the performance of your subsidiaries
- Difficulty complying with industry and government regulations

You are not the only one wrestling with these serious setbacks. They are systemic to corporate accounting performed for a corporate group—comprised of multiple entities—when support for master data governance is lacking. Data inconsistency and expensive manual rework of financial data are the results you can expect. The SAP Master Data Governance application allows you to centrally govern the financial master data used in your business applications by natively integrating with SAP Business Suite.

3.2.1 Management of Financial Master Data in SAP Business Suite

The SAP Master Data Governance application supports financial master data governance for usage in both SAP Business Suite software and non-SAP business applications. The application enables the integration of your corporate financial master data with your subsidiaries' financial master data. It facilitates the centrally governed maintenance of financial master data used in your corporate consolidation chart of accounts, general ledger accounts, cost elements, financial reporting structures, and organizational units—including "group companies," profit centers, and cost centers. The application supports the step-by-step creation of data in a staging area, up to the automatic distribution of validated and approved financial master data to your subsidiaries, and it eases maintenance of financial master data for your subsidiaries. The software can track all changes made to master data through auditable governance processes that comply with the Sarbanes-Oxley Act. In addition, the application provides flexible approval workflows that expedite and provide control over the change-request process. It also supports mandatory approval processes where at least two different people must approve actions. The maintenance process can be set up individually to embrace locally and centrally executed workflow steps such as requests, approvals, or data entry.You can see an example of detail associated with a specific account in Figure 3.3.

The software can enable mappings between consolidation and operational charts of accounts. Using replication methods such as enterprise services and Application Link Enabling (ALE), the software can distribute changes to other applications running throughout your company, including SAP ERP, consolidation applications, and non-SAP software. You can extract master data, import it into SAP NetWeaver Business Warehouse (SAP NetWeaver BW), and upload and download the data to other applications.

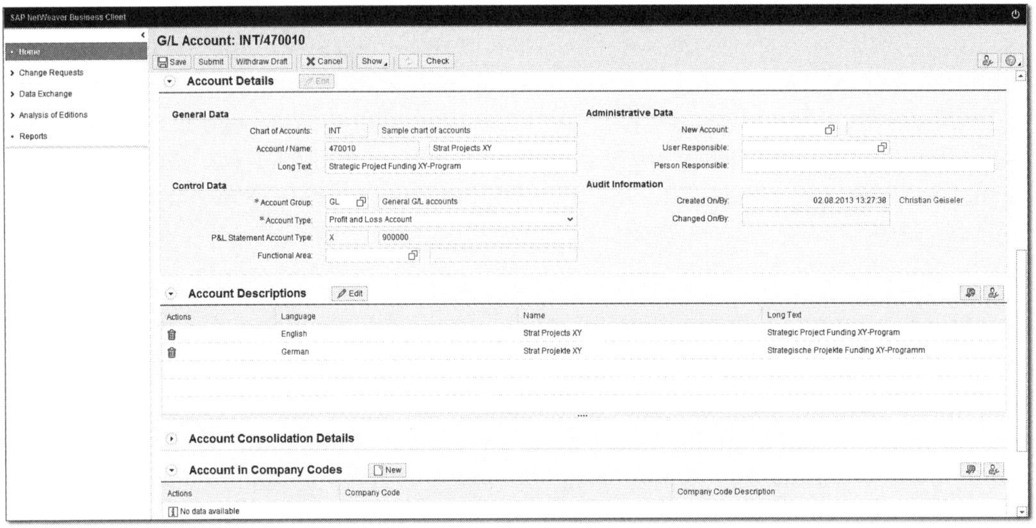

Figure 3.3 Master Data Governance- MDGF Account details

Integrated Financial Master Data Governance

The SAP software offers a number of features that automate the tasks of maintaining and distributing your financial master data, integrating the data more tightly, and increasing data consistency across the enterprise. These features include SAP Business Workflow, email notifications, automated rule validations, and the Data Replication Framework with its configurable replication mechanisms.

Flexible Data Model

The flexible data model supported by SAP Master Data Governance allows you to maintain your financial data centrally. A data model for standard financial objects used in SAP software is included, which can be refined through enhancements you define to meet your organization's specific needs.

Flexible and Robust Data Maintenance

With a user interface (UI) developed in the WebDynpro development environment, SAP Master Data Governance supports a very flexible UI model. You can define your own UI or extend the existing one to meet your business and end-user preferences. With the Business Rules Framework (BRF) tool within the SAP software, you can define business rules and build functions into the software to validate data input. You can set up the appropriate authorizations to enforce security and workflows across your enterprise. You can perform data maintenance on an individual business object or on a range of objects, and maintain business objects within hierarchies. With the ability to view the complete structure of your financial master data, you gain much-needed visibility and can drill down into the detail of any particular object you want to maintain.

Time-Dependent and Period-Dependent Versioning

To manage financial data competently and produce accurate, unambiguous reports, you must be able to version it. You must maintain the chart of accounts for the first quarter and for the second quarter simultaneously without any risk of confusion. SAP Master Data Governance supports versioning, which allows you to achieve transparency of your financial data. It also supports traceability of the data. If your approach to financial master data management is manual or homegrown—perhaps simply a spreadsheet—maintaining consistent data across the enterprise and governing that data is going to be a problem.

3.3 Transactional Data Management

In the previous section, we discussed the management of master data, so now let's delve into transactional data. First we discuss how to extract data from enterprise resource planning systems with SAP Rapid Marts, and then how SAP Financial Information Management can help your business users to manipulate that data so it can be consumed by other Enterprise Performance Management (EPM) solutions.

3.3.1 Extracting Data from ERP Systems with SAP Rapid Marts

ERP applications contain transactional systems with complex data schemas that span multiple functional modules and use thousands of relational tables. Names used for tables and columns in your transactional systems can be cryptic, making it difficult to understand the data. Vendors have proprietary application programming interfaces (APIs) for accessing transactional system security and business logic. Extracting data from these systems can be costly and time-consuming.

SAP Rapid Marts packages provide powerful and flexible data integration content to speed implementation, lower costs, and facilitate compliance. SAP Rapid Marts packages enable you to leverage SAP's domain knowledge, best practices, and prebuilt data models, as well as transformation logic and data extraction expertise for both SAP and non-SAP data sources—including Oracle applications. You also gain complete visibility into data lineage; for example, you can trace data back to its source even when integrating third-party data using connectors—and view transformations and applied rules. As a result, even when data comes from sources outside the SAP software landscape, you can see precisely what has been integrated.

SAP Rapid Marts address the need for fast, low-cost implementation with preconfigured extraction, transformation, and load (ETL) functionality, database schemas, semantic layers, reports, and dashboards.

SAP Rapid Marts packages accelerate access to your company's SAP ERP data and yield a wide range of business and IT benefits. You can realize fast time to value with prepackaged solutions that get you up and running in weeks rather than months. The packages reduce development costs with preconfigured ETL, database models, semantic layers, and reports that help reduce the load on your IT team and speed deployment.

3.3.2 SAP Financial Information Management

So now that you have extracted the data from the ERP system, you need to move the data to your Enterprise Performance Management (EPM) applications. Most businesses still rely on inefficient, manual, and error-prone processes to collect, map, and move data into their EPM software. Companies need to reduce the risk, cost, and effort of collecting, mapping, and loading data from systems running both SAP and non-SAP software directly into and between EPM solutions.

The SAP Financial Information Management application supports and enables an integrated process, giving you robust data collection functionality combined with strong finance controls, data validation, and comprehensive auditability. The result is quality financial data for your EPM applications, models, and reports.

Enabling Everyone to Work with Trusted Data

SAP Financial Information Management enables finance professionals to manage the process of accessing, mapping, and loading information from source systems to EPM solutions. The application combines ease of use with functionality that facilitates full compliance, builds trust in the data, and helps ensure data reliability—from source to report. All of this can be done without IT assistance. It features strong finance controls, data validation functions, and comprehensive auditability, enabling everyone in your organization to work with trusted, up-to-date data.

Simple Deployment and Intuitive Functionality

SAP Financial Information Management is designed for ease of use, enabling business users to set up and use repeatable, automated processes for managing enterprise financial data. Deployment and maintenance are simpler as well; because the software runs in a web browser, there's no need for client installations on employees' PCs. And the application can be easily distributed and maintained for enterprise users. The application makes it easier to access and use data; it shares a common "look and feel" with other SAP EPM solutions and is launched directly from within the applications it supports, including the following (and the chapters they are discussed in):

- SAP Intercompany (Chapter 8)
- SAP Financial Consolidation (Chapter 9)
- SAP Business Planning and Consolidation (Chapter 9)
- SAP Disclosure Management (Chapter 10)

Once deployed, the application provides business users with a familiar environment for managing enterprise financial data, acting as a staging room for all financial data across the enterprise.

Increased Productivity by Simplifying Data Integration

SAP Financial Information Management provides an intuitive environment for business users to define integration mappings and load validated data to a target EPM application. No manual coding is required; using an intuitive, wizard-driven integration interface, you simply select the source and target applications (SAP and non-SAP applications, as shown in the table) from a list. This interface dramatically simplifies and accelerates the mapping and load processes, helping business users work faster and more effectively.

Examples of Application Connectivity

- SAP Business Suite
- SAP NetWeaver BW
- J.D. Edwards software
- Oracle applications
- PeopleSoft software
- Siebel software

Examples of Database Connectivity

- Oracle
- DB2
- Sybase
- Microsoft SQL Server
- Informix
- Teradata
- Netezza

Key mapping activities supported by the software include the following:

- **Simplified mapping**
  Select targets from automatically generated pick lists available in a spreadsheet-like mapping area as seen in Figure 3.4. Options in pick lists are pulled directly from your SAP EPM solutions, and users can see only those options for which they have authorization.
- **Mapping rules for automation**
  Create mapping rules to automate entry patterns, such as wildcards and complex expressions. Rather than having to create and maintain countless individual rules, you can create one rule that applies to a broad set of data. The first row in Figure 3.4 uses the "*" wildcard so all accounts that start with 0004 in the source will map to E1610 as a target.
- **Mapping data reuse**
  Reuse mapping data contained in spreadsheets to simplify the configuration of SAP Financial Information Management. You can copy and paste individual cells, columns, or entire rows or grids directly from Microsoft Excel into mapping tables that the software uses to translate source data into target application data.

- **Multiple target-dimension mapping**
  Map accounts to multiple target dimensions by selecting up to six sources and six targets per mapping. As a result, you can dissect each general ledger account so that data can be mapped in a one-to-one, one to-many, or many-to-one fashion. Figure 3.4 illustrates mapping multiple dimensions.

After you map the data, you can specify a loading option. For example, you can do the following:

- Replace, aggregate, or delete data that has been loaded previously.
- Run any predefined application rules or controls.
- Filter by dimension to specify data for loading to a category (such as a budget or actual), reporting unit, or reporting period.

Improved Accuracy and Integrity

With SAP Financial Information Management, you can improve data accuracy and integrity while reducing risk. Users can launch and load tasks at will and monitor task execution in real time to verify a quick and successful integration, complete with validated results for auditing purposes. In Figure 3.4, you can see the easy-to-use interface. By reducing the need for manual intervention, there is less opportunity for human error to creep into the process (a common problem with other approaches to data integration), which can increase complexity and costs.

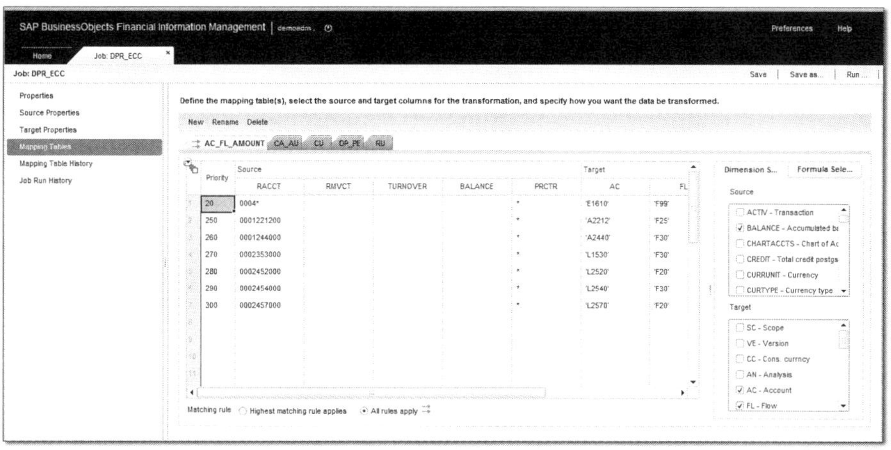

Figure 3.4 SAP Financial Information Manager Mapping Table

Reliable, Repeatable, and Lower-Cost Integration

SAP Financial Information Management supports a standardized process for EPM data integration that enables accurate, consistent, and repeatable information management across the enterprise. The result is easier access to trusted financial information—regardless of the source system or target EPM application. Due to the consistent integration approach the software supports, you can easily reuse and modify any integration process created using the application's wizard-driven environment. Because users can set up new integration links themselves—without the need for costly IT support each and every time they want to set up a new link—you can reduce integration costs substantially. Security is available so that you can define which users have the rights to create new mappings or to execute them. There is little or no requirement for writing complex integration scripts, as is the case with many integration applications, so there's little need for specialist coding skills and costly IT support. Additionally, because the software leverages SAP EPM solutions as the basis for powerful functionality for ETL data, you can reduce your IT integration systems landscape and total cost of ownership (TCO). For example, depending on what you want to integrate, you can use one integration system rather than multiple solutions. This can lead to a reduction in initial system costs, maintenance costs, and training costs because you no longer need to maintain skills in multiple systems. By itself, SAP Financial Information Management equips you to handle most integration requirements. By deploying this application and consolidating your integration systems to eliminate redundant functionality, you can potentially save software and maintenance costs.

Secure Access and Controls

From a user perspective, access to data, reports, and activities is controlled by role-based permissions. Your users see only what they should see, and their activities are restricted to those that support their role. In addition to working in a secure environment, users are directed to their activities from the point at which they enter the system. As a result, they do not waste time on areas or activities that are not relevant to their role.

Secure, Transparent Processes That Lower Costs

SAP Financial Information Management enables process transparency, resulting in greater clarity and confidence in integrated data, increased data accuracy, and faster auditing time frames—all while lowering compliance costs. As data is mapped, the software automatically creates an easily accessible audit trail for every data move. You can capture full mapping details, including the "from" and "to" values with time stamps for all affected dimensions. In addition, the audit trail tracks all details of the launch and load task, including task name, start and end time stamps, user, status, and detailed task feedback. Users can see their own audit trails, according to their role-based permissions, complete with mapping and load histories. Figure 3.5 shows a job log history in Financial Information Management. Audit users can see the audit history of all users. But because the audit trail history contains sensitive information, IT users, such as administrators, may not be able to view audit trails. SAP customers find that the increased process transparency enabled by SAP Financial Information Management—combined with the ability to accelerate audit time frames—helps build trust and confidence in financial data and EPM reporting generated by all integrated applications. At the same time, the software facilitates a smooth compliance process while lowering associated costs.

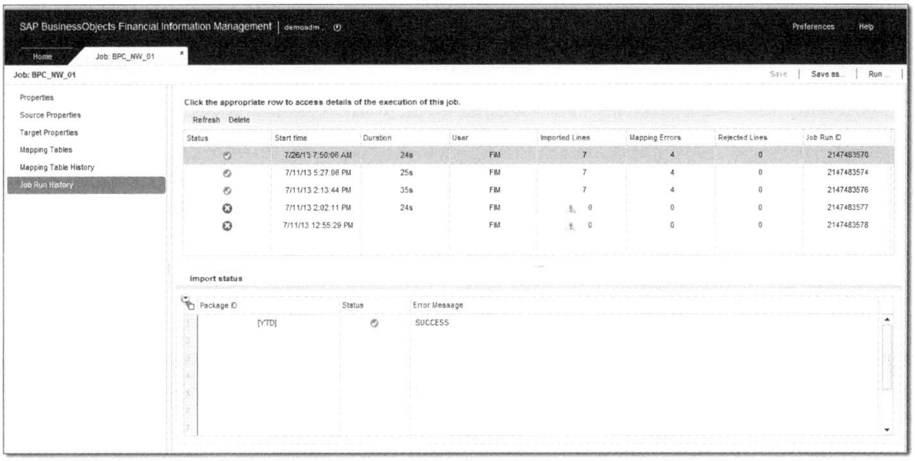

Figure 3.5 Information Management Job Run History

Greater Insights Enabled by Drill-to-Origin Functionality

After data from source systems is fed into one of your SAP EPM solutions, you can click any consolidated number to drill back to the source data. SAP Financial Information Management maintains a copy of actual source data. This functionality, which is enabled directly within SAP EPM solutions, is available through both web and desktop clients. As a result, you can view the breakdown of data at a more detailed level, such as the subaccount level, than is stored in the SAP EPM solution. You can also trace an aggregate amount across all contributing loading tasks. For example, after doing multiple loads via aggregation, you can access the contributing numbers because they are stored individually in the repository within SAP Financial Information Management. If you run a consolidation, you can trace from the consolidated number back to the source contributing numbers.

Data Integrity That Reduces Risk and Builds Trust

SAP Financial Information Management performs comprehensive validations before data is loaded to help ensure that error-prone financial data is loaded correctly the first time. The software automatically detects invalid mappings and missing dimensions and performs any additional validations that you define. During actual loading, the integrated, target SAP EPM solution also performs data validation activities, such as the following:

- SAP Financial Consolidation performs intelligent checks and applies filters and automated rules. The application also facilitates compliance with your centrally defined reporting framework. See Chapter 9 for more detail.
- SAP Business Planning and Consolidation performs validation activities related to dimension members, access security for dimension members and tasks, work-state checks, audit data updates, and more. See Chapter 9 for more detail.

Integration with SAP and Non-SAP Data Sources

SAP Financial Information Management can support the connectivity needs of large multinational businesses with thousands of reporting entities—each with data scattered across dozens of different source systems—and can provide a full audit trail for each. SAP Financial Information Management comes with (and fully integrates with) SAP BusinessObjects Data Integrator software, a robust data integration tool. You can integrate directly with heterogeneous application and database sources, such as your general ledger, and map data contained within them directly to your application. Because you no longer need to use intermediate flat files or manually rekey data to "move" data, the software saves time, reduces integration costs, and helps reduce the potential for human error. SAP Financial Information Management also supports best-practice implementations by leveraging predefined templates for integration and SAP Rapid Marts packages.

3.4 Summary

Financial information management is the glue that holds the financial closing process together. Both master data and transactional data are key building blocks. Obtaining solutions for your organization to gain better control, transparency, and automation to the information management process will save your organization both time and money and instill confidence to all that the information they are reporting is correct.

In the following chapters, you will go beyond the "put stuff in" part of information management as discussed as the beginning of this chapter, to the "doing stuff" and "getting stuff out" parts.

Throughout a period, financial postings are made to the General Ledger. To ensure accurate financial statements, you need to carry out period-end closing activities in the Finance module to ensure the correct valuation of the balance sheet and P&L statement for reporting and tax purposes for a legal entity.This chapter will explore the General Ledger and Subledger Close.

4 The General Ledger and Subledger Close

Within SAP, two modules allow you to manage your financial transactions. The Financial (FI) module encompasses General Ledger transactions, as well as subledger accounting to manage additional details, including accounts payable, accounts receivable, and fixed assets. Financial statements, including the balance sheet, P&L (profit and loss) statement, and cash flow statement are created from within FI. In parallel, the Controlling (CO) module provides you with the ability to perform management accounting, which enables you to manage your business. Both modules are at the heart of the SAP ERP system.

In this chapter, we look at the financial close processes that are required for FI. Keep in mind that both the FI and CO processes are necessary for the financial close. FI within SAP ERP allows you to manage General Ledger accounts and journal entries, as well as subledger accounting. You can also manage balance sheet valuation for items such as inventory to ensure correct valuation of products, and consistent financial statements as part of the financial close.

Several SAP Rapid deployment solutions (RDS) include both FI and CO processes; for examples, refer to the "Rapid Deployment Solutions for Finance" box in this chapter. For further detail on the CO activities required, please refer to Chapter 5.

4.1 SAP ERP Financials Concepts

Let's first look at the organizational elements that are available to you to support your various finance processes and reporting needs, and how the SAP ERP Financials module is closely integrated with the operational capabilities within SAP ERP. We review the organizational hierarchy within SAP ERP and then look at the document principle. This section closes with a customer story that demonstrates how these organizational elements can inform and support various finance processes.

4.1.1 The Organizational Hierarchy

At the end of a period, you need to ensure that you have a compliant closing process for each legal entity. A legal entity is the smallest organizational unit for which financial statements are legally required for tax and disclosure purposes. Most large organizations have many legal entities; within SAP ERP Financials, the company code represents the legal entity.

Each company code is linked to a chart of accounts, which defines all of the General Ledger accounts available for posting. The same chart of accounts can be used for multiple company codes; if this is the case, then multiple company codes can be assigned to the same controlling area, as shown in Figure 4.1. The controlling area is the link between the FI and CO modules; allocations can be made between company codes in management accounting as long as the company codes are linked to the same controlling area.

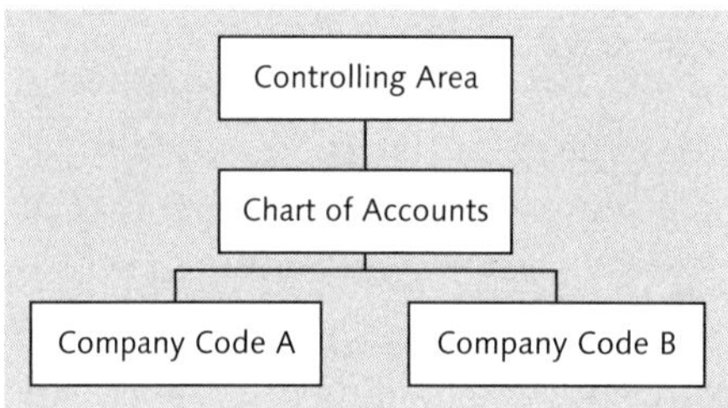

Figure 4.1 Multiple Company Codes Assigned to the Same Chart of Accounts and the Same Controlling Area

You may be tempted to define the company code at a different level than the legal entity, so that you can obtain financial statements. For that purpose, other organizational elements and fields are available that allow you to both maintain your complete financial statements at the company code level and obtain financial information across business units or at lower organizational levels; a common example is the requirement for financial statements at a plant level. For additional details, see the following "Managing Financial Results for Different Levels of the Organization" box.

Managing Financial Results for Different Levels of the Organization

While the company code represents a legal entity, you may want to generate financial statements for either larger or smaller organizational units. For example, your organization may have chosen to keep a legal entity of an acquired company separate for tax purposes, but you want to generate financial statements across company codes for a business unit or product line. Alternately, you may want to look at the financial results of smaller units within a company code. The following list describes these additional fields that are available to you to facilitate these types of reporting requirements:

- **Segments**
  If you are using the new SAP General Ledger (please refer to "The Classic and the New SAP General Ledger" box in Section 4.2.4), you can use segments, which are commonly used to support reporting by company divisions or geographies, which is a requirement for several international reporting standards. To use segments, you must also use profit centers.
- **Profit centers**
  Profit centers allow you to manage your business across company codes, or at lower levels of detail, for revenues, costs, payables and liabilities. You can also use profit center hierarchies for summary-level reporting. Beginning with SAP ERP 5.0, you can assign profit centers to a segment to support additional reporting requirements. For additional information about profit centers, see Chapter 5, Section 5.7.
- **Business areas**
  Both balance sheet (materials, receivables and payables, fixed assets) and P&L statement items can be assigned to business areas directly. However, you may need to execute additional processes; for example, when generating an invoice where different line items are assigned to different business areas, no business areas are assigned to the AR entry, so you must post a transfer to correctly assign the business area. Also, bank postings, equity, and taxes cannot be directly assigned, so business areas cannot be used for legal reporting.
- **Functional areas**
  Functional areas are designed to provide details related to the cost of sales, and they allow you to categorize operating expenses, such as production, sales, research and development, and administrative costs. Functional areas can be entered in a journal entry, or they can be derived from the master data of controlling objects; for more information about controlling objects, see Chapter 5.

4.1.2 The Document Principle

A document is created by the system to record every transactional activity that occurs within SAP ERP; this is true both in logistics and accounting. Examples of documents are sales orders, invoices, goods movements (into or out of inventory), and journal entries.

As part of the integrated nature of SAP ERP, when a transaction is posted in logistics—including in the Sales and Distribution (SD), Materials Management (MM), and Production Planning (PP) modules—a corresponding entry is automatically made to FI; for this reason, the financial account balances do not lag behind operations processes, and no reentry of financial journal entries is required. The appropriate accounts are configured and are typically determined from the master data in the transaction, including the master records for materials, customers, vendors, and assets. In addition, from any of these documents, for example a sales order, all subsequent documents can be displayed, such as a goods issue, invoice, and journal entry, as shown in Figure 4.2. Also, if there are controlling objects from the CO module that are associated with the posting, for example, a cost center or profit center, an additional CO document is created for each controlling object.

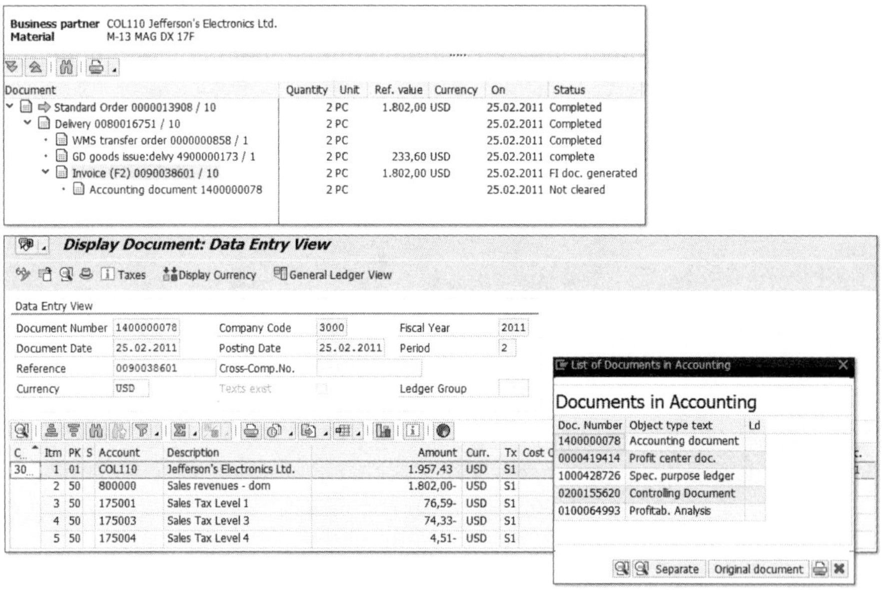

Figure 4.2 Document Flow from the Sales Order

Let's look at an example of the benefits that one customer, Cargojet Income Fund, achieved with the tight integration between SAP ERP Financials and the logistics modules of SAP ERP.

4.1.3 Customer Story: Cargojet Income Fund Soars to New Heights with Greater Financial Visibility

Founded in 2002 with a commitment to service and on-time reliability, Cargojet Income Fund grew rapidly to become Canada's leading express air cargo service, carrying more than 750,000 pounds of payload every night. But growth soon outpaced the capabilities of the company's legacy business systems, and it became increasingly difficult to access timely financial information. As a result, the airline decided to help clear the runway for future growth by implementing the SAP ERP Financials solution.

An analysis by the SAP Value Engineering group helped quantify the specific business benefits that the company could expect from the new SAP solution and provided benchmarks for Cargojet and its implementation partner, IDS Scheer Canada, to aim for. Their commitment and teamwork paid off with a rapid rollout of financial software to support General Ledger, controlling, accounts payable, and accounts receivable that was completed on time and within budget.

Previously, Cargojet relied heavily on spreadsheets to report and analyze business data, but greater automation now provides better visibility and understanding of the company's financial information with decision makers able to drill down through the latest data in any number of ways that make it easier to compare budgets against actuals and analyze performance across different periods. Cargojet has also established cost centers within the company that enable individual department leaders to view and manage their expenses, particularly the variable costs that are vitally important to the airline's financial success.

Cargojet is also seeing greater efficiency and productivity in its finance organization with the team delivering a 50% reduction in financial closing times while the time required to create new reports has been slashed by up to 60%. The effort for internal and external audits has also been reduced, helping to lower audit costs by an estimated 10% to 15%. While the value engineering study makes it easier to assess the return on investment, Cargojet thinks these accomplishments are just the beginning as it considers expanding its SAP software landscape in areas such as HR, maintenance, and sales.

User Interfaces

In addition to the SAP GUI and the SAP NetWeaver Portal, the SAP NetWeaver Business Client is a new user interface that provides a unified environment to harmonize access to various business applications. You can customize which information is displayed and collapsed, and you can combine both SAP and non-SAP information on the same page, as shown in Figure 4.3. This allows you to monitor external information, such as stock prices of your own and competitive companies.

Figure 4.3 Customer Master Data and Transactional Overviews Combined with External Web Information

One available option within the SAP NetWeaver Business Client is the use of role-based side panels for core SAP ERP transactions. Side panels provide an easy-to-navigate menu that give you access to all tasks that are relevant to your role. In addition, they enable context-sensitive displays of additional information about an application, such as business graphics that illustrate data from a table or the application which is shown in seperate tabs (see Figure 4.4).

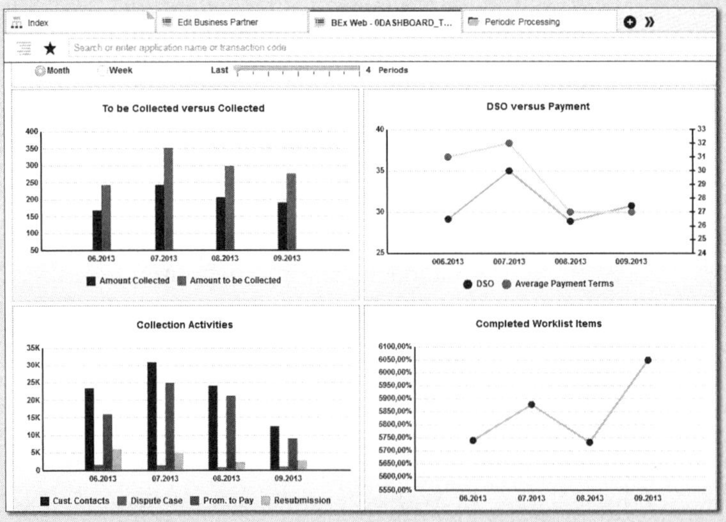

Figure 4.4 Context-Sensitive Business Information is Available Using Tabs.

This capability is useful leading up to the financial close; for example, a cost center manager can keep an eye on the departmental spend, and react to exceptions prior to the closing activities.

Now that we have reviewed some of the financial concepts that guide General Ledger and subledger processes, let's walk through the different aspects of the financial close of your legal entity, beginning with the core General Ledger application.

4.2 The General Ledger Close

General Ledger Accounting (FI-GL) allows you to create your chart of accounts, the General Ledger master records that are required for you to understand the financial health of your legal entity, and the financial statements for your organization.

The key master data record is the General Ledger account. First, you define the type of account, for example, whether it is a balance sheet or P&L account. You can decide whether manual posting is allowed on a particular account or whether posting is only done using automated processes, for example, from the logistics process described in Section 4.1.2. You can determine which fields are relevant for posting journal entries to the account; for example, for expense accounts, you can determine that certain accounts are used for orders and projects but not cost centers. In addition, you need to define whether an account is managed as an open item account, meaning that a clearing process must take place for each line item posted to the account; examples include accounts for bank postings, receivables and payables.

In this section, we look at the financial close processes that you need to carry out for the core General Ledger functions: posting periods, period-end journal entries, foreign currency valuations, and year-end close activities.

4.2.1 Posting Periods

In configuration, you set up the periods when you define your fiscal year. A period is usually a month. As part of the financial close, you need to open the next period to allow financial postings. In addition, you need to close the current period for posting, which prevents any additional financial entries from being made to a prior period. If you expect to make accrual entries in the prior period as part of your closing process, you may want to have both the prior period and the new, or current, period open simultaneously for a brief amount of time. Because posting periods can be opened and closed for account types and General Ledger account ranges, you can choose to close all accounts for posting in a prior period with the exception of those manual accrual accounts.

You can also define up to four special periods, which may also be open simultaneously. These special periods are typically used for year-end closing to create supplementary financial statements.

4.2.2 Period-End Journal Entries

There are many examples of journal entries that must be made during the financial close, such as accruals for interest or taxes, recurring expenses for rental costs, and deferrals of expenses for insurance premiums to allocate the cost to all periods even though the payment is made up front. These posting entries are made directly in the General Ledger, not through the integrated logistics processes.

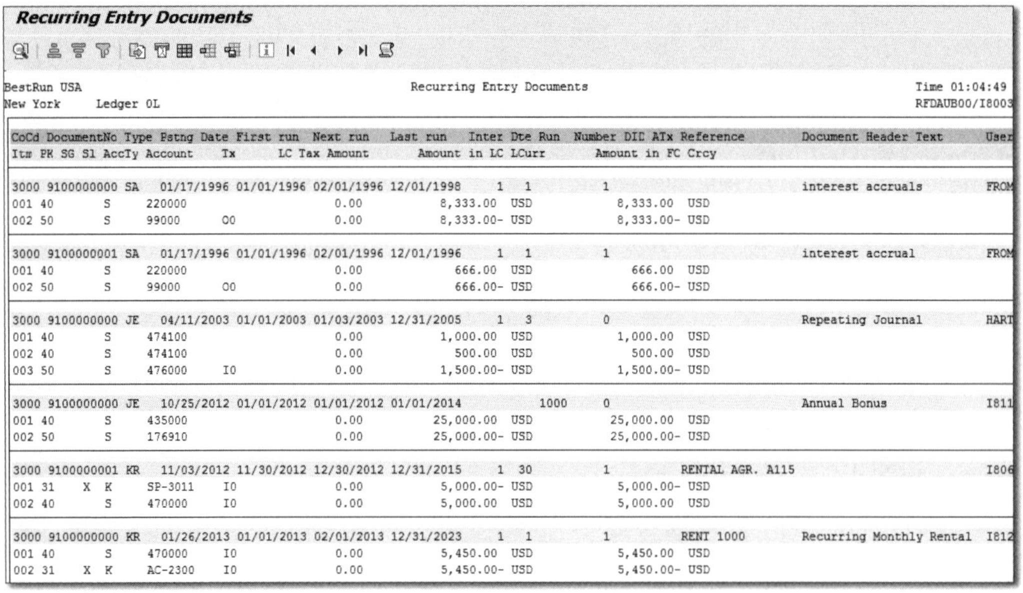

```
Recurring Entry Documents

BestRun USA                          Recurring Entry Documents                                  Time 01:04:49
New York     Ledger 0L                                                                          RFDAUB00/I8003

CoCd DocumentNo Type Pstng Date First run  Next run   Last run   Inter Dte Run  Number DIC ATx Reference       Document Header Text      User
Itm PK SG Sl AccTy Account    Tx       LC Tax Amount      Amount in LC LCurr      Amount in FC Crcy

3000 9100000000 SA   01/17/1996 01/01/1996 02/01/1996 12/01/1998     1   1           1                         interest accruals         FROM
001 40        S     220000                   0.00          8,333.00  USD          8,333.00  USD
002 50        S     99000      00            0.00          8,333.00- USD          8,333.00- USD

3000 9100000001 SA   01/17/1996 01/01/1996 02/01/1996 12/01/1996     1   1           1                         interest accrual          FROM
001 40        S     220000                   0.00            666.00  USD            666.00  USD
002 50        S     99000      00            0.00            666.00- USD            666.00- USD

3000 9100000000 JE   04/11/2003 01/01/2003 01/03/2003 12/31/2005     1   3           0                         Repeating Journal         HART
001 40        S     474100                   0.00          1,000.00  USD          1,000.00  USD
002 40        S     474100                   0.00            500.00  USD            500.00  USD
003 50        S     476000     I0            0.00          1,500.00- USD          1,500.00- USD

3000 9100000000 JE   10/25/2012 01/01/2012 01/01/2012 01/01/2014           1000      0                         Annual Bonus              I811
001 40        S     435000                   0.00         25,000.00  USD         25,000.00  USD
002 50        S     176910                   0.00         25,000.00- USD         25,000.00- USD

3000 9100000001 KR   11/03/2012 11/30/2012 12/30/2012 12/31/2015     1  30           1        RENTAL AGR. A115                           I806
001 31     X  K     SP-3011    I0            0.00          5,000.00- USD          5,000.00- USD
002 40        S     470000     I0            0.00          5,000.00  USD          5,000.00  USD

3000 9100000000 KR   01/26/2013 01/01/2013 02/01/2013 12/31/2023     1   1           1        RENT 1000        Recurring Monthly Rental  I812
001 40        S     470000     I0            0.00          5,450.00  USD          5,450.00  USD
002 31     X  K     AC-2300    I0            0.00          5,450.00- USD          5,450.00- USD
```

Figure 4.5 Automating Financial Entry Posting via Template

Different methods are available for posting these journal entries:

- **Manual entry**
  You can enter the accounting entry manually, as long as the General Ledger account has been set up to allow direct postings.
- **Templates for recurring entries**
  For transactions that are carried out repeatedly, you can set each up in a template, as shown in Figure 4.5, which you then run during the financial close.
- **Accrual engine**
  As part of the Financials Extension (EA-FIN), you can use the accrual engine to calculate and post accruals automatically. A common scenario is the calculation of revenue recognition values, for example, when the revenue of a sale should be distributed over the life of a contract.

4.2.3 Foreign Currency Valuation

During the General Ledger close, if you need to create financial statements in multiple currencies, you must perform foreign currency valuation. You may have open items that need to be revalued with the month-end exchange rate to ensure that balances are correct. Examples include vendor invoices, customer invoices, and General Ledger open item accounts. The system then also makes postings to unrealized gain and unrealized loss accounts.

In addition, you may be managing some of your General Ledger accounts in a foreign currency, most commonly balance sheet accounts. For gains and losses in the valuation based on the exchange rate, the system makes postings to expense and revenue accounts to reflect exchange rate differences.

Reorganizations

There may be business situations in which you have reorganized your company, for example, when introducing new product lines or restructuring business units. Such reorganization should be performed after a financial close so that you can start fresh in the new period. You may also have simply created new accounts or cost centers that you need to accommodate in your processes.

Many programs are available within SAP ERP Financials that help you carry out reorganizations. Examples include reorganizing the segments in the new SAP General Ledger, changing credit limits due to new policies, and reorganizing profit and cost centers due to a new organizational structure. The reorganization program also makes adjusting entries to the General Ledger where necessary.

4.2.4 The Year-End Close

During the year-end close, some additional activities take place. You may have chosen to create additional special posting periods to manage the year-end close, as discussed in Section 4.2.1.

In addition, you need to run the program to carry forward the balances to the new fiscal year, including the balances for balance sheet accounts, and a posting to the retained earnings account for the P&L balances.

Finally, year-end is the best opportunity to implement business reorganizations, as described in the "Reorganizations" box earlier.

The Classic and the New SAP General Ledger

The General Ledger has always been the cornerstone of the FI module. With the release of SAP ERP 5.0, the new SAP General Ledger was introduced, which includes the following features that help accelerate the financial close:

- **Parallel financial reporting through parallel ledgers**
  With the new SAP General Ledger, you can create multiple ledgers directly in the FI module, which allows you to create a ledger for various accounting principles, such as the International Financial Reporting Standard (IFRS) and various country-specific Generally Accepted Accounting Principles (GAAP) regulations. Also, standard reporting is available for all ledgers in the new SAP General Ledger. This effectively eliminates the need for special purpose ledgers (FI-SL) to handle parallel valuations, which also required creation of custom reports for its ledgers.
- **Balanced books by any dimension**
  The new SAP General Ledger enforces balanced books not only by company code but also by profit center, segment, and business area through a document splitting feature, which creates the appropriate balanced line items for these objects. This occurs when postings are made across the organizational hierarchy, for example cross-company code postings and cross-functional area postings. The classic General Ledger did not do this, as discussed in the "Managing Financial Results for Different Levels of the Organization" box.
- **Integration between financial and managerial accounting**
  Many fields in the Controlling (CO) module are also available in the new SAP General Ledger. In addition, for processes such as cost center assessments, described in Chapter 5, Section 5.2.6, which are only posted in the CO module, an FI document is now created to ensure that time-consuming reconciliations are no longer necessary.
- **Easier inclusion of customer-defined fields**
  If you define new fields for your organization, for example, based on industry requirements, these can be easily picked up by the standard reporting in the new SAP General Ledger.

Let's look at the story of one customer, the Automotive Group of Continental AG, which migrated from the classic General Ledger to the new SAP General Ledger.

4.2.5 Customer Story: Continental's Smooth Transition with the SAP General Ledger Migration Service

The Automotive Group of Continental AG with its three divisions, Chassis & Safety, Powertrain, and Interior, is present in more than 170 locations worldwide. Acquisitions resulted in a heterogeneous IT environment, and the company set about harmonizing platforms, including the financial accounting and controlling processes, by moving to the latest version of the SAP General Ledger application.

Previously, individual departments within the Automotive Group had to juggle various versions of the SAP General Ledger solution, which both hindered timely reporting and made assigning costs and revenues between different profit centers very difficult. What's more, different departments were using different terminology to refer to similar or even identical processes. To address these issues, the company used the SAP General Ledger Migration Service delivered by the SAP Active Global Support (AGS) organization to migrate data from 25 software systems and 34 clients to the latest version of SAP General Ledger.

The project was carried out within an extremely tight time frame of just 6 months and with minimal disruption to business processes. This is particularly important in the automotive sector because component suppliers' and customers' value chains are precisely aligned for just-in-time delivery, so a standstill at a Continental plant would have also stopped multiple OEM production lines.

The latest version of SAP General Ledger has replaced the multitude of ledgers previously in use at the Automotive Group, and today 360 employees at multiple sites across the globe use a single version of the software. The standardized framework allows staff to assign costs and revenues to specific departments, which greatly aids reporting, and the company is one step closer to realizing its vision of creating a standardized, integrated financial accounting and controlling environment. However, Continental is not there yet. The company acknowledges that its new General Ledger is just the starting point, and it also needs to standardize other core financial processes such as planning and budgeting, profit-center planning, and profitability analysis. Meanwhile, Automotive IT is looking into ordering further services from AGS, including implementing the SAP Financial Closing cockpit. See Chapter 6 for more detail on SAP Financial Closing cockpit.

Now let's look at the close process for the Accounts Payable and Accounts Receivable modules.

4.3 The Accounts Payable and Accounts Receivable Close

Both the Accounts Receivable (FI-AR) and Accounts Payable (FI-AP) modules have very similar processes for the financial close. Because these General Ledger accounts are managed as subledger accounts, the reconciliation is done using customer numbers for AR and vendor numbers for AP. The financial close activities are very similar.

AR and AP accounts are typically managed as open item accounts. Each line item that is posted to the account must be cleared, or offset, by another posting in the same account, usually for customer and vendor invoices. For example, the expected receivables for a customer must be offset by the actual customer payment. If these are not balanced, based on an underpayment, you need to take action, either by collecting the remaining amount of by writing it off.

The Accounts Payable (FI-AP) module is closely integrated with the procurement (MM-PUR) module. When a vendor invoice is posted, the AP subledger accounts are automatically updated. The organizational hierarchy relevant for the procurement module is primarily the procurement organization that is linked to the company code.

The Accounts Receivable (FI-AR) module is closely integrated with the SD module. When a customer invoice is posted, the AR subledger accounts are automatically updated. The organizational hierarchy relevant for the SD module is primarily the sales area within a company code; the sales area is a combination of the sales organization, distribution channel, and division that allows you to define your sales structure.

Within AP and AR, many of the processes discussed in Section 4.2 are also relevant, such as recurring entries and foreign currency valuation. In addition, the reconciliation of accounts, as well as postings to correctly reflect the valuation of your receivables and payables, must be carried out.

4.3.1 Reconciliation of Payables and Receivables Accounts

As part of the period close, you need to ensure that your financial documents are properly reconciled. Document reconciliation allows you to ensure that postings across company codes are correct and look at timing differences of postings. If you do find inconsistencies, these are corrected either through the automatic settings of the program or by using manual journal entries. The reconciliation program uses the Special Purpose Ledger (FI-SL). Alternately, a new intercompany reconciliation capability, leveraging SAP HANA, accelerates the reconciliation process and does not require the Special Purpose Ledger, and instead works with the original documents posted in the FI module.

4.3.2 Valuation of Payables and Receivables Accounts

To ensure that you have the correct balances of your payables and receivables, you can run several programs to help you ensure this correct valuation. These postings may include the following:

- **Open item clearing**
  For both payables and receivables, while most organizations run this program on an ongoing basis, you should ensure that you have cleared all open items prior to sending any balance confirmations to your vendors and customers.
- **Interest calculation**
  For your receivables, you can calculate interest either on the balance of the receivables for a customer or on the interest in arrears of overdue items only.
- **Balance confirmations**
  For your payables and receivables, during the close, you evaluate the outstanding payables for your vendors and customers, and identify any discrepancies between your organization's records and the records of these business partners. You may request your vendors and customers to respond to you, or you can send a notification with the request to contact you only if the vendor or customer disagrees with your balance statement.
- **Reserve for bad debt**
  For your receivables, this program applies a percentage against open receivables and posts these to the General Ledger to adjust the expected receivables; this is also referred to as provisions for doubtful receivables. Different countries have their own rules as to when an open receivable can be classified this way.

In addition to the period-end processes, an additional step at year-end is to carry forward the balances of both AR and AP accounts, as shown in Figure 4.6.

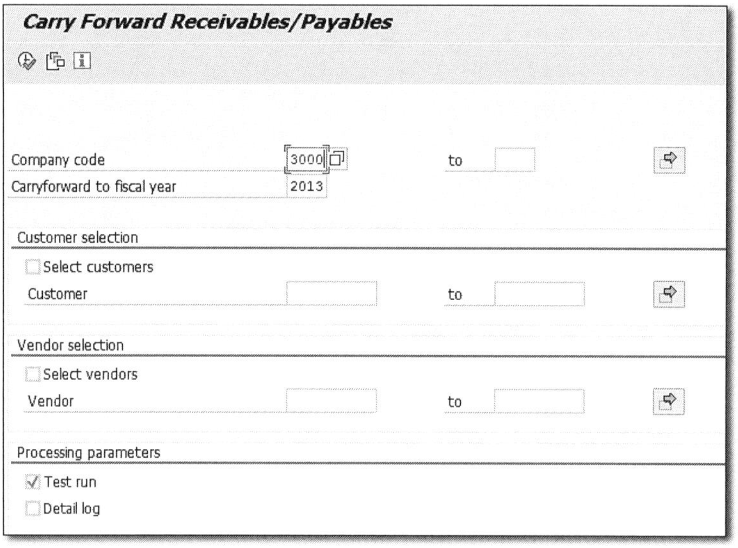

Figure 4.6 Carrying Forward Receivables and Payables Balances at Year-End

4.3.3 Collections and Dispute Management

Although there is no requirement to run dunning processes at period end, it is common for companies to use the financial close as an opportunity to send reminders to customers for outstanding payments, which can be scheduled to run automatically based on the parameters that you define.

In addition, the extended Receivables Management capabilities allow you to manage credit, collections, and dispute cases; now known as Receivables Management, these modules were formerly known as SAP Financial Supply Chain Management (FIN-FSCM). Although these processes can be executed throughout the month, your company may want to ensure that outstanding collections and dispute items are dealt with at the period close. On the collections side, you can create work lists, which are used by the finance team to contact customers who have outstanding receivables. On the dispute management side, you can automatically create dispute cases during the close, based on open receivable items or based on discrepancies that arise during the processing of incoming payments.

4.3.4 Travel Management

The SAP Travel Management application (FI-TV) allows you to manage the entire trip lifecycle, from pre-trip approval to online booking, expense reporting, and reimbursement. You can consider the payment of travel expenses to employees as a special case of the AP process; from the expense report, you execute posting runs that transfer the approved expenses to accounting. Many companies schedule these posting runs on a weekly basis. While there are no specific period-end processes required, you may have internal procedures to ensure that outstanding travel expenses are reimbursed before closing a period, meaning that you can schedule an additional posting run for the end of the period to reduce the outstanding liabilities for travel expenses. You can also configure a workflow that reminds employees to submit outstanding expense reports prior to the period close. Next, we take a look at the financial close for your fixed assets.

4.4 Asset Accounting Close

The Asset Accounting (FI-AA) module allows you to manage your fixed assets such as buildings and equipment. The main organizational element for a company code is the chart of depreciation, which contains the types of depreciation that needs to be posted for fixed assets, including book deprecation, tax depreciation, and group depreciation, and the rules that govern the calculation of each type of depreciation. The primary activities for the financial close are the posting of depreciation and the capitalization of costs incurred for an asset under construction.

4.4.1 Posting Depreciation

Within asset management, every asset master record is created as part of an asset class, for example, production machines, buildings, real estate, and computers. For each asset class, you can define different default depreciation parameters, including the useful life of an asset and the type of depreciation, for example, straight-line depreciation, unit-of-production depreciation, sum-of-year method, and double-declining balance. Based on the depreciation method, you may smooth out the depreciation of the asset evenly over the course of its useful life, or you may have a more aggressive depreciation schedule where you depreciate more of the asset value at the beginning of its useful life. You can run planned depreciation at the end of a period; if you have skipped a posting run, you can post unplanned depreciation, which posts the depreciation value for all skipped periods as well as the current period. A report of the depreciation values for the depreciation run, as well as the cumulative depreciation for an asset, is available, as shown in Figure 4.7.

Depreciation Posting Run for company code 3000

Asset	SNo.	Acct.det	BusA	Cost Ctr	Real Estate Key	Profit Ctr	Name	Ref. Document	Description	Σ Plan.Amt	Σ Amt Posted	Σ Amount TBP	Σ Cumul.Amt	Crcy
1113	0	10000	1000	4230		3010	Assembly Building, New York Plant	17	Ordinary deprec.	66,181.70-	26,575.00-	5,314.00-	31,889.00-	USD
1153	0		2000				Equipment			80.00-	21.00-	9.00-	30.00-	USD
1116	0			4290		3300	Production Building, Los Angeles Plant			21,260.00-	8,858.00-	1,772.00-	10,630.00-	USD
1134	0			4290		3300	Elevator			2,120.00-	884.00-	176.00-	1,060.00-	USD
1149	0			4290		3300	Elevator			4,167.00-	1,250.00-	417.00-	1,667.00-	USD
1150	0			4290		3300	Equipment			3,969.00-	1,191.00-	397.00-	1,588.00-	USD
1152	0			4290		3300	Equipment			500.00-	209.00-	41.00-	250.00-	USD
1155	0			4290		3300	Elevator			3,959.00-	1,042.00-	417.00-	1,459.00-	USD
1179	0			4290		3300	Elevator			28.00-	0.00	3.00-	3.00-	USD
1180	0			4290		3300	Elevador			30.00-	0.00	3.00-	3.00-	USD
1181	0			4290		3300	Elevador			325.00-	0.00	25.00-	25.00-	USD
1112	0		3000	4200		3000	Production Building 1, New York Plant			20.00-	9.00-	1.00-	10.00-	USD
1130	0			4200		3000	Production building			795.00-	332.00-	66.00-	398.00-	USD
1124	0			4215		3005	Production Building 2, New York Plant			30,000.00-	12,500.00-	2,500.00-	15,000.00-	USD
1117	0		4000	3120		3100	Plant I - Warehouse Central Street			9,692.00-	4,039.00-	807.00-	4,846.00-	USD
1114	0			4240		3100	Production Building, Chicago Plant			42,519.00-	17,717.00-	3,543.00-	21,260.00-	USD
1126	0		6000	4258		3070	Production Building 2, Chicago Plant			340,000.00-	141,667.00-	28,333.00-	170,000.00-	USD
1115	0		7000	4275		3500	Production Building, Atlanta Plant			51,023.00-	21,260.00-	4,252.00-	25,512.00-	USD
1129	0			4275		3500	Production building			4,495.00-	1,873.00-	375.00-	2,248.00-	USD
1164	0			2-1001		3402	Building asset Internal SAP			1.00-	0.00	1.00-	1.00-	USD
1133	0		9100	9130		9130	Building: 1435 Parkway Hall			287,107.00-	119,628.00-	23,925.00-	143,553.00-	USD
1135	0				BE 3000/999	9110	Office Center			220,000.00-	91,667.00-	18,333.00-	110,000.00-	USD

Figure 4.7 Report of Depreciation Values for Fixed Assets

The depreciation value can also be posted to management accounting, such as a cost center or order, which is often captured as overhead. For more information about cost centers, see Chapter 5, Section 5.2, and for more information about internal orders, see Section 5.3.

4.4.2 Assets Under Construction

The Investment Management (IM) module helps you to plan, invest, and finance investment projects, such as capital investments, research and development, and maintenance programs. Investments initially incur costs and may result in revenue at a later time, but not all investment projects must be capitalized.

Specifically for fixed assets, you can use investment programs to collect costs for assets under construction (AUC). The IM module leverages the CO module to capture these costs. For smaller assets where you don't need sophisticated project management, for example, for a piece of equipment, you can use internal orders to collect these costs. (For more information about internal orders, see Chapter 5, Section 5.3.) For more complex AUCs, such as building a plant or another new facility, you can use the Project System (PS) module both to collect costs and to manage the project and its resources. (For more information about projects, see Chapter 5, Section 5.4.)

The costs for an AUC are collected throughout the period. During the financial close, the standard close processes in the respective CO module are applied. The difference is that a calculation takes place using results analysis, which determines how much of the costs should be capitalized to an AUC; the settlement rule for those internal orders and projects is to the AUC, which is an asset master created with a specific asset class for AUCs.

4.4.3 Year-End

Because the fixed asset accounts are balance sheet accounts, additional activities are required during the year-end close:

- **Fixed assets fiscal year change**
  To post asset transactions in the new fiscal year, you need to execute a fiscal year change within the AA module. You can still continue to post to the prior period as part of the financial closing process.
- **Account reconciliation**
  This program provides a list of accounts that have differences that need to be reconciled for asset balances and depreciation postings.
- **Opening a new approval year for investments**
  In a new fiscal year, a new investment program is created based on the structure of the prior year. When you then close the prior approval year, any open investment measures and appropriation requests are moved to the new investment program.
- **Carry forward the budget for investment programs**
  This program allows you to carry forward any unused budget from the previous approval year.

Next, we look at ensuring the correct balance sheet valuation of your inventory.

4.5 Inventory Management

In the Inventory Management (MM-IM) module, from a financial perspective, you need to ensure that your inventory is valued correctly on your balance sheet. There are different ways that you can choose to value your inventory, and these can be used in combination with each other, depending on the type of material in question. See the "Inventory Valuation Methods" box for additional information.

Inventory Valuation Methods

You can value the units of material that you have in your inventory in the following ways:

- **Standard cost**
  A standard cost is the estimated cost of labor, machine time, materials, and overhead, typically for a semifinished or finished good. All units are valued at this standard cost, regardless of whether the actual production costs were lower or higher. The standard cost is developed based on manufacturing data such as routings and bills of material (BOMs), and the associated costs of these resources.
- **Moving average**
  The price of material, typically commodities including raw material and supplies, is recalculated each time additional inventory is received and each time old inventory is used, so the cost in the material master can change daily. This should only be used if there is no need to analyze detailed variances of the materials.
- **Actual costing**
  Many companies are looking at valuing their inventory using actual costs. The material ledger initially values inventory at standard cost, while other costs incurred during the period are posted to the material ledger. These additional postings are used to calculate a periodic unit price, which is an average price you can use to valuate the material stock at period-end.
- **Lean accounting**
  As the accounting counterpart to lean manufacturing, lean accounting assigns actual costs to value streams and eliminates the concept of manufacturing orders. Because actual costs are assigned to value streams directly, there is no ability to analyze variances; instead, KPIs are defined as measurements. The most common tool for lean accounting in the SAP portfolio is the use of SAP Profitability and Cost Management (PCM) module that is part of SAP solutions for enterprise performance management (SAP solutions for EPM).

Many companies continue to use standard costing for their inventory valuation, but there is an increasing trend toward getting a view of actual costs. Although the material ledger provides actual costs, this is still an average cost for the period. The difference from moving average is that this revaluation occurs at the end of a period, not as each transaction is posted during the period.

As part of the inventory valuation during the financial close, we will look at the goods receipt/invoice receipt clearing; inventory valuation, including work in process (WIP) and units in inventory; and the closing of the posting period for materials.

4.5.1 GR/IR Reconciliation

The goods receipt/invoice receipt (GR/IR) clearing account contains the value of goods that you have received but for which have not yet been invoiced, and invoices for goods which you have not yet received. When you receive the missing goods or invoice, the system makes an offsetting posting to the GR/IR clearing account.

The system does not clear the items from this account. Instead, a GR/IR program determines an item balance for each reconciliation account and reference, or assignment number. If the account has a credit balance, goods have been received but not invoiced; if the account has a debit balance, goods have been invoiced but not yet received. The program then prepares adjustment entries to ensure correct valuation; for example, if you have received goods into inventory but have not yet been completely invoiced, a debit posting is made to the GR/IR adjustment account with a credit to an account used to track the value of goods delivered but not invoiced. These postings are reversed after the close is complete and financial statements have been generated.

A new dashboard is available for GR/IR clearing, powered by SAP HANA, that provides real-time charts and calculated KPIs for GR/IR information including open items, account balances, mismatches in the clearing process, and drill-down to vendor and line item information.

4.5.2 Work in Process

Within SAP ERP Financials, the CO module is leveraged for the actual production process, which means that production costs for materials actually reside on the P&L. To ensure correct inventory valuation, you need to run a program that calculates the WIP for all open production items, which you then settle, creating an offset posting on the P&L, and debiting the actual work in process costs to an inventory WIP account. For additional information, see Chapter 5, Section 5.5.1.

4.5.3 Inventory Valuation

Different companies vary on how often they revalue their inventory. With a more volatile economic environment, most companies are no longer revaluing inventory on an annual basis but have moved to revaluations as often as monthly. Two processes are available, one using a costing run to develop a standard cost, and the other using the material ledger to calculate a periodic unit price.

Standard Cost

If you are using standard cost for your inventory valuation, you use the costing run to develop your standard costs. The costing run looks at the value of the components in the BOM; the value of the resources in a routing, including set-up time, labor, and machine time; and overhead that will be allocated the product. The costing run calculates the estimated standard cost of the product, as shown in Figure 4.8. After the cost estimate has been created, the follow-on processes are marking, then releasing, the costing run, which then updates the standard cost in the material master and revalues inventory at the new standard cost.

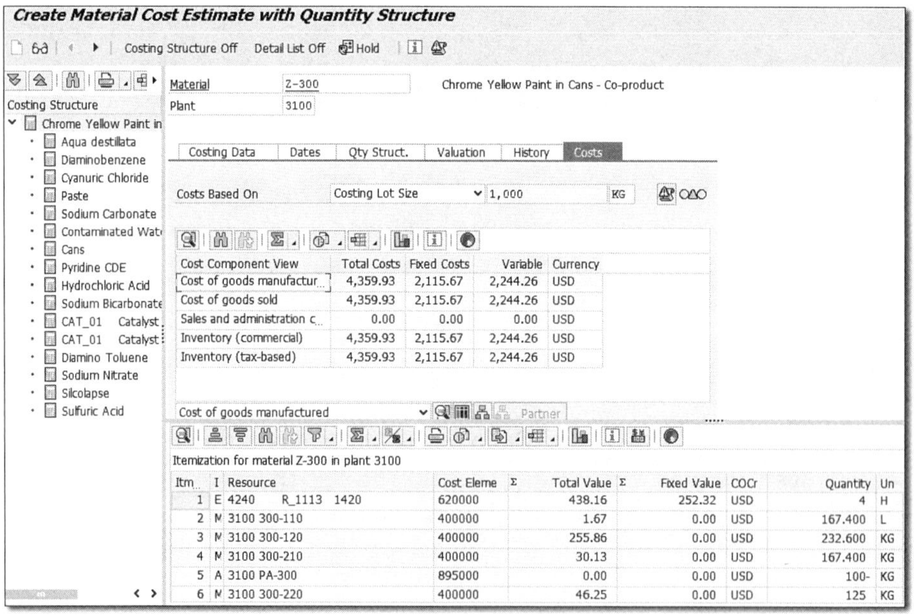

Figure 4.8 Material Cost Estimate Using Manufacturing Master Data

The material master also contains other price fields that you may wish to update, such as material prices for tax and commercial valuation. As an example, the FIFO (First In, First Out) calculation updates the tax price field in the material master.

Material Ledger for "Actual Costs"

The material ledger (CO-PC-ACT) allows you to come closer to actual costing by calculating a periodic unit price. The other benefit to the material ledger is the ability to manage material prices in up to three currencies and valuations.

During the period, the material in inventory is valued at standard cost. The material ledger then leverages the costing run to calculate the periodic unit price, which includes the actual costs incurred during the period for a material. This results in the determination of the periodic unit price; this periodic unit price can then be used to revalue inventory at that price and is also updated in the material master to be the standard cost for the preliminary inventory valuation in the subsequent period.

Another use case of the material ledger is to carry out an alternative valuation after the initial costing run, using a longer time period than one period, in order to smooth out seasonal variances, and to accommodate for timing differences such as vendors whose invoices to you are delayed.

4.5.4 Posting Periods

As part of the closing, you need to ensure that postings within MM are not made to prior periods. Similar to the period close described in Section 4.2.1, you need to close the prior period for material master postings after you have completed all financial close activities for materials and inventory management.

Rapid Deployment Solutions for Finance

SAP Rapid Deployment Solutions (RDS) contain a combination of preconfigured software, plus implementation services, to help you accelerate your implementation. You can choose modular RDS solutions, so you can scale your implementation and maintain control of your scope. Several RDS solutions are available for different parts of the finance portfolio:

- SAP ERP Financials contains capabilities for the financial close for the FI and CO modules, including the SAP ERP Finance and Controlling rapid-deployment solution; the

SAP ERP Finance and Controlling for Subsidiaries rapid-deployment solution; and the SAP HANA Accelerated Finance and Controlling rapid-deployment solution.

- For the SAP solutions for EPM, additional RDSs include the SAP Financial Close and Disclosure Management rapid-deployment solution (for more information, see Chapter 9, Section 9.4.1) and the SAP HANA Profitability Analysis rapid-deployment solution (for further information, see Chapter 5, Section 5.6).

Next, let's look at a ConAgra Foods' story on how it leveraged two SAP rapid deployment solutions (RDS) for the FI and CO modules to gain value in a short amount of time.

4.5.5 Customer Story: ConAgra Foods Improves Financial Business Processes with In-Memory Computing

Omaha-based ConAgra Foods Inc. is one of North America's leading food companies with its brands found in 97% of America's households. The company sells nearly 12.3 million packages of food products each day to grocery, convenience, mass merchandise, and club stores as well as to a variety of well-known restaurants, foodservice operators, and commercial customers.

Having a large portfolio of brands and products that are sold through such a wide range of outlets means there is a vast of data about both material costs and the profitability of products, brands, and divisions that the company needs to report on at period ends to prepare accurate and reliable segmented P&L reports. Accelerating the production of these month-end material ledger and cost and profitability reports would clearly expedite the financial close and provide more timely information for forecasting, so the company partnered with hardware supplier Hewlett-Packard and SAP Consulting to leverage the in-memory calculation power of SAP HANA.

Implementing the SAP HANA Profitability Analysis RDS took four weeks and implementing the SAP ERP Finance and Controlling RDS with SAP HANA took 8 weeks. Both of these were considered to be low-risk projects because they benefitted from a tried and tested best-practice methodology that would enhance the transfer of knowledge and expertise to ConAgra's own staff, enabling them to extend the use of the SAP HANA platform in the future.

Today, the transfer of vast amounts of material ledger data into the SAP NetWeaver Business Warehouse (SAP NetWeaver BW) that previously took 7 hours has been reduced to a mere 30 minutes—effectively a 92.9% reduction—and this helps accelerate period end closing. At the same time, detailed cost and profitability reports are substantially quicker and easier to access so that the month-end forecasting cycle has been reduced by 3 days, giving ConAgra the agility and insight it needs to make better decisions in its fast-moving business.

Shared Services for Streamlined Financial Processes

A shared services organization is an internal business unit that provides a service to other areas of the company. Shared services are often implemented for support of administrative functions, including finance, human resources, procurement, and IT, to name a few. For finance, you can think of this as eliminating a finance department in each location and consolidating that function on a global or regional basis; many global companies have created multiple shared service centers, each covering a different geographic area, such as the Americas, Europe, and Asia. The benefits of shared services include standardizing processes across the company, consistent application of policies, and reduced costs.

While many companies leverage SAP ERP Financials as described, a recent innovation is the SAP Shared Service Framework, which allows you to use the SAP CRM Interaction Center capabilities—but without the need to implement SAP CRM—to enable communication such as inbound and outbound call center and email capabilities, to use skill-based routing (e.g., to route receivables questions and payroll questions to different teams with the appropriate expertise), to create service requests when an issue surfaces, and to provide self-services for employees to access information themselves.

Several predefined scenarios are available; those related to finance include the following:

- **Accounting Interaction Center**
  Service agents can access FI and CO module capabilities, as well as Receivables Management capabilities, including electronic bill presentment and payment (SAP Biller Direct), SAP Collections Management, and SAP Dispute Management.
- **Travel Interaction Center**
  Service agents leverage SAP Travel Management, together with the Interaction Center, to process expense reports, view credit card receipts, and update employee master data.

For companies that have implemented a shared services organization, the financial close is usually processed by these shared services business units, leveraging the same core finance capabilities discussed here. Although there are no additional period-end processes specific to shared services, through the SAP Shared Services Framework, an additional capability for processing at period end is the automatic creation of service requests based on batch jobs, for example, errors in payment runs. If you choose to run this process, you can ensure that the shared services organization can proactively be involved in the resolution of these issues.

Next, we consider reporting, which is a key element to ensuring that the processes have been executed correctly as part of the close.

4.6 Reporting

Reporting is an integral part of the financial close. For FI, different types of reports are available that allow you to monitor the financial close, as well as make business decisions based on financial results. Reports that are available as part of FI include the following:

- **Master data reports**
  These reports allow you to get a listing of the master data records in your SAP ERP Financials, such as a list of General Ledger accounts in your chart of accounts, or a listing of changes made to the General Ledger master records.
- **Account balances**
  These reports allow you to see the balance of your General Ledger and subledger accounts at any time and break down those balances by other types of organizational elements, such as segments, cost centers, and profit centers, as shown in Figure 4.9.
- **Line item reports**
  These reports allow you to see the individual postings made to specific accounts. Line item reports also include open item reports, which help you manage your subledger and clearing processes.
- **Document reports**
  These reports provide information on specific journal entries and changes made to those entries, as well as consistency checks, for example, to highlight gaps in document numbers.
- **Financial statement reports**
  These reports of the balance sheet, income statement, and cash flow statement are the primary financial statements that must be produced. Options include comparisons of actuals to planned data, and actual comparisons across periods.

To ensure that these reports are analyzed as part of the financial close, you can incorporate them into the SAP Financial Closing cockpit as tasks that need to be executed, with instructions for the types of reviews that are necessary; for additional information, please refer to Chapter 6.

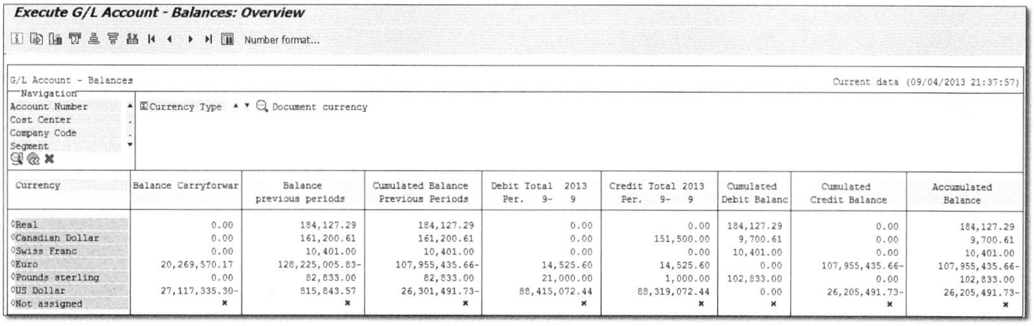

Currency	Balance Carryforwar	Balance previous periods	Cumulated Balance Previous Periods	Debit Total 2013 Per. 9- 9	Credit Total 2013 Per. 9- 9	Cumulated Debit Balanc	Cumulated Credit Balance	Accumulated Balance
Real	0.00	184,127.29	184,127.29	0.00	0.00	184,127.29	0.00	184,127.29
Canadian Dollar	0.00	161,200.61	161,200.61	0.00	151,500.00	9,700.61	0.00	9,700.61
Swiss Franc	0.00	10,401.00	10,401.00	0.00	0.00	10,401.00	0.00	10,401.00
Euro	20,269,570.17	128,225,005.83-	107,955,435.66-	14,525.60	14,525.60	0.00	107,955,435.66-	107,955,435.66-
Pounds sterling	0.00	82,833.00	82,833.00	21,000.00	1,000.00	102,833.00	0.00	102,833.00
US Dollar	27,117,335.30-	815,843.57	26,301,491.73-	88,415,072.44	88,319,072.44	0.00	26,205,491.73-	26,205,491.73-
Not assigned	×	×	×	×	×	×	×	×

Figure 4.9 GL Account Balances Overview with Drill-Down

In addition to the reporting available directly within SAP ERP Financials, other tools are available for reporting, including the SAP NetWeaver BW and the SAP BusinessObjects Business Intelligence (BI) tools. For additional information, please refer to Chapter 11.

The story of KazStroyService Group illustrates the benefits of SAP ERP Financials as an integrated part of SAP ERP, in combination with SAP BusinessObjects BI solutions, to facilitate the reporting across finance and operations that is a crucial aspect of each step of the financial close.

4.6.1 Customer Story: KazStroyService Group Streamlines and Consolidates Business Processes

When it comes to construction and logistics for oil and gas and other industries, KazStroyService Group (KSS) is a world-class leader. But with operations in Kazakhstan, India, and Turkmenistan, as well as plans to expand into other sectors such as roads, power plants, and ports, the company needed a single IT platform to consolidate and streamline crucial business and financial processes.

KSS initiated a project to install a single IT platform that would unify all group companies, improve operational visibility across projects, and provide accurate management reporting in real time by engaging with Highbar Technologies to upgrade to the latest version of the SAP ERP application and deploy SAP BusinessObjects BI solutions across multiple lines of business.

Using the SAP RDSs that expedite the adoption of BI for specific lines of business, such as sales, financial reporting, procurement, and plant maintenance, in timescales as short as three months meant that the project team could successfully complete more than 40 separate rollouts spanning all 3 companies in the group within 11 months—and on budget.

With its portfolio of SAP solutions in place, KSS is now using a single enterprise platform to consolidate and streamline all business and financial processes across projects and subsidiaries. This has allowed the company to increase operational efficiency and gain better control over projects with increased productivity, accelerated process cycles, and reduced costs. For instance, the company estimates that its financial close cycles have been reduced by 60% and its procurement-to-pay processes are an amazing 99.99% faster. At the same time, the pervasive use of SAP BusinessObjects BI solutions that incorporate real-time dashboards means managers have access to reliable and up-to-date information that enables them to make quicker and more informed decisions.

Meanwhile, the finance teams need considerably less time to prepare management reports, which improves productivity and releases resources for more value-added analysis—something that would not have been possible without a unified platform based on SAP ERP and SAP BusinessObjects BI solutions.

4.7 Summary

The FI module within SAP ERP allows you to manage General Ledger accounts and journal entries, as well as subledger accounting, including accounts payable, accounts receivable, and fixed assets. You can also manage balance sheet valuation for items such as inventory to ensure correct, consistent financial statements as part of the financial close.

In the next chapter, we show how management accounting is handled in the CO module, how it is tightly integrated with the FI module described here, and the closing activities that are necessary as part of the financial close.

Management accounting breaks down account-level information into more detail to enable managers to make better business decisions and plan for the future. In SAP ERP, this is handled in the Controlling (CO) module, which requires that additional information be incorporated into the financial close activities to enable management reporting and to ensure compliance with accounting standards. This Chapter will explore the financial close in controlling.

5 The Financial Close in Controlling

The balance sheets and P&L statements that are often top of mind during the financial closing activities do not tell the entire story. While the chart of accounts reflects the categories that are required for external reporting, it is not the appropriate level of detail for managing departments or projects. This lower level of detail typically involves departments, which are represented by cost centers; projects, which are represented by work breakdown structures (WBS elements) and networks; simple, short-term activities, which are represented by internal orders; and manufacturing processes that capture the cost of producing a product or product line, which are represented by manufacturing cost objects.

In SAP ERP, the General Ledger (GL) accounts reside in the Finance (FI) module, while management accounting processes are handled within the Controlling (CO) module. As a result, it is not necessary to explode the number of GL accounts to manage the lower level of detail.

This is a different approach than many legacy systems where the chart of accounts—the actual GL account coding block—includes the cost center as part of the account number. For example, if we take the GL accounts 123 and 456, and cost centers AB, CD, and XY, which are allowed to post to these accounts, the coding block of these legacy chart of accounts includes both the account and the cost center, requiring an exponential increase in the number of GL accounts, as shown on the left side of Figure 5.1. It also means that each time a new cost center is created, the updates to the master data can be very time-consuming because many new accounts need to be created.

By separating financial (FI) information from management accounting (CO) information, the chart of accounts contains only the "pure" GL accounts. The organizational entities (in this example, the cost centers) are represented by their own master data. In a journal entry in SAP ERP, the GL account and the cost center are represented by two different fields, as shown on the right side of Figure 5.1. Reporting in SAP ERP on the cost centers, then, does not involve reporting directly on the GL accounts in FI but instead on the cost centers in CO.

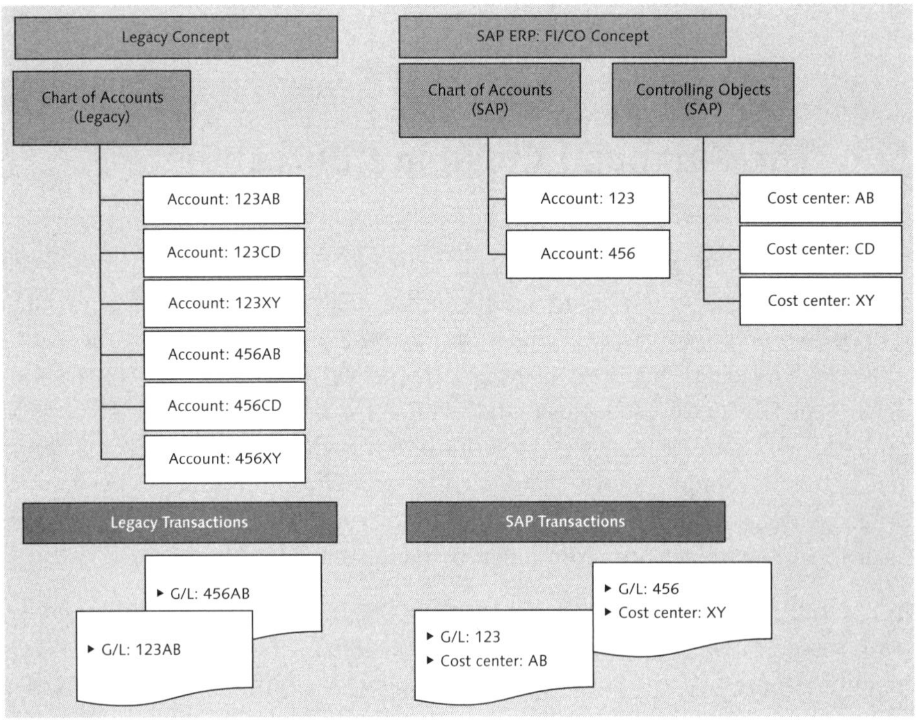

Figure 5.1 Separating Data between FI and CO

The Organizational Hierarchy within Controlling

The organizational hierarchy determines how costs can be moved. Unlike journal entries between legal entities (company codes), there are limitations within CO when the controlling objects do not fall within the same top-level hierarchy:

- The operating concern is the organizational entity used in Profitability Analysis (CO-PA). Multiple controlling areas can be assigned to an operating concern; postings between operating concerns are not possible.

- The controlling area is the highest entity within all CO processes below CO-PA. Multiple company codes are mapped to the controlling area; it is not possible to post allocations between controlling areas.

Figure 5.2 shows how an organization is represented within SAP in relation to the controlling area in the left column; the right column highlights the fields that are relevant for profitability segments in the operating concern.

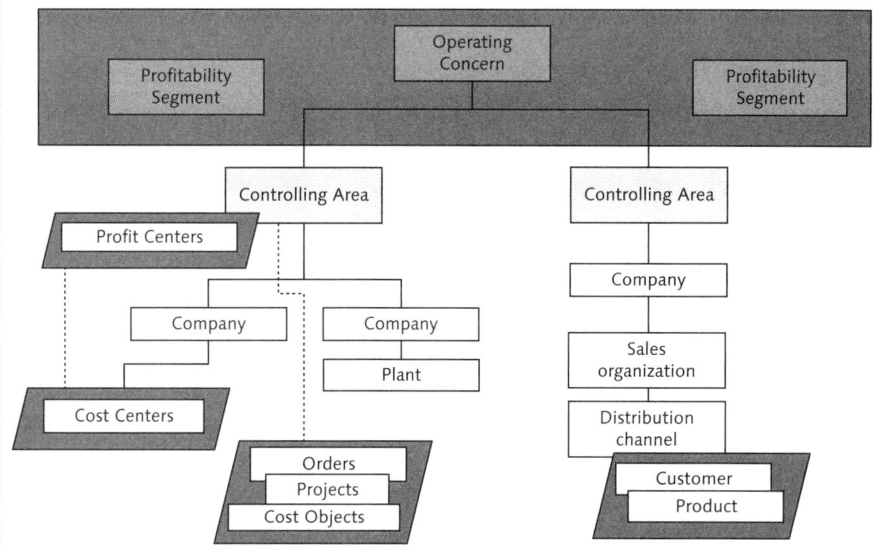

Figure 5.2 Organizational Elements and Master Data Mapped to the Operating Concern and Controlling Area.

In this chapter, we will cover the master data in the CO module that is relevant for the financial close processes, as well as the period-end activities that you need to perform.

5.1 Cost Element Accounting

Often, accountants talk about GL accounts, while the department managers speak about cost elements. There are two main categories of cost elements, primary and secondary, in Cost Element Accounting (CO-OM-CEL). We will discuss each of these cost element types in further detail.

5.1.1 Primary Cost Elements

A primary cost element is a master record in the CO module, which represents a Profit & Loss (P&L) account; this cost element uses the same account number as its GL counterpart. Each time a posting is made to a P&L account, the system checks to see whether a primary cost element exists. If so, it requires that a controlling object is entered. Controlling objects are master records, such as cost centers or projects, which provide the capability of tracking the costs associated with these P&L accounts on a more detailed level.

To illustrate this logic, Figure 5.3 shows an example of a manual journal entry. A posting is made to account 123, which has a corresponding cost element; therefore, the system requires a controlling object to be referenced, in this case, project (WBS element) XYZ. If, instead, the posting is made to account 456, there is no primary cost element, and no controlling object is entered.

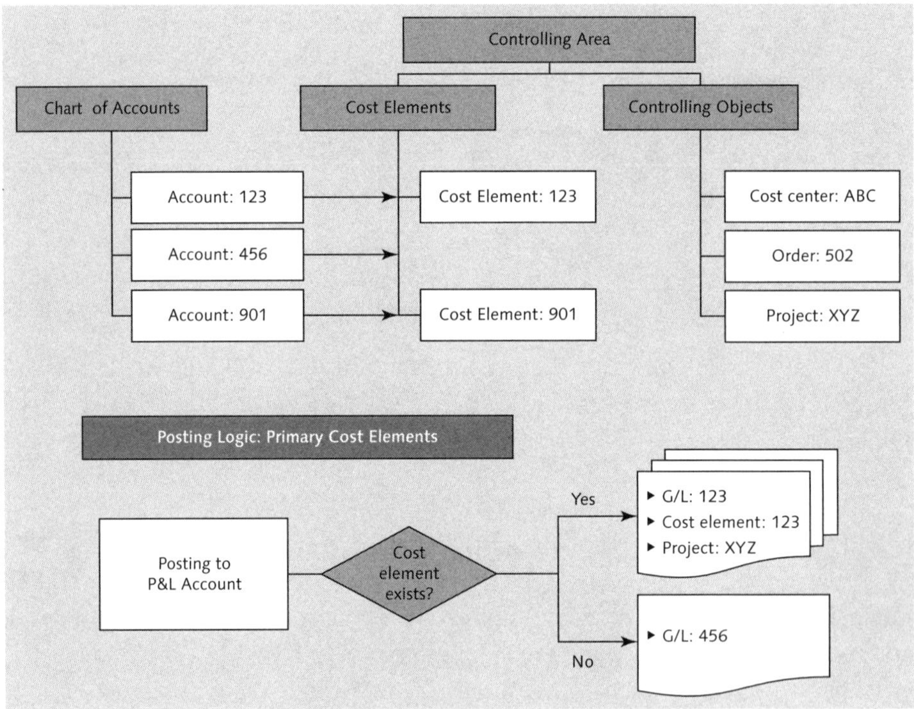

Figure 5.3 A Manual Journal Entry With and Without a Primary Cost Element

For many financial entries, the controlling objects are entered manually during the creation of a journal entry. To ensure control of these postings, you can limit which cost elements can post to particular controlling objects; for example, costs related to marketing activities should not be posted to a utilities cost center.

Note that a single line item in a journal entry only posts to a single controlling object; if more than one controlling object is required, then you need additional line items in the journal entry. Each line item then includes the same primary cost element but a different controlling object.

5.1.2 Secondary Cost Elements

When moving costs between controlling objects, in most legacy systems, a financial journal entry would have been required, for example to allocate costs from one cost center to another. Within the Controlling module, costs can be moved between controlling objects without affecting the GL. These cost movements are tracked with secondary cost elements; they are essentially accounts that exist only in the CO module, not in FI. When costs are moved, for example to apply overhead to a production order, a CO document is created to capture the debits and credits between the controlling objects.

Figure 5.4 shows a very simple example to illustrate the difference between primary and secondary cost elements. Costs are posted to cost center AB using two different primary cost elements, as shown in the left column, FI Documents. These costs are then allocated out to other cost centers; while the same secondary cost element could have been used for all allocations, the more common approach, shown in the center column, CO Documents, is to use a different secondary cost element for each primary cost element in use, so you can more easily trace the flow of costs across controlling objects in reporting.

From a FI module point of view, the costs still reside in the original P&L GL account. They were only moved within the CO module. From the point of view of a cost center or other controlling object, reporting must include both primary and secondary cost elements to ensure a complete view of all associated costs, as shown in the right column, Cost Center Reports.

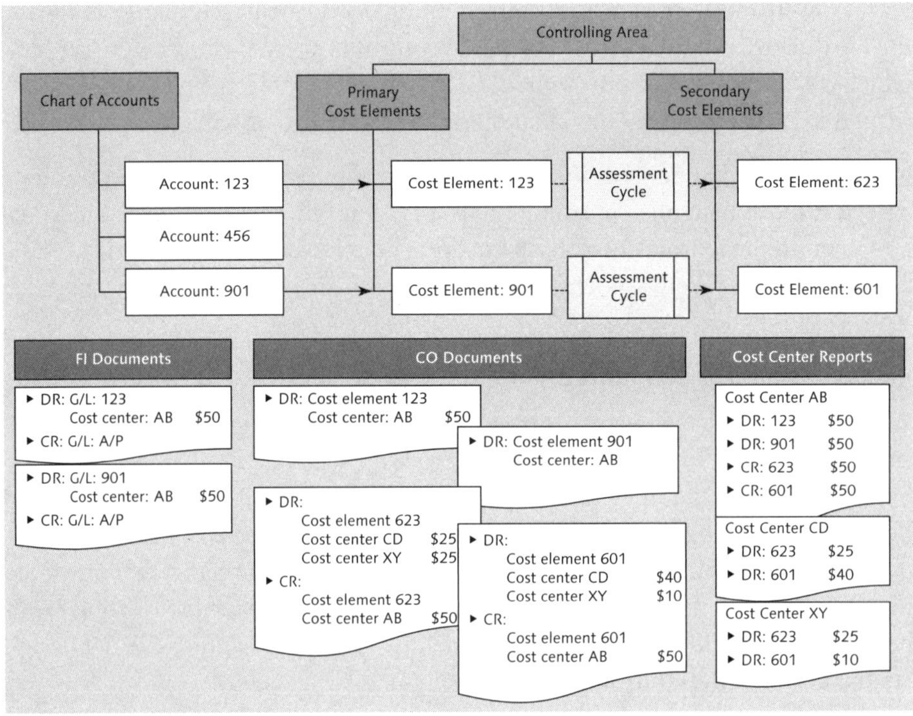

Figure 5.4 Secondary Cost Elements Capturing How Costs Flow between Controlling Objects

5.1.3 Integration between Operations and Controlling

We have covered direct postings made to the CO module from journal entries and the movement of costs between controlling objects. Other postings originate from other operational processes, which automatically post to controlling objects. For example, fixed asset depreciation is posted to either cost centers or orders; payroll expenses are posted to cost centers; purchase orders are posted against cost centers, orders, or projects; and the costs of manufacturing a product are posted to orders, projects, and sales order items.

In these cases, you can configure these cost elements so that no manual postings are allowed. This is common for manufacturing and product costing processes, where you do not want manual postings to skew the results of analyzing production costs.

In each of the other modules within SAP ERP, including Materials Management (MM), Production Planning (PP), and Sales and Distribution (SD), as well as the SAP ERP Human Capital Management solution (SAP ERP HCM), configurable logic is available to determine the correct accounts and controlling objects. The most common method is to use the master records in question. For example, the asset master record contains both an account determination key that drives the postings to primary cost elements, as well as the controlling object (cost center, order) to which deprecation postings will be made.

The following customer story illustrates how the Korea Exchange Bank was able to leverage the integration of operational and finance processes to achieve significant results.

5.1.4 Customer Story: Korea Exchange Bank Benefits from Standardized Business Processes

Founded in 1967, Korea Exchange Bank (KEB) has pioneered both personal and commercial financial services with a network that includes more than 350 domestic branches and 25 international locations. Like many Asian banks, KEB once managed with multiple systems that it had developed in-house, resulting in staff having to manually gather information from different systems to perform standard business operations such as budgeting and expense allocation. In addition to becoming a burden for the bank's IT staff, this home-grown environment resulted in critical concerns over data consistency and reliability.

KEB decided that standardized and integrated solutions from SAP offered a better way to do business and implemented SAP ERP for operations such as enterprise-wide budgeting, asset management, taxation, and logistics, followed by SAP Supplier Relationship Management (SAP SRM) to manage the entire purchasing lifecycle from purchase requests to asset termination to become the first major bank in Korea with an integrated ERP-based management system.

The SAP solutions enabled budget planning and execution to become highly efficient with all of the information stored in one system, which greatly improved process reliability and transparency. At the same time, KEB reports 100% accuracy in cost accounting and improved cost traceability. And historical data is always available with just a few mouse clicks.

Automated operations are eliminating paper, increasing efficiency and reducing costs. For example, employee expenses once submitted using paper receipts are now handled electronically via an interface between the corporate credit card system and SAP ERP. As a result, approval times have been cut by 90%. Other improvements, such as a new electronic bidding process, have helped KEB save about 7% in total purchasing spend in the first year alone, saving more than US$10 million. This improved efficiency has enabled KEB to redeploy more than 30% of its purchasing personnel to more strategic sales positions.

Other than core banking processes, KEB estimates that it now manages up to 90% of its operations on SAP solutions, making it easier for staff to manage end-to-end processes with more accurate and consistent data.

Now that we have looked at the cost elements, let's take a look at the different controlling objects, including cost centers, orders, projects, and the cost objects associated with product costing processes, and the period-end process that is required for each. We will also look at how profitability analysis and profit centers are handled as part of the financial close.

5.2 Cost Centers

Departments within an organization are typically represented by cost centers (CO-OM-CCA) with a responsible owner, or department head, that is responsible for the expenses of a specific part of the organization. Cost centers collect costs associated with the department; these costs are then allocated to receivers, which are represented either by other cost centers or other controlling objects such as orders and projects. As part of the financial close, you need to carry out a series of steps for cost centers, including posting any necessary accruals, calculating overhead, clearing cost centers through allocations, and calculating variances for cost centers. Let's look at each of these steps in further detail.

5.2.1 Accruals

Accrual entries can be made through journal entries in FI by posting to GL accounts and referencing a controlling object. Alternately, you can process accruals for cost centers directly in CO. You can choose to use the logic for applying overhead costs based on actual costs posted to an individual cost center, or you can create special accrual calculation cost elements to smooth out seasonal costs across periods.

5.2.2 Basis for Cost Center Allocations

Costs that are collected in cost centers are typically allocated to other controlling objects so that they can be included as part of a fully absorbed product cost, and they should be considered to more accurately show true profitability. Methods to allocate costs include the use of cost elements, activity confirmations, and statistical key figures.

5.2.3 Cost Elements

Both primary and secondary cost elements that are posted to a controlling object can be used as a basis for allocations. If cost elements are defined at a detailed level, the allocation can be very specific. As an example, you may want to allocate overhead based on the labor costs that have been posted to the receiving controlling object.

5.2.4 Activity Types

An activity type is used to define an activity, or resource, that is produced by a cost center. For a manufacturing process, activities can be categorized as setup time, labor and machine time. For services such as utilities and computer access, an activity can be computer usage or the amount of energy produced.

Activities can be directly allocated to a receiver as they are executed, usually by indicating the quantity of the activity that was used, such as confirming the hours of labor time used in the manufacturing process based on time entry of the production workers. This credits the sending cost center and debits the receiving controlling object, such as another cost center or a production order. The unit of measure, such as hours, is multiplied by the planned activity rate. These activity type postings occur throughout the period.

While activity rates are often entered manually during planning, you can also choose to calculate an actual activity rate at period-end based on the actual consumption of the activities. Alternatively, activities can be indirectly allocated at period-end by defining calculation rules and weighting factors of the activity usage that occurred throughout the period.

5.2.5 Statistical Key Figures

Statistical key figures can also serve as an allocation basis. Some of these key figures are fixed and remain the same in subsequent periods until a change is entered, for example, the square footage of a plant, or the number of employees in a particular department. Other key figures are based on volume, which varies by month, such as number of orders or number of telephone minutes used.

The Logistics Information System (LIS) is available to track key figures that can also be used for allocations. Each type of logistics process has its own information system that is delivered as part of SAP ERP; examples include procurement, sales, inventory management, production (shop floor), plant maintenance, and quality management. You can analyze the performance of your logistics processes using the key figures in these information systems, such as the quantity of raw materials or supplies that are purchased, quantity of products sold, number of returns processed, and so forth. In addition to being used for the analysis of logistics processes, you can transfer the values of these key figures to the corresponding statistical key figures in the CO module to ensure consistency and reduce manual data entry.

5.2.6 Allocations

The primary mechanisms for allocations from a cost center are distributions and assessments in cases where there is no direct activity that can be confirmed. Allocations are normally performed using cost center groups; for example, sales and marketing costs will be allocated to production cost centers for the absorption of overhead costs. Most organizations define a progression of allocations, for example, from administrative cost centers to production cost centers, using cost center groups in the cost center hierarchy, as shown in Figure 5.5. You should ensure that as you define the hierarchy of allocations, you do not allocate back to a cost center that has already been cleared.

You can create rules for these allocations, which contain the logic of the amounts that will be allocated from one cost center to another. You can define a fixed amount that is allocated. Alternately, you can use a percentage split, by cost element or for total amounts. And finally, you can base the allocations on postings in the receiver, such as statistical key figures.

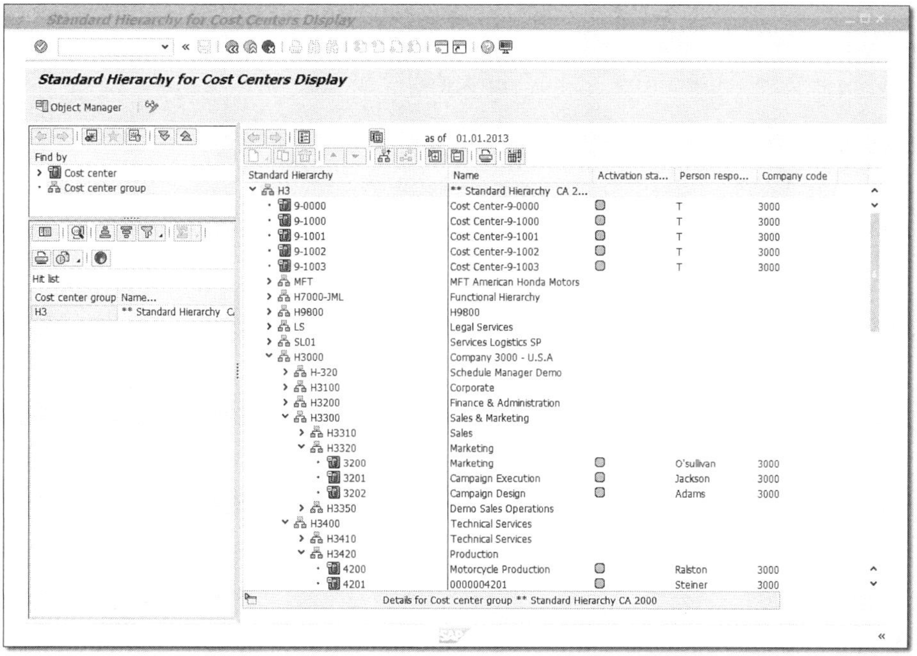

Figure 5.5 Cost Center Hierarchy Containing Cost Center Groups Useful for Performing Allocations

There are two types of cost center allocations: distributions and assessments. The main difference between them is in how the cost elements are handled for the period-end postings:

- Distributions use the original primary cost element that was used in the original posting to the cost center. Secondary cost elements that were posted to the sending cost center cannot be allocated using distributions.
- Assessments use a secondary cost element to post allocations, for both primary and secondary cost elements that were posted to the sending cost center. This approach provides you with the maximum visibility of both incoming and outgoing posts to the cost center.

5.2.7 Variances

To effectively manage a cost center, a variance calculation provides a department head with the information about the difference between the actual and planned (or target) costs, and the overabsorption or underabsorption of costs. While some companies simply use a report for this analysis based on cost elements posted to the cost centers, the SAP ERP system has a variance calculation that determines variance categories. The variance calculation determines two types of variance categories, the input variances and output variances:

- The input variance calculation compares actual debits and credits to the cost center and to the target costs. Target costs are determined during planning, based on planned debits and credits, and the planned activity level.
- The output variance calculation looks at the activity allocations that took place during the period and compares the actual activity allocations with the target costs.

These calculations help cost center managers analyze the reasons for the differences. These variances can then be cleared, for example, through an assessment to the operating concern in the CO-PA module. Please refer to Section 5.6 for further details on CO-PA.

Overhead Allocations for Orders and Projects

In addition to the allocations between cost centers, overhead is also applied from cost centers to controlling objects such as orders and projects. In addition to the direct costs that are attributable to a product or to a project, indirect costs are incurred that are not directly associated with the production process, such as sales and marketing costs, machine depreciation, and nonmanufacturing supplies. Because these costs cannot be directly associated with a particular product, allocation methods are used to distribute these costs based on an algorithm.

Several options enable you to allocate indirect costs to reflect a fully absorbed cost. How these allocations occur, and to what level of detail, directly influence the reported profitability of customers, products, channels, and geographic areas. The following options are available:

- Allocation of overhead between controlling objects within the CO module (CO-OM), for example, between cost centers, or more commonly from cost centers to orders and projects. The method used is either a percentage of direct costs, for example, by expense type, or quantities, for example, of raw material issued to a production order. The overhead is allocated using secondary cost elements.
- The Activity-Based Costing module (CO-OM-ABC) uses master data referred to as a business process, which allocates resources using process drives to the receivers. Receivers can be any type of profitability segment, including products, customers, and sales channels.
- Allocation can be settled from the cost centers directly to profitability segments within the Profitability Analysis (CO-PA) module at a higher level, for example, to a product line. A top-down allocation can then take place within the CO-PA module.

In cost-based profitability analysis, these allocations remain within the CO-PA module and are not reflected in the GL.

- As part of the SAP solutions for enterprise performance management (SAP solutions for EPM), the SAP Profitability and Cost Management (SAP PCM) application uses cost drivers to perform these top-level allocations, which can also be used for both activity-based costing as well as lean accounting. The cost drivers are set up directly within SAP PCM; this is a standalone application that is separate from SAP ERP, which enables more flexible modeling and allows data to be easily incorporated from both SAP systems and non-SAP systems.

Next, we will take a look at the period-end processes necessary for the different types of controlling objects that typically receive overhead allocations from cost centers, as well as the most common usage of each controlling object.

For each of these controlling objects, the calculation and posting of overhead described in the "Overhead Calculations for Orders and Projects" box is the first step. The posting of overhead is performed using secondary cost elements. The processes described next assume that overhead is allocated directly within the CO module and not using the other profitability solutions described in the "Overhead Allocations for Orders and Projects" box.

5.3 Internal Orders

Costs often need to be tracked at a lower level of detail than that of a department. This is the case for special projects where more detailed control is necessary, for example, a capital investment such as new equipment for a production line. Alternatively, multiple departments may collaborate on projects, such as a trade show or a research project, so the costs should not be tracked by a single cost center. You can also use an internal order to track more detailed overhead costs, such as maintenance or utilities.

Internal orders (CO-OM-OPA) are used to capture such costs primarily when the task is not complex. Throughout the period, you post costs directly to the internal order, either through a direct posting of a primary cost element, or by confirming an activity that results in a posting through a secondary cost element. Figure 5.6 shows the balance of an example internal order.

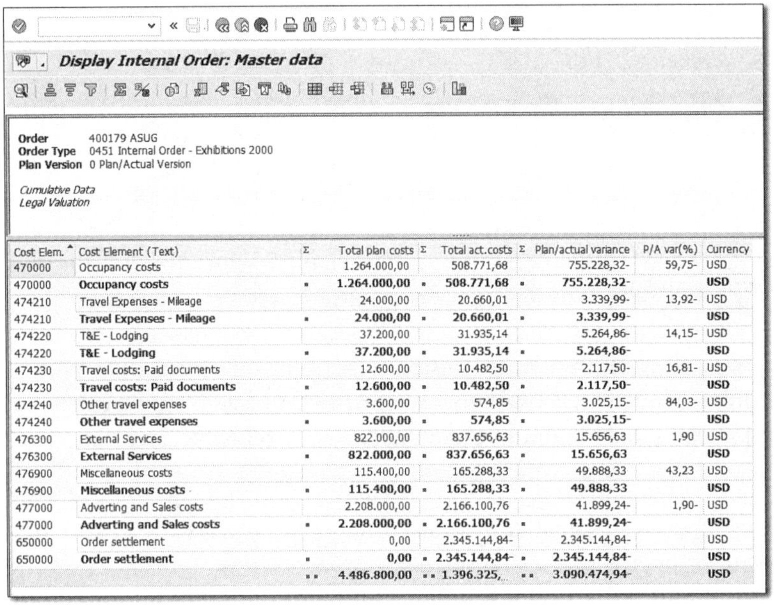

Display Internal Order: Master data

Order 400179 ASUG
Order Type 0451 Internal Order - Exhibitions 2000
Plan Version 0 Plan/Actual Version

Cumulative Data
Legal Valuation

Cost Elem.	Cost Element (Text)	Σ	Total plan costs	Σ	Total act.costs	Σ	Plan/actual variance	P/A var(%)	Currency
470000	Occupancy costs		1.264.000,00		508.771,68		755.228,32-	59,75-	USD
470000	**Occupancy costs**	▪	**1.264.000,00**	▪	**508.771,68**	▪	**755.228,32-**		**USD**
474210	Travel Expenses - Mileage		24.000,00		20.660,01		3.339,99-	13,92-	USD
474210	**Travel Expenses - Mileage**	▪	**24.000,00**	▪	**20.660,01**	▪	**3.339,99-**		**USD**
474220	T&E - Lodging		37.200,00		31.935,14		5.264,86-	14,15-	USD
474220	**T&E - Lodging**	▪	**37.200,00**	▪	**31.935,14**	▪	**5.264,86-**		**USD**
474230	Travel costs: Paid documents		12.600,00		10.482,50		2.117,50-	16,81-	USD
474230	**Travel costs: Paid documents**	▪	**12.600,00**	▪	**10.482,50**	▪	**2.117,50-**		**USD**
474240	Other travel expenses		3.600,00		574,85		3.025,15-	84,03-	USD
474240	**Other travel expenses**	▪	**3.600,00**	▪	**574,85**	▪	**3.025,15-**		**USD**
476300	External Services		822.000,00		837.656,63		15.656,63	1,90	USD
476300	**External Services**	▪	**822.000,00**	▪	**837.656,63**	▪	**15.656,63**		**USD**
476900	Miscellaneous costs		115.400,00		165.288,33		49.888,33	43,23	USD
476900	**Miscellaneous costs**	▪	**115.400,00**	▪	**165.288,33**	▪	**49.888,33**		**USD**
477000	Adverting and Sales costs		2.208.000,00		2.166.100,76		41.899,24-	1,90-	USD
477000	**Adverting and Sales costs**	▪	**2.208.000,00**	▪	**2.166.100,76**	▪	**41.899,24-**		**USD**
650000	Order settlement		0,00		2.345.144,84-		2.345.144,84-		USD
650000	**Order settlement**	▪	**0,00**	▪	**2.345.144,84-**	▪	**2.345.144,84-**		**USD**
		▪▪	**4.486.800,00**	▪▪	**1.396.325,..**	▪▪	**3.090.474,94-**		**USD**

Figure 5.6 Costs Posted to the Internal Order throughout the Period

During the financial close, you can apply overhead to the internal order from one or more cost centers (please refer to the "Overhead Allocations for Orders and Projects" box in Section 5.2.7). After all costs have been applied to the internal order, it is settled to one or more receivers (please refer to the "Settlement" box in Section 5.5.2). Again, it is important to map out the progression of the settlement, so that a settlement does not occur to an internal order that has already been cleared.

5.4 Project Systems

For large-scale projects, as well as for smaller projects that require additional planning activities in addition to cost collection, you can use the Project System module (PS) to include logistics and timeline planning to help you with your project management. Examples of more complex projects include engineer-to-order projects such as the design and build of a new airplane, and investment projects such as the construction of a new building that will be capitalized. For more information on the valuation of investment projects, please refer to Chapter 4, Section 4.4.2.

The following types of master data used to represent projects allow you to manage project revenues, costs, and resources:

- WBS (work breakdown structure) elements represent the hierarchical structure of your project's phases. You can designate which WBS elements are used for collecting costs, which WBS elements act as summary nodes that may or may not allow a direct posting, and which WBS elements allow billing and postings of revenue. Figure 5.7 shows a graphical representation of a project; from this view, you can drill down into the project master data to see additional details.
- Networks control the individual activities and resource assignments of a project. The use of networks is optional; you can think of them as more sophisticated production orders, which give you the ability to link to activities in other networks for particular tasks. Figure 5.8 shows a list view of how network activities are linked to WBS elements. The use of resources is posted directly to the networks as you execute these tasks.

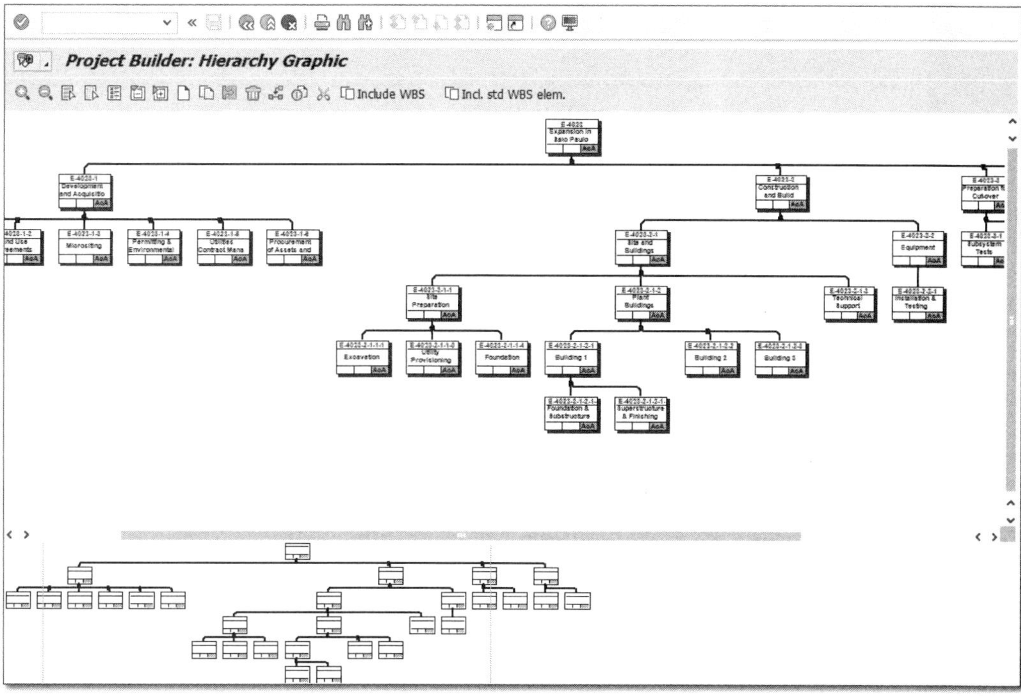

Figure 5.7 The Graphical View of a Project's Hierarchical Structure

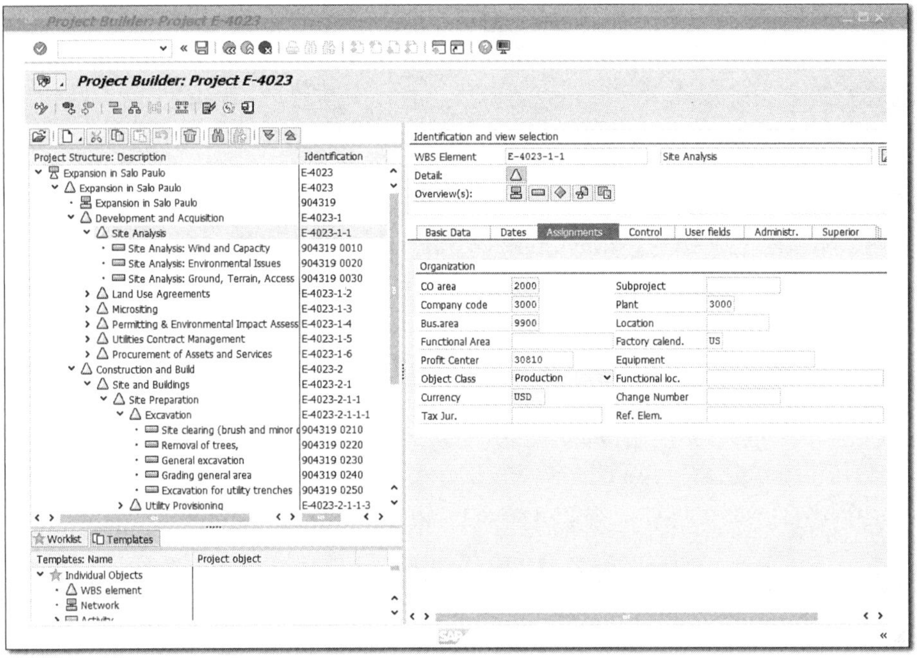

Figure 5.8 A Project Overview with both WBS Elements and Networks

After any relevant overhead application to the project (please refer to the "Overhead Allocations for Orders and Projects" box in Section 5.2.7), a results analysis calculation takes place to determine the value of the project. A project is typically open across several periods, so a financial close process is necessary to ensure that the revenues and costs that have been posted to the project are recognized correctly in the GL.

You need to choose the type of results analysis calculation that most accurately values the work in process (WIP) for each project.The different types of results analysis are:

- **Revenue-based results analysis**
  The system uses planned and actual revenues of the project to determine the associated cost of sales that should be posted. If the actual expenses incurred are higher than what should be recognized as the cost of goods sold (COGS), as is often the case in the early stages of a project, a posting is made to WIP for the difference.

- **Percent of completion results analysis**
  The system determines the completion of the project by comparing the planned and actual costs of the project. The revenue that needs to be recognized on that basis is calculated based on the percentage of completion of the project. For projects in which there is a significant cost overrun, it may be the case that more revenue must be recognized than has been billed.

Remember that the costs posted to a project reside on the P&L. The results analysis process stores the calculated values using a special type of cost element, referred to as results analysis cost elements. The settlement process (please refer to the "Settlement" box in Section 5.5.2) then posts these calculated values back to balance sheet GL accounts, such as WIP and deferred revenue, which ensures compliance with financial accounting regulations.

5.5 Product Costing

In SAP ERP, the cost to manufacture products is managed on the P&L in product costing (CO-PC), to leverage the CO module. This approach differs from most legacy systems, where costs associated with manufacturing a product remain on the balance sheet, moving from the raw material account into a WIP account, and from there into the finished goods inventory account; only the variances are written off on the P&L. Because the approach in product costing is different in SAP ERP, you need to execute closing processes to ensure correct valuation of inventory and WIP.

From an inventory valuation perspective, many organizations use standard costing, meaning that for each product, the standard cost is calculated based on the value of the expected resources required to manufacture a product. If the actual production process takes additional, or fewer, resources, these values are written off as variances. For information about inventory valuation with a costing run and using actual costing with the material ledger, please refer to Chapter 4, Section 4.5.3.

Cost objects are used to collect the costs associated with producing a finished good. Different cost objects are used based on the type of manufacturing processes used. These include production orders for discrete manufacturing; production cost collectors and the cost object hierarchy for repetitive manufacturing; process orders for process manufacturing; production orders and sales order items for make-to-order and assemble-to-order manufacturing; and projects for engineer-to-order manufacturing.

Whenever a posting is made in the Production Planning (PP) module, a posting is made in FI and CO at the same time, referencing the appropriate cost object. Direct costs include resources, such as the raw or semi-finished materials needed for the manufacturing process, as well as activities, including setup, labor and machine time. Each of these resources is tracked using cost elements, as shown in Figure 5.9.

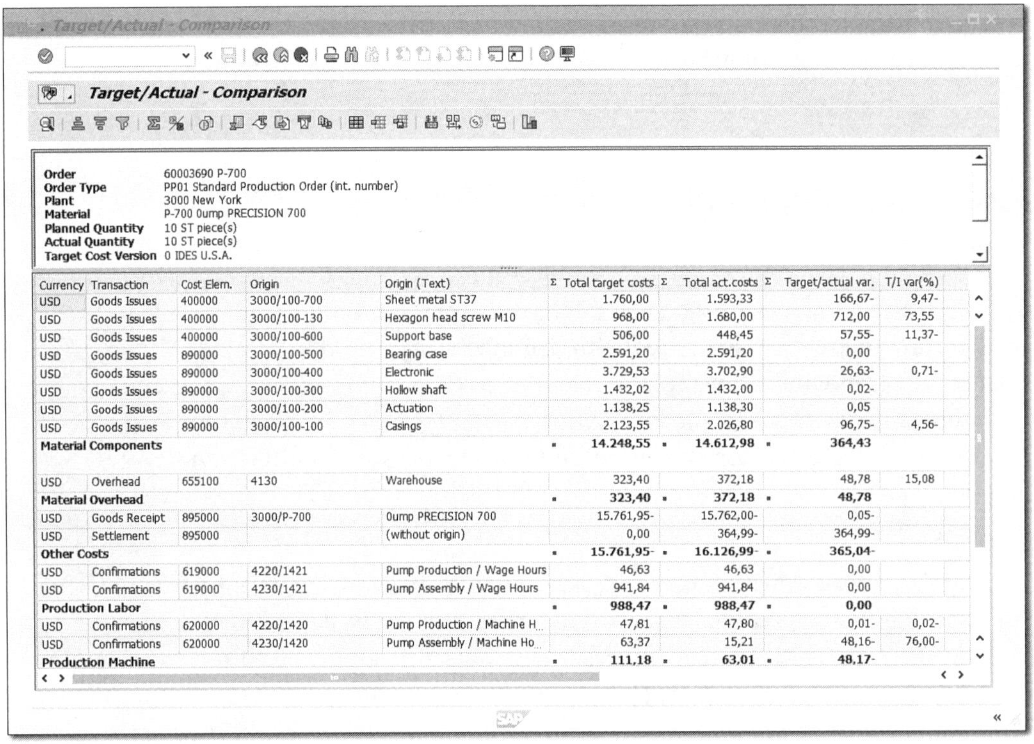

Figure 5.9 Target and Actual Costs on a Production Order Shown by Cost Element

At period-end, overhead is applied to these cost objects (refer to the "Overhead Allocations for Orders and Projects" box in Section 5.2.7). Subsequently, a series of processes must be run on the cost objects, including the calculation of WIP and variances, and posting those values through a settlement process (please refer to the "Settlement" box in Section 5.5.2). These processes are run typically while production work is still ongoing; for the values in the GL to remain as clean as possible, the WIP and variance calculations should be run immediately after one another.

5.5.1 Work in Process

If a cost object is still open at the end of a period—meaning that production for the entire quantity is not yet complete—the production costs still reside on the P&L. The system calculates the work in process (WIP) to determine the balance on the cost objects: all costs debited to the cost collector, minus all costs credited which is the standard cost of all completed finished goods. A special type of cost element, called a results analysis (RA) cost element, tracks the WIP amounts. If WIP was calculated for a cost object in a prior period, and the cost object is still open, then any additional WIP that should be posted is calculated. If WIP was calculated in a prior period, but the manufacturing process is complete and the cost object is closed, the WIP amount that needs to be canceled is calculated. The WIP values will be posted to the balance sheet, with an offsetting entry on the P&L, when you run settlement on the cost objects.

5.5.2 Variances

Variances are the difference between the standard cost of the finished products and the actual costs posted to the cost objects. These costs still reside in the various cost elements on the P&L. Variances can be analyzed by comparing the actual costs on a cost collector with the target costs, which are the planned costs (typically the standard cost of a finished product) multiplied by the quantity that was expected to be manufactured. This calculation categorizes the variances so that you can perform further analysis on your manufacturing processes, including input variances, output variances, and scrap:

- Input variances are caused by the differences in the price and quantity of the materials (such as raw materials) and resources (represented by activity types) that were used during production.
- Output variances are caused by a difference in the quantity of products that were manufactured or a difference in the valuation of the completed products due to a change in the standard cost. A remaining variance, which cannot be assigned to another category, is also classified as an output variance.

- Scrap variances result from scrap due to a lack of quality. For some products, a planned scrap value is expected due to the manufacturing process.

These variance calculations help production managers analyze the reasons for the differences and can also be used as input when it is time to create a new standard cost for materials that are being produced. Please refer to Chapter 4, Section 4.5.3 for more details.

The variances are posted during settlement; one account offsets the P&L accounts in which the resource costs are consumed during production, while the other side of the posting is to the actual variance account on the P&L. If you are using CO-PA, the variances can also be posted to the operating concern. For further details, please refer to Section 5.6.

Settlement

The concept of a settlement is the same throughout the CO module for all types of orders (sales order items, cost objects in product costing, internal orders) as well as for projects (both for WBS elements and networks). Note that cost centers are an exception to the use of settlement; instead, they use the allocation methods of distributions and assessments.

Settlement is the mechanism used to post the values calculated in previous steps—RA, WIP, and variances—to the GL. Settlement can occur from one controlling object to one, or multiple, receivers. Specific scenarios include the following:

- Clear, or zero out, the expenses (and revenues, where applicable) of specific controlling objects. If you have chosen to use a fully absorbed product cost, all costs collected in the CO module will be allocated to a product eventually.
- Within product costing for make-to-stock and repetitive manufacturing processes, the settlement rule refers to the finished product that is being manufactured to process the goods receipt. During settlement, any previously calculated WIP and variances are posted to the GL accounts. For make-to-order and engineer-to-order scenarios, the settlement receiver is the sales order item or project through which the configuration specifications were captured.
- For capital investments, whether managed with an internal order or a project, the settlement is to a fixed asset to ensure proper capitalization.

In designing the progression of settlement between controlling objects, you need to ensure that you do not settle to a controlling object that has already been cleared, as this will result in inconsistencies.

While settlement is normally the last step of the financial close for a controlling object, settlement does not prevent future postings to the controlling objects. Settlement can be run at any time, not only during the close process; each time, only the changes are posted, ensuring that entries are not double-posted.

If you have activated cost-based Profitability Analysis (CO-PA), the last step in your progression is a settlement to a profitability segment within the operating concern.

Let's look at how a customer, Qingdao TKS Sealing Industry, was able to leverage the tight integration between the logistics and financial modules, including the link between production and product costing, in SAP ERP.

5.5.3 Customer Story: Qingdao TKS Sealing Industry Achieves Transparent Reporting

As its product range grew, Qingdao TKS Sealing Industry Co. Ltd., (TKS), a well-established manufacturer of oil seals and other components used in automobiles, locomotives, machinery, and domestic appliances, needed to break down its monolithic organization into divisions and departments. Despite years of good service, its legacy software was unable to provide these newly autonomous business units with the unified finance management functionality that would help managers drive competitiveness and improve their results. Particular issues that needed to be addressed were optimizing the size of inventories that had escalated with a growing product line, improving cash flow that suffered from production being out of step with orders, and increasing the accuracy of costing products.

After assessing the products of a number of well-known software vendors, TKS selected the SAP Business Suite and selected Neusoft Group as its implementation partner while educating staff and skillfully positioning its most effective people into appropriate positions to support the implementation.

The project progressed rapidly, and the first sets of monthly accounts and operational reports were produced to schedule after seven months. The reports gave all of the divisions and departments within TKS complete transparency into their businesses covering areas such as financial accounting, cost control, production planning and control, procurement and inventory management, sales and distribution, and quality management in operations.

After several months of operation, the benefits of running SAP ERP became increasingly evident, and TKS was able to strengthen its supervision and control of finances in all aspects of its business as well as dramatically improve financial planning and analysis. More accurate cost analysis has both reduced operating costs and enabled more accurate internal transfer pricing while improved lean manufacturing has reduced both inventory and occupancy costs while improving customer satisfaction.

Although TKS now has the information needed to support effective decision making, there is still work to be done to achieve full IT transformation with the company expanding its range of SAP applications into areas such as manufacturing and human resources.

5.5.4 The Material Ledger

For the controlling processes that we addressed in this chapter, the assumption is that materials being produced are valued at a standard cost. However, some companies prefer to use actual costing or need to manage multiple valuations of products or multiple currencies. The material ledger provides you with this capability and can be used for the revaluation of materials that affect the balance sheet accounts. For further details, please refer to Chapter 4, Section 4.5.3.

Now that we have looked at the controlling objects used for collecting costs, let's turn our attention to how these costs are associated with revenues to determine profitability and margins.

5.6 Profitability Analysis

The Profitability Analysis (CO-PA) module allows organizations to measure their profitability based on business segments, which includes products and product lines, customers and customer groups, geographies, and channels. You create the operating concern by defining the business segments that you want to measure, as well as the values that are relevant for analyzing profitability. You then create reports; the system provides the capability to allow you to dynamically drill down from the summary level down to lower levels of detail, as well as switching the order of fields in a report. For example, you may look at all customers and drill down to the products they purchased; you can then flip the order and look at all products and drill down to all customers who purchased each product. For the CO-PA module, reporting is available from within SAP ERP, as shown in Figure 5.10, or through SAP NetWeaver BW InfoCubes.

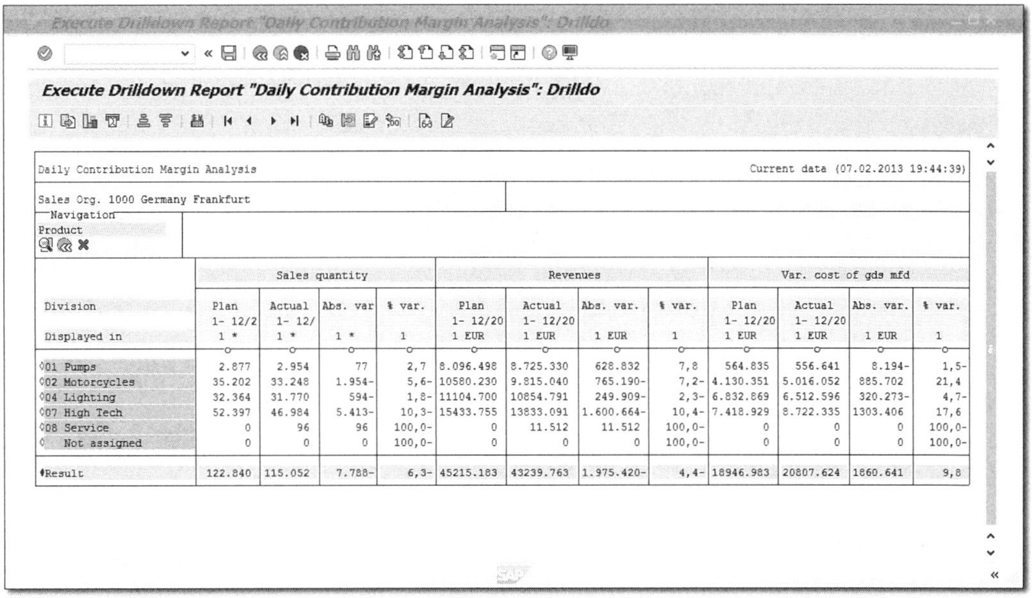

Division / Displayed in	Sales quantity Plan 1- 12/2 (1 *)	Sales quantity Actual 1- 12/ (1 *)	Sales quantity Abs. var (1 *)	Sales quantity % var. (1)	Revenues Plan 1- 12/20 (1 EUR)	Revenues Actual 1- 12/20 (1 EUR)	Revenues Abs. var. (1 EUR)	Revenues % var. (1)	Var. cost of gds mfd Plan 1- 12/20 (1 EUR)	Var. cost of gds mfd Actual 1- 12/20 (1 EUR)	Var. cost of gds mfd Abs. var. (1 EUR)	Var. cost of gds mfd % var. (1)
01 Pumps	2.877	2.954	77	2,7	8.096.498	8.725.330	628.832	7,8	564.835	556.641	8.194-	1,5-
02 Motorcycles	35.202	33.248	1.954-	5,6-	10580.230	9.815.040	765.190-	7,2-	4.130.351	5.016.052	885.702	21,4
04 Lighting	32.364	31.770	594-	1,8-	11104.700	10854.791	249.909-	2,3-	6.832.869	6.512.596	320.273-	4,7-
07 High Tech	52.397	46.984	5.413-	10,3-	15433.755	13833.091	1.600.664-	10,4-	7.418.929	8.722.335	1303.406	17,6
08 Service	0	96	96	100,0-	0	11.512	11.512	100,0-	0	0	0	100,0-
Not assigned	0	0	0	100,0-	0	0	0	100,0-	0	0	0	100,0-
Result	122.840	115.052	7.788-	6,3-	45215.183	43239.763	1.975.420-	4,4-	18946.983	20807.624	1860.641	9,8

Figure 5.10 Contribution Margin Analysis Report Showing Plan vs. Actual Revenues and Costs

An operating concern can be cost-based, account-based, or both:

- Cost-based CO-PA is used for cost of sales accounting, in which the costs are matched to the revenues that were booked in a particular period. Value fields are used to capture this information; these value fields can be mapped to cost elements, but they can also be defined at lower levels of detail, for example, the fixed and variable components of the same cost element.
- Account-based CO-PA is used for period accounting and allows an organization to easily reconcile the values in the CO-PA module with the values in the GL. Some accounts, such as balance sheet accounts that should be captured in account-based CO-PA, can be defined as statistical cost elements to enable a posting for reporting purposes but without moving costs into a true controlling object, in this case a business segment.

Values flow into the operating concern throughout the period. For example, information from sales orders and invoices is captured, which includes information about the customer, products sold, and channel. Additional rules can be set up to group products, customers, and regions for a summarized analysis. Postings can also be made to a business segment with journal entries.

At period-end, costs are typically posted to an operating concern through the closing activities of the other controlling objects. For information that comes from sales and manufacturing processes, these postings are made at the stock keeping unit (SKU) level. For postings that originate from cost centers, orders, and projects, many organizations choose to allocate to a business segment at a higher level. For example, marketing costs are often posted to a region, so you can then use the top-down distribution capability to allocate down to a lower level, such a to a sales office, from where these costs are in turn distributed down to products. This distribution can be based on either planned or actual data that has already been posted within the CO-PA module. This allocation is reflected in reporting only in the operating concern and is not posted back to the GL.

SAP CO-PA Accelerator

The information in the CO-PA module allows you to generate detailed financial reports and to make decisions about the product mix in various regions, sales, and pricing. The faster that CO-PA reports run and the more data that is included in the reports, the more valuable the results to enable real-time decision making. To support such detailed decisions, the volume of data becomes very high. Traditionally, organizations needed to schedule batch runs overnight to enable better reporting performance the next morning. With the SAP CO-PA Accelerator, powered by SAP HANA, the CO-PA allocation and reporting capabilities leverage in-memory computing, enabling faster top-down allocations during the close, as well as real-time access to information, both through predefined profitability reports as well as ad hoc analysis and what-if analyses. From SAP's own implementation, an analysis involving 85 million records was accelerated from over 1 hour to less than 30 seconds.

5.6.1 Customer Story: Promivi, a Leader in Animal Nutrition, Utilizes SAP HANA and Gains Profitability and Growth Insight

To sustain its growth, Rotterdam-based Provimi Holdings, a leader in animal feeds and nutrition solutions, transformed itself into a real-time organization by using the in-memory capabilities of the SAP HANA platform to power the existing investment in the SAP Business Suite, which was already deployed in the 26 countries across 4 continents where the company operates.

Increasing the performance of reporting was a priority, and Provimi can now mine a wealth of consistent operational data to gain new business-relevant insight in fractions of a second. Using a Rapid Deployment Solution (RDS) that enabled the implementation to be complete within 3 weeks with minimal disruption, the company accelerated the speed of its Controlling and Profitability Analysis (CO-PA) and operational reporting by a factor of 15,000. In addition to giving business users immediate insight into the financial performance of products, customers, brands, and territories through interactive analytics, the ability to run core financial reports much faster has also reduced the cycle times for repetitive financial processes so that the finance team anticipates a 40% reduction in the time taken to complete a month-end close.

But in addition to these improvement in operational productivity that have resulted in some incremental cost savings, Promivi has enjoyed very real financial benefits with the rapid insight into business performance helping to identify an opportunity to reduce working capital by half a million euros within the first week of going live.

Rogier Jacobs, CIO of Provimi Holdings, talks about "3-3-3 for SAP HANA" because it only took the implementation team 3 days to successfully complete a proof of concept using their CO-PA data; they were live and running in 3 weeks; and now it only takes 3 seconds to run any CO-PA analysis.

5.7 Profit Centers

Profit centers allow you to analyze internal costs according to business units and organizational responsibility. Profit Center Accounting (EC-PCA), part of Enterprise Controlling (EC) within SAP ERP, is an account-based method of looking at profit from an organizational standpoint, independent of the legal entity structure.

PCA is integrated with the CO module through a linkage of the profit center hierarchy to the controlling area. Many master records—including cost centers, projects, orders, material masters, and fixed assets—can be mapped to profit centers to ensure postings that include these master records will also reference a profit center. Certain balance sheet accounts—payables, receivables, inventory, and assets—can also be analyzed from a profit center perspective.

By default, PCA uses the period accounting method, in which profitability is based on the revenues and expenses incurred during a particular period. It can also support cost of sales accounting, meaning the COGS is recognized only in the period in which the corresponding revenues are recognized.

For PCA, you need to generate an opening balance for those balance sheet accounts that you want to analyze, which determines the balance for the profit center according to profit center assignments in master and transactional records. Examples include receivables, payables, inventory, and assets.

Although there are special cases in which closing activities should be carried out, for the most part, PCA benefits from the closing activities in other modules. For example, cost center distributions and assessments are already reflected for profit centers. You may need to run the allocation process directly in PCA in cases where a profit center has been defined to collect costs instead of a cost center, for example, for services.

When using the classic GL, if you choose to post balance sheet items to profit centers directly in transactions throughout a period, you need to carry the balances in the accounts forward for the profit centers, again for example for receivables, payables, fixed assets, and inventory accounts. Also, when reporting at higher levels in the profit center hierarchy, consolidation processes should be carried out to ensure accurate data.

When using the new SAP GL, because it is already integrated with PCA, you will not need to take the extra steps of posting balances for inventory accounts. You can also leverage the additional benefit of being able to generate financial statements on the profit center dimension. For further information about the SAP GL, please refer to Chapter 4, Section 4.2.4.

Now that we have covered the period-end processes, let's take a look at additional processes that are required at the end of the year.

5.8 Year-End Closing

At the end of the fiscal year, after the normal period-end close is complete, you need to perform additional activities. These activities include carrying forward commitments to the new fiscal year, which you need to perform for cost centers, internal orders, and projects. Also, for internal orders and projects, you need to carry forward budgets. Finally, you need to carry forward profit center balances to the new fiscal year.

The other controlling objects covered do not require additional steps to be carried out for the year-end close.

5.9 Reconciliation Between the FI and CO Modules

With the differentiation between financial and management accounting, you need to ensure that you reconcile postings that occur across organizational entities. For example, often more than one company code is linked to a controlling area. If an allocation takes place within the controlling area but cuts across different company codes, a reconciliation posting to the FI module is necessary. The same is true of allocations across business areas and functional areas.

If you are using the classic GL, these types of postings are captured in the reconciliation ledger. You can show a report of the required postings, and then use an automated program, which posts the reconciliation entries back to the financial module using reconciliation accounts that you create for this purpose.

If you are using the new SAP GL, the use of the reconciliation ledger is no longer necessary. Each time a cross-organizational allocation is made, for example, between profit centers, a financial posting is automatically created. For further information, please refer to Chapter 4, Section 4.2.4.

5.10 Summary

The Controlling (CO) module within SAP ERP allows you to manage cost centers, projects, and orders, which reflect a lower level of detail than in the chart of accounts. This module is designed to capture the details behind accounts in the P&L statement. The financial close processes for management accounting allows you to process both direct and indirect costs and allocations, and ensures the correct valuation of products, projects, orders and profitability segments.

In the next chapter, we will look at the process for governing the close for a legal entity, or company code. The SAP Financial Closing cockpit provides one place to control the close, for both financial and management accounting processes.

Managing the legal entity close means ensuring that each step is carried out successfully and that all steps are executed in the correct order. The SAP Financial Closing cockpit manages the entire close process for the entities of a group across both finance and operations tasks. This chapter will review the management of the entity close.

6 Entity Close Management

The first financial close activity that you need to process is the entity close. Each entity within an organization needs to close their books and this involves many steps and often multiple people. Often different parts of an organization will manage subsets of the close, for example by division or by geographical location. For statutory purposes, each legal entity must close their books. A legal entity is represented by the company code within SAP ERP Financials. But regardless if you have and SAP ERP or any other general ledger system, you must close down to the entity level.

Typical closing cycles for an entity involve time-consuming manual tasks, such as journal entries, accruals, reconciliations, and the gathering of financial data from across different systems. These manual tasks are often interspersed between automated system jobs that must be run before the next task can be carried out. In larger companies, the closing cycle can be even more complicated because the work of numerous people must be coordinated across different subsidiaries, divisions, time zones, and software systems. Each closing task must be performed correctly and in the proper sequence; otherwise, you may encounter delays in your closing process.

In most companies, the progress of the close is monitored by using spreadsheets, which rely on manual updates to maintain the status. Maintaining spreadsheets manually introduces risk in the process such as people not working on the proper version. Also, spreadsheets are not able to assist in either collaboration between teams or in automating the scheduling and monitoring of a system transaction or program.

The SAP Financial Closing cockpit application allows you to leverage best practices across your organization to define a standard close process, manage both manual and system tasks, enable collaboration between team members, automate batch jobs, and monitor the progress of the entity close. The application can be installed either alongside SAP ERP or stand-alone on SAP NetWeaver. It can be accessed from the SAP graphical user interface (GUI), or through a web-based user interface (UI) using either the SAP NetWeaver Portal or the SAP NetWeaver Business Client. The SAP Financial Closing cockpit also enables you to work across multiple SAP ERP or SAP R/3 backend systems, other SAP systems (including SAP NetWeaver Business Warehouse), and non-SAP systems, eliminating the need to log in to multiple systems to complete the legal entity close.

Each task in the template is given a date and time relative to the close date. So certain tasks will happen on the day before the close or two days after. Therefore when you create the actual task list off of the template you enter the actual close date, May 31st for example, and each task is assigned the actual date based off the template. Let's look at how this application can help you plan and execute your financial close tasks, and monitor the results of the close.

6.1 Plan and Prepare the Entity Close

To standardize the financial close across your organization, you first create templates that contain the tasks, in order, that need to be executed as part of the financial close (see Figure 6.1). The tasks are typically sorted based on the organizational hierarchy, including company code, plant or controlling area (for additional information, refer to Chapter 4, Section 4.1.1). Since each task has a date and time associated with it as mentioned, you can also organize your tasks by time.

You may have differences in your close tasks depending on the timing, such as year end, quarter end, and period end, or depending on regional differences, for example, to handle local tax processes or to handle a plant close for different types of manufacturing methods. You can choose to create multiple templates, or you can create one template to handle multiple types of closing cycles. If you choose to use one template, you can flag each task to designate to which closing type it belongs.

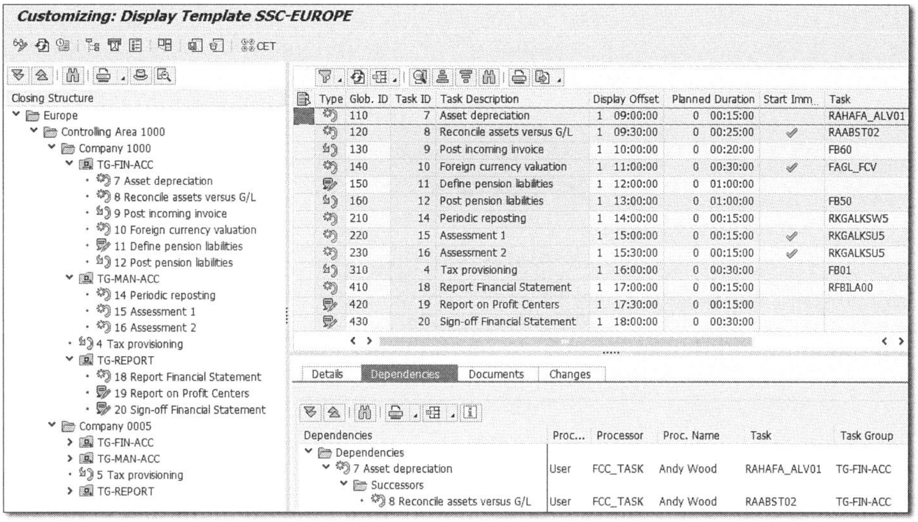

Figure 6.1 Using a Template to Standardize the Close Process

You can create different types of tasks within a template, including the following:

- Notes to document instructions for manual tasks outside of any system or for sign-off tasks.
- Calling up a transaction that needs to be executed, such as opening the next period for posting or posting journal entries for accruals.
- Calling up programs that you want to run online, such as a balance sheet report
- Batch jobs including passing over of values of standard and customer-definable variables from SAP Financial Closing cockpit to the native SAP scheduler, such as fixed asset depreciation—a huge gain in efficiency and quality by reducing the maintenance effort for variants
- Process flows that include dependencies between programs and system jobs, for example, in product costing where the sequence of calculating work in process (WIP), then calculating variances, then a settlement run for posting the results to the appropriate accounts must be maintained.

As discussed, you can create templates for different periods, different entities or different locations, but also deal with diversity within the same template. Not only does this help you manage your tasks but it also allows you to share best practices across the organization. Templates are easy to maintain and you can share task groups across different templates.

You can also create tasks using the SAP Central Process Scheduling application by Redwood. For additional information about scheduling automated jobs, see the "Scheduling Automated Financial Close Tasks" box in the following section.

6.2 Execute the Entity Close

When you are ready to begin the close, you then choose the appropriate template that contains the tasks that are required. As mentioned at the end of the first section in this chapter, each task in a template has a date and time associated with it relative to the actual close date. The system will track both the planned and actual start and end date and time of a task. At any time in the close, you can see the status of each task, as shown in Figure 6.2, as well as any dependencies between the tasks. You can set up event based close such that whenever all predecessor tasks are done, either the user of the next manual task is notified or the automatic task is started immediately.

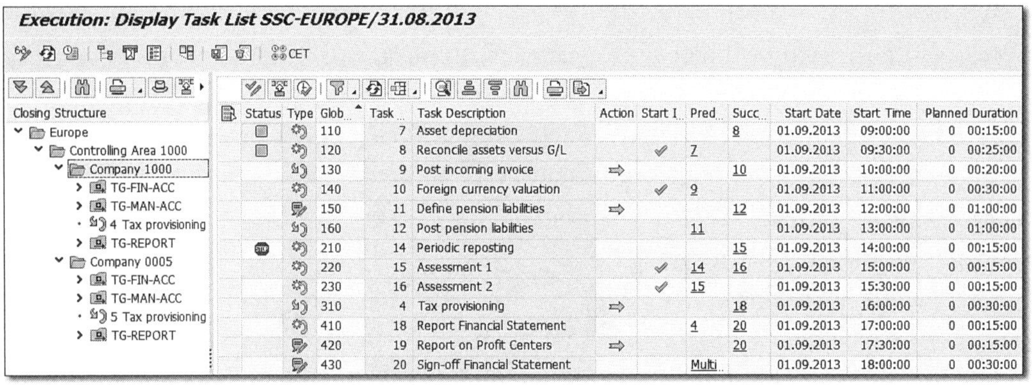

Figure 6.2 The Entity Close Progress in the SAP Financial Closing cockpit

You can also define alerts that are sent to enable better collaboration and facilitate a faster close. These alerts can be sent to proactively inform a task owner when there is an issue with a particular task, such as errors that occurred in a scheduled program or as an indication that an automated system job has completed and that it is time for a manual step to be executed. Notifications can also be very useful to inform about delays.

SAP Central Process Scheduling by Redwood (SAP CPS)

The SAP Central Process Scheduling application by Redwood is a partner solution that has been tightly integrated in the SAP Financial Closing cockpit to automate enterprise process management. Via the SAP Financial Closing cockpit, you define system jobs that need to be run as part of the financial close, schedule their execution, and monitor the results.

As for other tasks, you can indicate the start time and the parameters for running each job. In addition, the application allows you to define process chains and pass parameters from one process step to another, such as identify reconciliation accounts with balance unequal zero, create correction postings via batch input, and reversal postings into the next period.

For each job, you can see both the parameters and the results of the job run within the SAP Financial Closing cockpit, as shown in Figure 6.3.

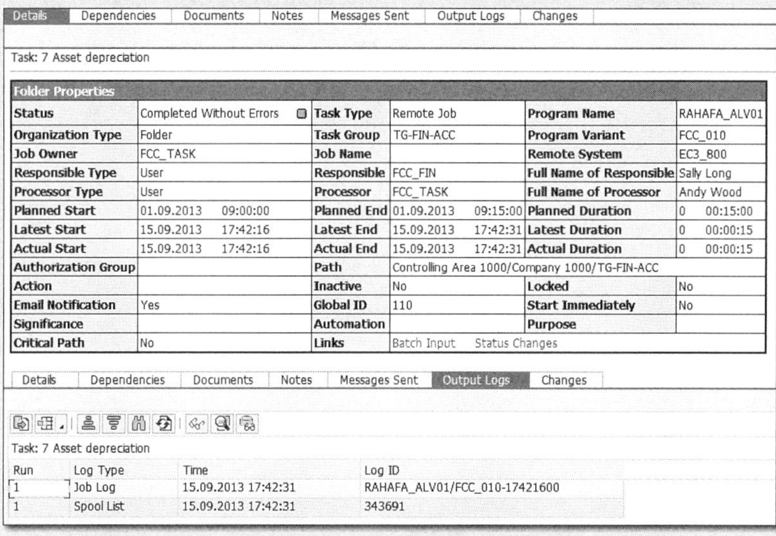

Figure 6.3 Results of the Execution of Automated System Jobs Viewed within the SAP Financial Closing cockpit

In addition to the straight-forward scheduling of jobs, you can also use conditional process intelligence to define dependencies between jobs. For example, if a batch job finishes with errors, these need to be corrected before the next job can be run; an example of this is in product costing (please refer to Section 5.5), where you would want to correct errors in the work in process and variance jobs before running the settlement to post the results to the General Ledger.

You can also monitor the performance of the batch jobs across periods. Each task has an estimated runtime. As shown in Figure 6.4, the performance of the jobs can be monitored across time, where exceptions are prominently highlighted. An analysis of the batch job performance may indicate that system performance tuning is required; alternatively, if the longer runtimes are due to a growing volume of data, you may want to adjust the expected time, or investigate whether archiving of data may be necessary.

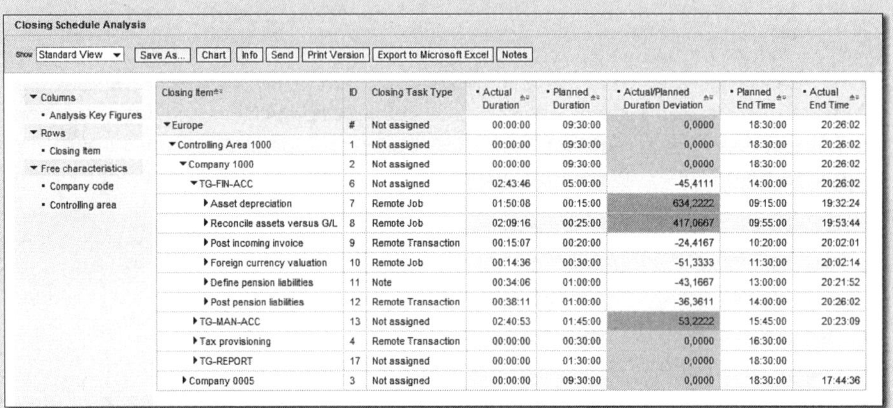

Closing Item	ID	Closing Task Type	Actual Duration	Planned Duration	Actual/Planned Duration Deviation	Planned End Time	Actual End Time
Europe	#	Not assigned	00:00:00	09:30:00	0,0000	18:30:00	20:26:02
Controlling Area 1000	1	Not assigned	00:00:00	09:30:00	0,0000	18:30:00	20:26:02
Company 1000	2	Not assigned	00:00:00	09:30:00	0,0000	18:30:00	20:26:02
TG-FIN-ACC	6	Not assigned	02:43:46	05:00:00	-45,4111	14:00:00	20:26:02
Asset depreciation	7	Remote Job	01:50:08	00:15:00	634,2222	09:15:00	19:32:24
Reconcile assets versus G/L	8	Remote Job	02:09:16	00:25:00	417,0667	09:55:00	19:53:44
Post incoming invoice	9	Remote Transaction	00:15:07	00:20:00	-24,4167	10:20:00	20:02:01
Foreign currency valuation	10	Remote Job	00:14:36	00:30:00	-51,3333	11:30:00	20:02:14
Define pension liabilities	11	Note	00:34:06	01:00:00	-43,1667	13:00:00	20:21:52
Post pension liabilities	12	Remote Transaction	00:38:11	01:00:00	-36,3611	14:00:00	20:26:02
TG-MAN-ACC	13	Not assigned	02:40:53	01:45:00	53,2222	15:45:00	20:23:09
Tax provisioning	4	Remote Transaction	00:00:00	00:30:00	0,0000	16:30:00	
TG-REPORT	17	Not assigned	00:00:00	01:30:00	0,0000	18:30:00	
Company 0005	3	Not assigned	00:00:00	09:30:00	0,0000	18:30:00	17:44:36

Figure 6.4 Monitoring Programs and Batch Jobs through a Comparison to Planned, or Expected, Execution Time.

Although the SAP Financial Closing cockpit allows you to schedule remote jobs in multiple SAP ERP systems even without the partner solution, SAP Central Process Scheduling by Redwood is required if you need to run jobs in other SAP systems such as SAP Customer Relationship Management (SAP CRM) or SAP NetWeaver BW, as well as incorporate tasks to be executed in non-SAP systems.

Let's look at how Dow Chemicals was able to standardize and streamline its financial close with the SAP Financial Closing cockpit and SAP Central Process Scheduling by Redwood.

6.3 Customer Story: Dow Chemicals' Faster, Less Costly Financial Close Process with SAP Solutions

Since it was founded by Herbert Henry Dow in Midland, Michigan, in 1897, innovation has enabled Dow Chemical to grow into a global company with a portfolio of more than 5,000 science-based products that it delivers to customers in approximately 160 countries. Today, with annual sales of nearly US$54 billion, the company runs 188 manufacturing sites in 35 different countries. And with close to 50,000 employees, it operates more than 750 subsidiary companies around the world.

But the spirit of innovation at Dow does not stop with its products and services; it also extends to back-office functions such as the financial close. Growth caused this process to become exceptionally complex and time-consuming with more than 1,000 different month-end jobs that were being manually coordinated by emails and spreadsheets.

During the 20 years that Dow has been an SAP customer, it has established a strong, trusting relationship with the company now helping to determine some of the functionality in recent SAP software releases. So when SAP suggested that the issues with the financial close process could be resolved with the SAP Financial Closing cockpit, the finance team listened. This solution centralizes the financial close process, automates key tasks, measures closing-cycle efficiency, and facilitates collaboration with an intuitive interface that gives real-time visibility throughout the process. At the same time, Dow also implemented the SAP Central Process Scheduling application by Redwood, which automates the batch processing of data during the close process.

Today, Dow has a single point of entry for all of its financial closing activities with a single global template that standardizes the financial close process across all its subsidiaries. Accessing this through Dow's corporate portal, finance staff can track progress with a complete, real-time overview of closing status and drill-down functionality for more details. Because all of the steps in the close are now automatically scheduled, the finance team is free for more value-adding work, but should any issues arise with the close, they can be quickly resolved using the solutions' collaboration functionality.

Since implementing the SAP Financial Closing cockpit and SAP Central Process Scheduling, Dow completes its month-end closes in a fraction of the time with improved efficiency, better visibility, and reduced costs—all helping the company keep a step ahead of the competition, even in its back-office processes.

6.4 Monitor the Entity Close

The SAP Financial Closing cockpit provides you with a single environment with a real-time view of every closing cycle task and its status. In addition to monitoring the automated jobs, as described in the "Scheduling Automated Financial Close Tasks" box in the previous section, you can also monitor the entire entity close process.

From a macro perspective, you can view the execution of the close using the task list, as shown earlier in Figure 6.2, or you can use a graphical Gantt chart view, as shown in Figure 6.5. By monitoring the entity close closely, you can identify issues, overdue tasks, and resource bottlenecks early in the close cycle before the overall close schedule is impacted.

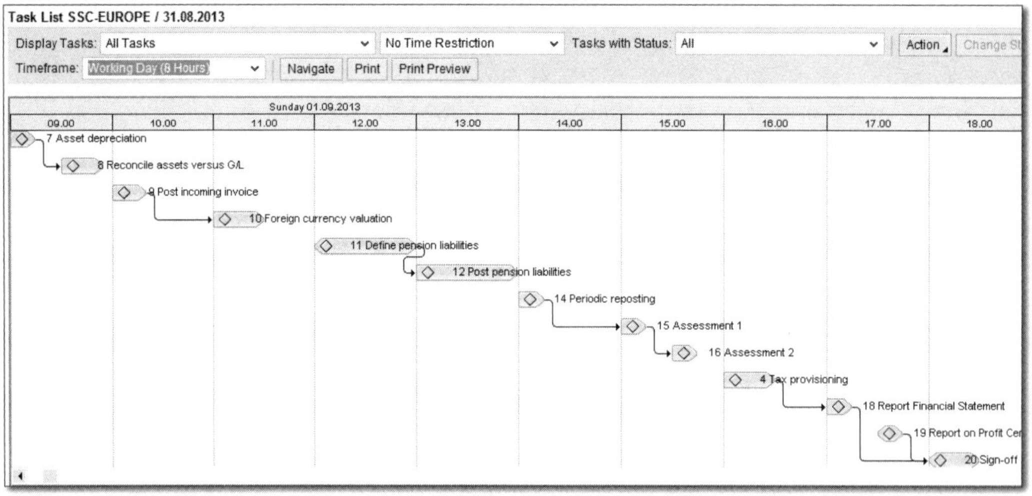

Figure 6.5 A Gantt Chart View Monitoring the Progress of the Period-End Tasks to Ensure the Timeliness of the Financial Close

From a micro perspective, you can drill down on each task to view its status and other details that have been documented about the task. You can use notes and attachments to document any collaboration or the resolution of any issues that you encountered. For automated tasks, such as programs that were run, you can directly access system logs and spool lists from the SAP Financial Closing cockpit without needing to search for them. The system provides a complete audit trail for configuration and execution. You can easily analyze any kind of status change, how often a task was executed, or who added or changed notes and attachments.

Finally, you can create a graphical dashboard to obtain an overview of the financial close, as shown in Figure 6.6. In this dashboard, which leverages SAP BusinessObjects Business Intelligence capabilities, you can create key performance indicators (KPIs) and calculate statistics, such as the percent of completion of the close, to allow you to quickly monitor the overall progress across regions and time frames.

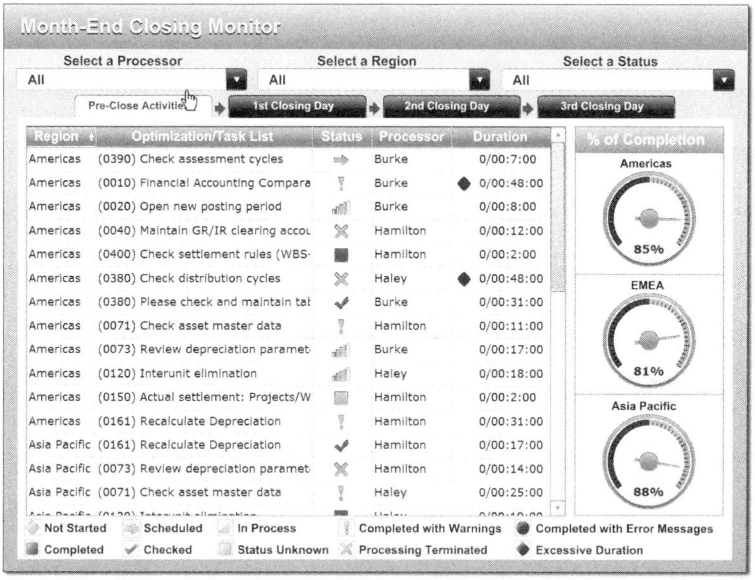

Figure 6.6 Using a Dashboard to Monitor the Legal Entity Close by Region

6.5 Summary

The SAP Financial Closing cockpit allows you to centralize, automate, and accelerate the steps that you need to process the financial close each of your entities, and it enables you to ensure that the steps are executed in a repeatable manner for consistency and auditability. The steps include manual tasks as well as scheduling transaction and programs that need to be run as part of the close. In addition, you can monitor the status of the close, drill down to the task level for additional details if you encounter an issue, and obtain KPIs of the status of the close at any time. All this enables compliance and provides stronger governance.

Now that we have looked at the entity close, in the next chapter, we will cover the extended controls you can use to ensure that the close is compliant and auditable, which are available using SAP solutions for governance, risk, and compliance (GRC).

Putting appropriate internal controls in place ensures a compliant financial close and enables external auditors to audit and report on these controls as part of the required disclosures in financial statements. This chapter will explore internal controls and their value in compliance.

7 Enhanced Internal Controls for Better Compliance

The financial close culminates with the issuance of reports that highlight the financial outcomes for the business. Many companies must also report on the health and integrity of their business. For these companies, a part of the financial close is accumulating and reporting on information about the orderly execution of your business, especially your financial processes. For many, the periodic financial close includes routine reports that internal controls are in place and effective. This is done to provide assurances to management, investors, and regulators that your business processes are well designed, and executed as designed and in an orderly way. Regulators in many countries require that management assess and publicly report on the internal controls related to the preparation and issuance of financial statements. Beyond this, external auditors may be required to independently audit internal controls. Depending on your business and industry, you may have a number of regulatory compliance requirements related to your internal controls.

Internal controls are rules or standards that dictate how a business process is to be executed. The controls ensure that this is done with integrity and in a predictable, transparent, and repeatable way. Controls are also designed to ensure that an affected business process follows all of the rules set by regulators. There may be a focus on particular controls where there is a risk that a business process step may not be executed as desired or required.

There are many ways to categorize the various types of controls. For this discussion, consider these different types of controls:

- Access controls that dictate who executes steps in a business process, what business systems they have rights to, and what types of data they can view and update. Ultimately, these controls ensure that employees have access to the data and systems that enable them to fulfill their responsibilities.
- Segregation of duties (SoDs) controls that ensure the execution of multiple steps in a business process are performed by different people to minimize the opportunity for fraud and abuse.
- Business process controls that outline the expected or proper way for a series of business process to execute. For example, a purchase order must be issued to a supplier to purchase goods or services, and the purchase order must be issued prior to the delivery of those goods or services. Another example is a business process that requires approvals at defined stages in a process, for example travel and expense approvals.
- Account reconciliations that require a person to explain the difference between multiple collections of related transactions.
- Physical inventories that ensure the amount of materials on hand is as expected based on a system-maintained inventory.

Controls should be in place and executed as business processes proceed. A routine examination, commonly referred to as a control test, should be completed at a predefined frequency. Any test failures must be corrected. The results of all control tests should be aggregated and reported to senior management, investors, and regulators. The ultimate goal is to report that controls are in place and effective. For many companies that publicly issue financial reports, this report of control effectiveness is done at the same time and, therefore, considered an integral part of the financial close.

Technology, specifically software solutions, can play a considerable role in helping companies and other organizations manage controls programs and execute control testing. SAP solutions for governance, risk and compliance (GRC) allow you to address compliance and controls requirements and, ultimately, ensure that your financial close more compliant. These solutions help you automate both access controls and process management to prevent unauthorized access to sensitive and key corporate information, as well as detect fraud and abuse. Once configured, these solutions provide continuous monitoring of key risk indicators and compliance effectiveness across enterprise systems, business processes, and IT infrastructures that enable you to align risks and compliance programs to strategic initiatives, plans, and execution.

Let's take a look at a customer story. Natura had identified weaknesses related to the control of access to information and implemented SAP Access Control to resolve these issues.

Customer Story: Natura Consolidates a Governance Model to Lower the Information Security Risk

Faced with a high level of information security risk, Brazilian personal care specialist Natura began a process to strengthen its governance model. An audit identified a number of weaknesses, particularly the lack of a solid strategy for managing access. Additionally, the company did not have a culture of governance and information security, and the low level of involvement of business areas in the process of risk assessment made the situation even harder to manage. A change in corporate culture was necessary.

Natura finished creating a risk matrix in 2009. That year, it also implemented SAP Access Control and adapted its processes to conform to the Sarbanes-Oxley (SOX) Act, which requires the creation of reliable mechanisms for auditing and security to mitigate a company's business risks. The new governance model that Natura established allowed for a more accurate assessment of security risks as well as the fulfillment of compliance regulations resulting in the company obtaining SOX certification. With the support of SAP software, Natura saw its level of information security risk drop by an estimated 69%.

But as the company grew, it needed to further strengthen the governance model and the strategy for managing access. So, in 2010, Natura upgraded SAP Access Control to consolidate its governance model while at the same time benefitting from simpler interfaces and better integration with the existing SAP architecture. This upgrade has allowed for more complete, compliant reporting as well as reducing the time needed to prepare reports for auditing by 60%. The upgrade also required a reassessment of access, allowing inactive profiles to be excluded. Thus, the access matrix used by SAP Access Control became leaner, with a resulting 30% drop in transaction volume per profile. Natura also experienced lower maintenance costs with 50% fewer support calls being made to customer service.

Raising the business areas' understanding of processes related to the governance model has created a new culture of risk management at Natura. The time needed to maintain controls for employee compensation has fallen by 15–20%, and, the consolidation of the governance model at Natura has achieved a total reduction of 87% in information security risk overall. Now let's take a look at how effective access risk management plays an important role in the finance organization.

7.1 Access Risk Management

If we look specifically at the financial close process, team members need access to both information and transactions in order to execute financial close activities. Managing access manually is time-consuming and increases the risk that team members are unable to perform their responsibilities if access isn't granted, as well as the risk that team members will have too much access to sensitive data.

With SAP Access Control, you can automate processes to detect, remediate, and prevent access violations; streamline and automate user provisioning; and centralize role management. This helps reduce the cost of access management, audit, and ongoing compliance activities while minimizing the risk of internal fraud.

Automating user access management tasks makes it easier for users to obtain the access that they need in a timely manner while maintaining compliance.

SAP Access Control provides a standardized and centralized framework for users to request the access that they need and approvers to review and manage those requests. Team members can create access requests, as shown in Figure 7.1.

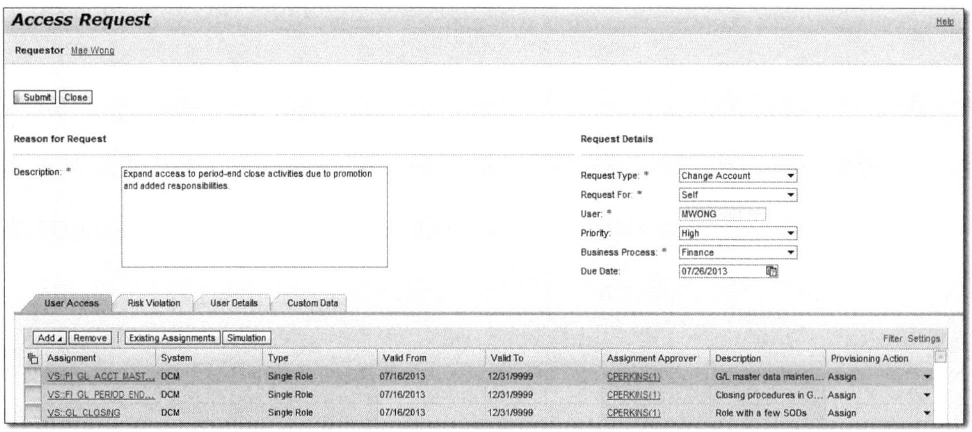

Figure 7.1 Requesting Roles through SAP Access Control

After a request is submitted, an automated workflow engine sends the request to one or more approvers for processing. Analyzing the risks associated with the requested access is a critical step in the process, which should be addressed before access is assigned to ensure identified risks are adequately mitigated. Here, risks may be identified due to a segregation of duty (SoD) or critical access violation (see Section 7.1.1 for more on SoD). During the workflow process, a risk analysis can be made mandatory to check for risks that are introduced by the roles requested in conjunction with any roles that are already assigned to the user. These requests can be accepted or rejected either online or through a mobile app (see Figure 7.2) as discussed in the "Mobile Apps for Faster Response to Risk" box.

At times, a user may need temporary access outside of normal job responsibilities. Also, a team member may need access that is sensitive in nature and must be tracked for audit purposes, for example, maintaining posting periods during the close process, or updating vendor accounts as part of the accounts payable close while a colleague is on vacation. The emergency access management capability of SAP Access Control allows employees to execute tasks under a firefighter ID in an auditable manner. The application provides a closed-loop process for managing emergency access—automating the request, approval, access monitoring, and review of activities performed—in a centralized location with a full audit trail.

Mobile Apps for Faster Responses to Risk

When you make your compliance processes mobile, your finance teams have the tools they need to manage risks and policies on their mobile devices in real time. For example:

- **SAP GRC Access Approver mobile app**
  This app helps you ensure that the right employees have access to the right systems. Finance officers can review and approve time-sensitive access requests on their mobile devices, allowing requests to be answered quickly without an increase in compliance risk. The app leverages automated rules in SAP Access Control and flags requests that have been evaluated as being risky, as shown in Figure 7.2.
- **SAP GRC Policy Survey mobile app**
  This app helps you keep track of the latest policy changes within your organization. Managers can minimize compliance risk while taking surveys to help understand the full implications of new policies. An example is distributing corporate codes of conduct documents, with survey questions asking employees to acknowledge their acceptance of these policies; these policies are often referenced in an annual report.

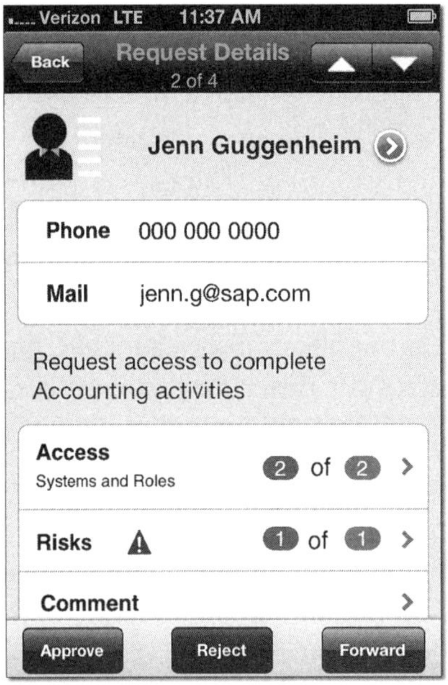

Figure 7.2 Approve or Reject Access Requests on Mobile Devices

Ultimately SAP Access Control enables the finance organization to have real-time visibility into the access that team members have and the risk that is presented as a result. Without an automated solution, it is nearly impossible to have an accurate view of access governance and to ensure that any access risk violations are effectively mitigated.

7.1.1 Segregation of Duties

Segregation of duties (SoD) is a primary internal control intended to prevent internal fraud and error by separating tasks within a business process between multiple users. An example of this in the financial close process is separating the responsibility for depositing cash and reconciling bank statements, or the ability to receive checks as payment and the responsibility for write-offs.

Implementing SoDs can be challenging for companies small and large, as many times it is impossible to completely segregate incompatible duties. In these cases, mitigating controls should be implemented to minimize the risk.

Let's take a look at a customer story. Infosys Limited was able to practically eliminate SoD violations with SAP Access Control.

7.1.2 Customer Story: Infosys Treats Governance and Compliance Strategically with SAP Access Control

Infosys Limited is one of the largest technology services companies in the world with a staff of 150,000 in 64 offices and 63 development centers providing technology-enabled business solutions for Global 2000 companies.

With a stated vision to become a globally respected corporation and a mission to build an enterprise prepared for tomorrow, the executive team at Infosys prioritized the need to embrace robust corporate governance and implement vigorous risk management practices, viewing them not just as an obligatory obligation but as something that could drive competitive advantage and business performance.

Recognizing that they lacked a systematic and efficient way of handling governance, risk, and compliance across the enterprise, the management team endorsed the need for investment. As a first step, Infosys integrated the SAP Access Control application into their existing SAP ERP application backbone. A multidisciplinary team made up of business process owners and individuals from enterprise audit, IT, and enterprise risk management was assembled to identify enterprise SoD risks. The team analyzed risks from a number of business units against the end-to-end business processes, the responsibility of users involved in the business operations, and a standard SoD rule set provided by the SAP software—and after several iterations, identified and categorized SoD risks based on the business impact. This provided the basis for revoking unnecessary access permissions and remapping those that were really needed.

Through SAP Access Control, the team mapped out governance policies for role management so that SoD risk analysis could be performed before roles were released to the test and production environment. This eliminated the ability to create roles that resulted in SoD violations. With SAP Access Control up and running, Infosys has successfully embedded compliance into its core business processes with automated and real-time monitoring of access permissions and conflicts in the system resulting in the early detection of potential risks and proactive prevention of possible SoD conflicts. In fact, the organization has reduced the human effort associated with user access provisioning and deprovisioning by 80% and has entirely eliminated SoD violations.

Let's now take a look at managing not just access to individual transactions and data, but how controls are implemented across business processes.

7.2 Identifying Controls across a Business Process

The need for controls goes beyond effective access risk management. Compliance requirements often dictate that you document your collection of controls and execute periodic controls testing. For many compliance programs, the execution of and reporting on control testing coincides closely with required financial reporting. There is, therefore, a need to incorporate compliance and other associated tasks into the prototypical close process. The controls and associated control testing relate to various business processes. The controls integral to financial business processes, including general accounting, revenue recognition, accounts payable and receivable, and financial statement preparation, are always in scope.

SAP Process Control technology can and, especially for larger companies, should enable the documentation of controls, control testing, and aggregation of required signatures or approvals. SAP Process Control is an application for compliance and policy management. It helps you by focusing resources on key risks—the most critical regulatory requirements and high impact processes—and by providing continuous insight into your compliance and controls status for better decision making. Automated control testing can be executed via a connection to the SAP ERP system.

Let's look at how controls are created and the remediation that can be used when the control is violated.

7.2.1 Control Monitoring and Remediation

Internal controls are rules or standards that dictate how a business process is to be executed. The controls ensure that this is done with integrity and in a predictable, transparent, and repeatable way. Controls are also designed to ensure that an affected business process follows all of the rules set by regulators. There may be a focus on particular controls where there is a risk that a business process step may not be executed as desired or required.

A control is created where a step in a business includes risk that that activity will not be completed as required. These controls need to be tested on a periodic basis so that any violations can be identified and resolved. Depending on the control, testing may need to be done manually, or in a semi-automated or automated fashion.

The following types of automated and semi-automated controls monitor information in SAP ERP:

- Configuration controls to identify unauthorized configuration settings.
- Master data controls to identify suspicious settings in master data records.
- Transaction data controls to identify unusual business transactions.

For example, in the context of the financial close, the change in the useful life for large capital investments, such as buildings, can have a dramatic impact on the depreciation that is posted. For such a control, as shown in Figure 7.3, automated monitoring and testing is possible through a connection with the SAP ERP system where the fixed assets module has been implemented.

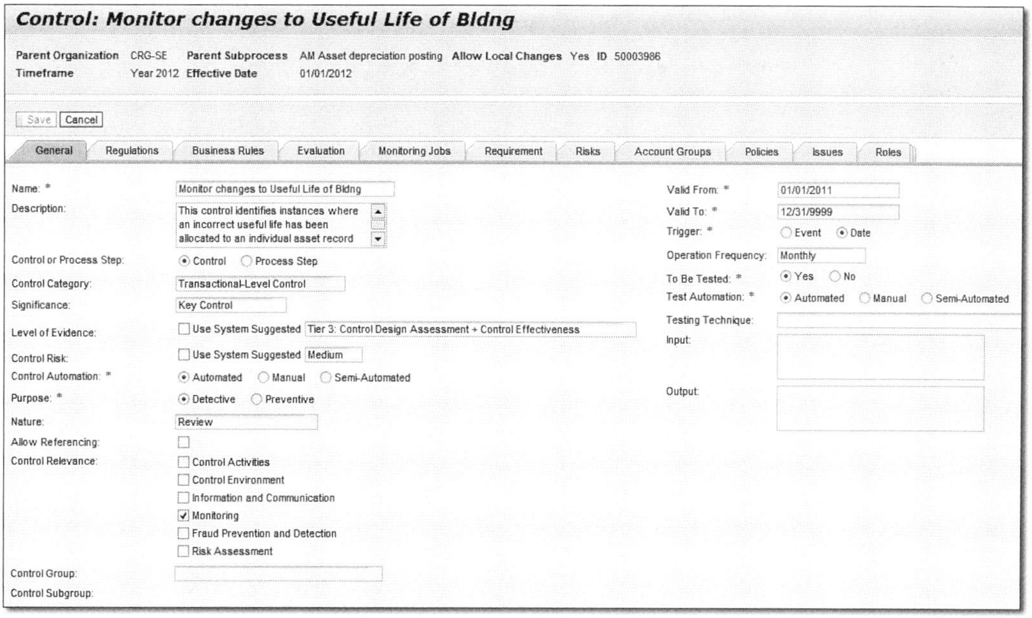

Figure 7.3 Defining a Process Control

When a control test fails, it is highlighted as part of the comprehensive monitoring available with SAP Process Control. The workflow capabilities then route the violation to the owner, who can determine the needed remediation steps. This plan can include activities to mitigate any risk and may involve changing a policy or a configuration setting in order to maintain compliance. For example, if a violation has been identified due to a manual journal entry, as shown in Figure 7.4, you may want to disallow manual entries on particular accounts or implement other safeguards for reviewing such entries in the future. Similar controls are in place for other financial business process steps. Correspondingly, control tests are in place and executed routinely. The results of the control tests and any outstanding remediation tasks must be reviewed during the financial close process. This is done to ensure that all controls related to financial business processes are in place and effective. Ultimately, management may issue a statement affirming this to comply with regulatory reporting requirements.

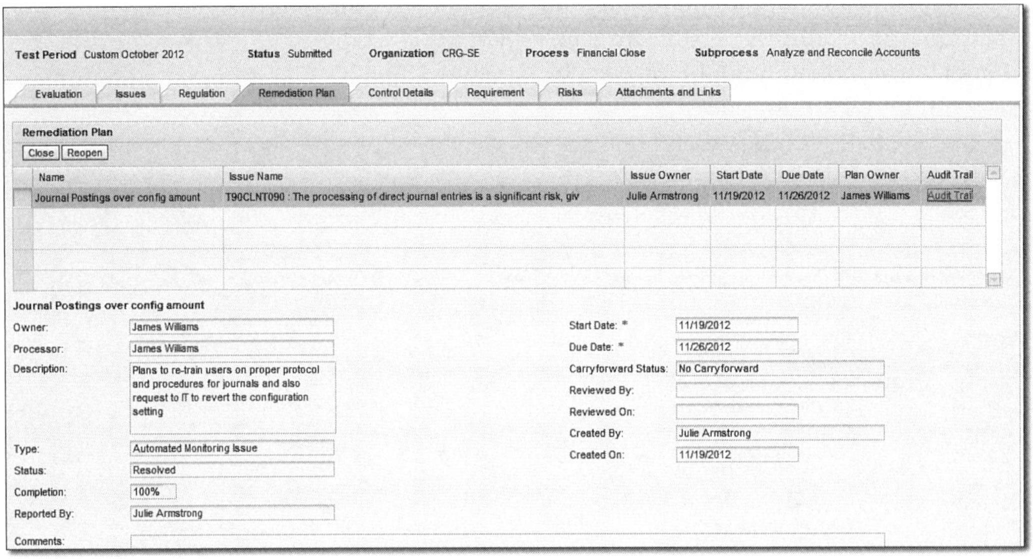

Figure 7.4 Defining a Remediation Plan

In the next section, we will look at a customer, REC Silicon, who was able to increase visibility into its processes using SAP Process Control.

7.2.2 Customer Story: REC Silicon, Inc. Leverages Enhanced Process Controls

At its production facilities in Moses Lake in the state of Washington and Butte in Montana, REC Silicon, Inc., produces silane gas and electronic and solar-grade silicon that are used by its sister companies in the REC group and third parties in the manufacture of solar panels.

The company needed to improve its management of financial business processes, which were entirely manual and paper-based, in order to further enhance the group's ongoing commitment to regulatory compliance regarding process control monitoring. At the same time, it hoped automation would reduce the internal workload associated with process controls and the cost of external auditing. The REC group had recognized the benefits of creating an IT foundation to support a more global, complex organization and had already implemented standard integrated SAP applications in areas such as financials, sales, manufacturing, procurement, and reporting. Into this now uniform environment, a project team made up of REC Silicon staff and SAP Consulting introduced the SAP Process Control application, which effectively provided information system controls for the existing financial applications and delivered the compliance reporting functionality that was required.

Running the business using a single instance of SAP applications meant fewer overall systems in operation so the IT team could develop deep expertise and focus dedicated resources on projects that supported ongoing improvements across the business, including the management of core financial processes. The introduction of the SAP Process Control application into this standardized environment allowed essential financial processes during closings, reconciliations, and account postings to be monitored and reviewed well in advance of quarterly discussions with the external auditors. This substantially improved existing application and process controls and enabled the company to put the required governance frameworks into practice on a monthly, weekly, and even daily basis with tools that enabled the necessary monitoring.

Having better visibility into financial processes also reduced the number of ad hoc reporting requests that were typically required to meet compliance needs during audits, and it is anticipated that both the impact and cost of external audits will be reduced. Next, let's consider a special case for the use of SAP Process Control: the management of internal audits.

7.3 Audit Management

For the annual internal audit, your challenges are maintaining audit quality standards, managing work papers, and audit reporting—often with scarce resources. To help you manage the auditing process, SAP Audit Management, powered by

SAP HANA, leverages several components, including SAP Process Control, SAP Audit Management from SAP ERP and SAP NetWeaver, and SAP Multiresource Scheduling. These tools help you standardize the audit documentation and test procedures, create workflow functionality, and identify the required reporting. You may also choose to use SAP Risk Management to prioritize audit activities.

With SAP Audit Management, you can use existing GRC data on risk assessment results to facilitate risk-based scoping for the annual audit plan, including audit planning, preparation, execution, and reporting.

You then create the audit plan by copying an audit plan template. Figure 7.5 shows an initial audit plan structure. You may want to create different templates, depending on the timing of the audit (quarterly and annually), or the type of audit, for example, a SOX (Sarbanes-Oxley) audit, tax audit, or fraud audit. Other information includes the dates of the audit, documentation that needs to be completed, and question lists.

You can also identify the resources that are required for the audit. If you are using the scheduling component, then you can check on the availability of the resources during the period of time that the audit is taking place.

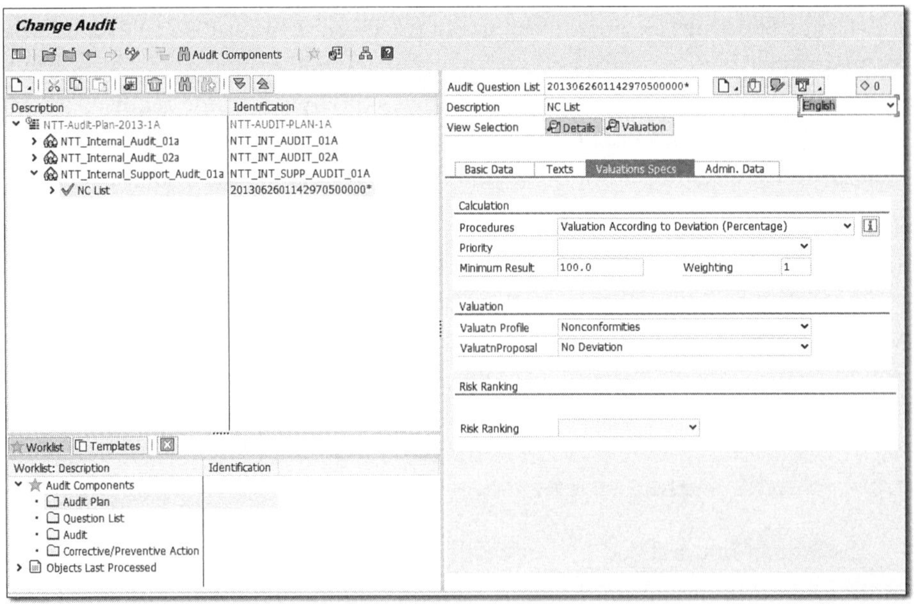

Figure 7.5 Control Audit Steps with an Audit Plan

After the audit has been released, work can begin. The resources that are executing the audit can document their work, include test results from predefined procedures, and respond to internal controls and risks that were previously identified. Work papers can be attached so that all documentation is in one place. As each step is completed, an employee can then set the status of that step.

Managers can enter review notes for the audit procedure, providing the ability to review the audit file to ensure that it has been prepared in accordance with internal audit's methodology and IIA (Institute of Internal Auditors) standards, for assurance that the work performed has addressed all risks identified within the scope of the audit. It also provides the ability to input reviewer comments and provide approval.

After all of the test procedures are complete, the audit lead then enters an overall assessment and rating for the entire audit. The degree of fulfillment and the overall assessment is automatically calculated based on the valuation assignment in the individual audit steps.

From within the audit plan, you can generate the audit report, which includes background information on the business unit under audit, scope of the audit, and identification of key issues, findings, and internal control weaknesses that need to be addressed, as well as the key stakeholders accountable to address them.

Now let's take a look at advanced reporting and analytics capabilities that you can use to analyze your compliance effectiveness.

7.4 GRC Analytics

Prior to the availability of analytic solutions, many compliance officers spent the majority of their time running reports, collating the results, managing spreadsheets, calling other employees, and sending emails to analyze the state of access compliance. By using analytics capabilities, you can be more proactive in identifying risks and monitoring risk violations.

With SAP BusinessObjects Business Intelligence (BI) solutions, dashboards, such as the one shown in Figure 7.6, are available to allow you fast access to compliance information. Dashboards provide the following information:

- **Access risks** allow you to identify overall risk violations and identify business processes at the highest risk.
- **Alerts** allow you to identify which acts were actually performed and by which users.
- **Review of access rules** includes looking at how access risks are defined and how functional rules are mapped to the transactions being monitored.
- **Role reviews** identify which users are assigned to which roles, as well as which roles are orphaned, or not in use.
- **Review of emergency access** allows you to monitor the audit trail and the frequency of use of the firefighter ID.

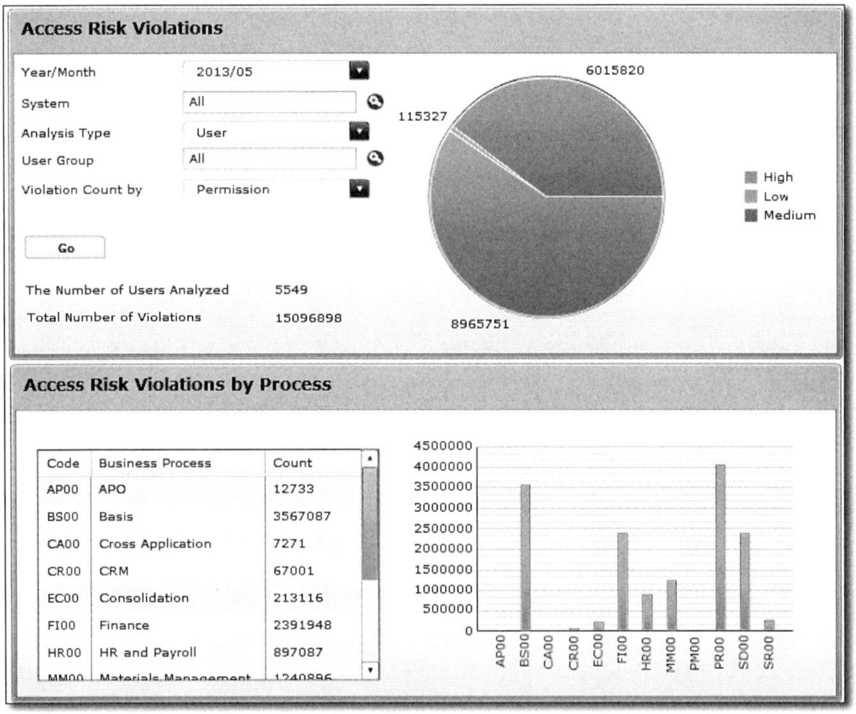

Figure 7.6 Monitoring Access Risks and Violations with Dashboards

As the workforce becomes increasingly mobile, you need to be able to access risk and compliance information quickly. With SAP Access Control dashboards, which are available on a desktop browser as well as on mobile devices, you can access all of the information you need while on the go to ensure your company is within access compliance, for example, for a quarterly internal audit. In the dashboard shown in Figure 7.7, you can analyze the trends related to access risk to determine whether one business process has increased or decreased violations, for example, on a quarter over quarter basis. In addition, you can analyze violations of your SoD rules. For each area, you can drill down to more detailed information.

The information provided may lead you to make decisions related to user access. For example, you can remove critical or sensitive access from an employee's everyday role and instead have the employee perform the activities through a firefighter ID. This allows the users to do the job they need to, while giving compliance officers and auditors the extra layer of reporting for sensitive information.

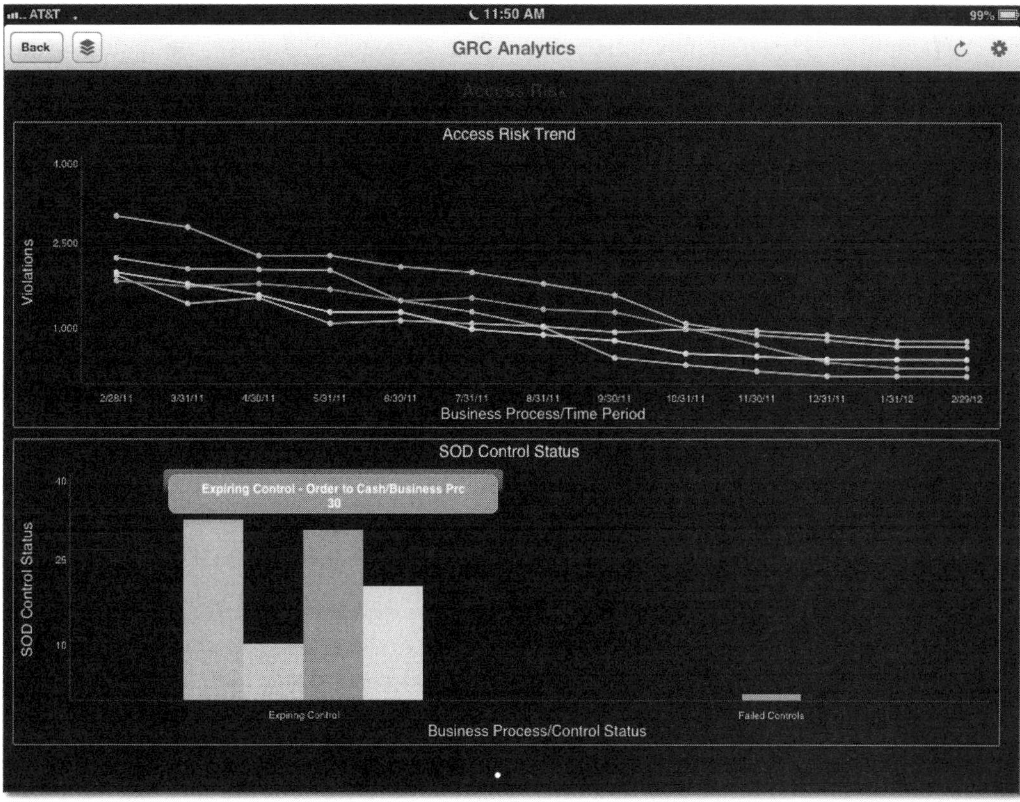

Figure 7.7 Mobile Access from the Apple iPad

Leveraging SAP HANA for Compliance

Using the SAP HANA platform, SAP solutions for GRC benefit from greater and timelier access to data for monitoring and reporting purposes. The following are two examples where the real-time power of SAP HANA is leveraged in these solutions:

- With the SAP HANA Live for SAP solutions for GRC and integration with the SAP NetWeaver Business Warehouse (SAP NetWeaver BW) application, you can create a virtual data model. This enables custom reporting through the SAP BusinessObjects portfolio and increases the speed of your access to information for analysis.
- The SAP Fraud Management application, powered by SAP HANA, allows you to uncover hidden trends and patterns in large amounts of data to detect fraud in near real time. In addition to the advanced analytic capabilities, the application includes simulation features to reduce false positives and enables you to proactively develop fraud-prevention strategies.

7.5 Summary

The financial close includes critical activities to affirm that key controls throughout the business are in place and effective. These tasks must be completed in conjunction with other well-known tasks that are considered part of the financial close. Technology should play a role to ensure that these tasks are repeatable, independent, and objective. SAP solutions for GRC allow you to effectively automate all of the required activities. By doing so, you can better manage your risk and compliance programs, protect your revenue streams and reputation, optimize business operations, and improve financial performance. In the next chapter, we will look at preparing for the group close by exploring how to process intercompany reconciliations.

Intercompany reconciliation has been cited for many years as one of the most common and frequently occurring barriers to a fast, high-quality close. The question is: what can you do about it? This chapter aims to provide you with some answers.

8 Intercompany Reconciliation

In this chapter we will discuss the challenges and possible solutions surrounding intercompany reconciliation. We will begin by defining intercompany reconciliation then discuss the solutions SAP has to offer. We will discuss not only how these common challenges can be addressed with software solutions but also how addressing the overall process can improve business results and showcase improvements. This chapter covers the intercompany reconciliation process at a high level and showcases the options and business benefits of SAP's solutions for today's enterprises. Let's start by defining what we mean by *intercompany reconciliation*.

8.1 Defining Intercompany Reconciliation

During the financial close process, business organizations must eliminate intercompany activity so they do not overstate account balances. For example, if Entity A has a $100 accounts payable (AP) transaction due to Entity B, Entity B should have a corresponding accounts receivable (AR) transaction on its books. These amounts need to be eliminated before the total AP and AR amounts are calculated for the entire organization so they are not overstated. Before these accounts are eliminated, they first need to be reconciled. The intercompany reconciliation process is often referred to as intercompany matching (see Figure 8.1).

There are many reasons intercompany account balances between entities might not match, including timing of recording the transactions, exchange rate differences, or even outright mistakes. Typically, the reconciliation process starts at the account level by comparing intercompany AP against intercompany AR. When the intercompany account balances don't match, then detailed transactional or invoice level data is consulted.

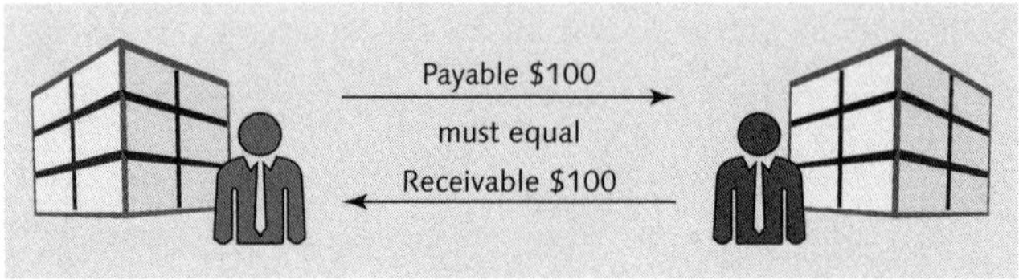

Figure 8.1 Intercompany Reconciliation

Each entity's transactional and invoice level details are typically captured in the General Ledger (GL) system. Most GL systems allow for the recording of the trading partner. Most transactional systems can record the intercompany trading partner when the transaction is recorded. This level of detail is required to automate intercompany reconciliation and elimination. Now we have defined the issue, the following sections will introduce different solutions to address these challenges, both from a technology and a process angle.

8.2 SAP Solutions for Intercompany Reconciliation

As discussed in the prior section, during the consolidation process, intercompany data must first be reconciled at the account or balance level. These balances are made up of transactions, so to reconcile the balances, you must dive into the details.

Challenges around intercompany reconciliation vary based on the structure of your source systems that capture transactional intercompany data. Source intercompany data typically comes from a GL system. If your organization has many disparate sources systems, there will be more challenges when reconciling intercompany data than if you have one source system.

SAP offers two solutions specifically for intercompany reconciliation:

- Intercompany Reconciliation (ICR): Cross-company Intercompany Reconciliation is a part of the Financials Extension (EA-FIN) business function.
- SAP Intercompany: SAP Intercompany is part of the Enterprise Performance Management (EPM) suite.

SAP Intercompany Licensing Note

Although SAP Intercompany can be licensed separately for use with non-SAP consolidation systems, it is included with the license rights of SAP Business Planning and Consolidation and SAP Financial Consolidation.

The following sections will discuss which solution is better suited for different environments.

8.2.1 One Source System

Many organizations are moving toward one standard transactional system. In the event that your organization has one instance of an enterprise resource planning (ERP) system, intercompany reconciliation has fewer moving parts. When all the transactional or invoice data is contained in one system it makes it easier to manage.

For organizations who are centralized on once instance of an SAP ERP there is an intercompany solution included. Intercompany Reconciliation (ICR) is part of the SAP ERP. ICR can be used for transactional matching when *all* reconciling entities are on SAP ERP and *all* relevant data is stored in SAP ERP. Cross-company ICR is a part of the Financials Extension (EA-FIN) business.

The purpose of ICR is to ensure that intercompany documents from accounting transactions within the corporate group correspond to one another. It contains tools that check whether documents have been correctly assigned to a business transaction, tools that enable you to find corresponding documents easily, and tools to make additional assignments. ICR operates on the level of companies and partner companies (trading partners).

If the reconciliation process is successful, this will ultimately lead to reduced differences in corporate group consolidation.

SAP Intercompany, on the other hand, is part of SAP's EPM suite. SAP Intercompany is a peer-to-peer web based solution. See Table 8.1 which defines the differences between the two solutions.

	SAP Intercompany	Intercompany Reconciliation (ICR)
Product details	Part of the enterprise performance management (EPM) suite	Cross-company Intercompany Reconciliation is a part of the Financials Extension (EA-FIN) business function as part of the SAP Business Suite.
Requirements for SAP ERP customers interested in transactional level detail	▸ NOT ALL reconciling entities are on SAP ERP OR ▸ Reconciling entities use multiple SAP ERP systems	▸ ALL reconciling entities are on SAP ERP AND ▸ ALL relevant transaction data is stored in the same SAP ERP system
Suitable for non SAP ERP Customers	Yes	No
Suitable for customers with multiple or disparate ERP systems	Yes	No
Further detail	Discussed further in Section 8.3	Further detail for SAP ICR can be found *http://help.sap.com*. Search on key words "EA-FIN: Intercompany reconciliation."

Table 8.1 Differences between SAP Solutions for Intercompany Reconciliation

8.2.2 Multiple Intercompany Source Systems

Many organizations have multiple instances of source transactional systems. Different divisions or geographical regions may be using different GL systems. They could be different instances of an SAP ERP system, for example, or there could be Oracle in Europe, JD Edwards in Latin America, and SAP in Japan.

In this case, the ability to reconcile between entities that are on different source systems becomes more challenging. SAP Intercompany is a solution perfect for this type of landscape.

8.2.3 Leveraging Consolidation Systems for Intercompany Reconciliation

As discussed both ICR and SAP Intercompany are leveraged for reconciling intercompany information at the transactional or account detail level. Consolidation systems such as SAP Business Planning and Consolidation and SAP Financial Consolidation (discussed further in Chapter 9) reconcile intercompany information at the account level and not at the invoice or transactional level. As such, additional tools are required to reach that lower level of detail.

8.3 Managing the Intercompany Process

In the previous section, we introduced how different technology landscapes can affect the intercompany process; let's now explore options for varying the intercompany process.

8.3.1 Traditional Intercompany Reconciliation Process

Traditionally, the reconciliation process is managed by corporate headquarters. They collect data from the various reporting units and, in some cases, need to normalize the data. Once collected from all reporting units, a reconciliation process is run that matches all of the intercompany data against the corresponding entities. Many organizations rely on financial consolidation systems as their intercompany reconciliation tool, which are usually designed to capture account balances, rather than the transactional detail required, as discussed in Section 8.2.3. Reports are created that highlight the out-of-balance information and are then returned to the reporting units (see Figure 8.2).

The reporting units then drill back to the transactional detail manually to understand what makes up the account balances. After retrieving the detail, they correspond with the other entities via phone, fax, or email to determine why the discrepancies exist. Not only is this manual reconciliation time consuming, but it is also difficult to trace as much of the unstructured data contained in emails that are not easily audited.

Reporting units wait until the end of the period and rely on communications from corporate before they begin to look at the intercompany balance. Corporate becomes not only the intermediary but also the policing agent to ensure that the balances are reconciled. Headquarters become overwhelmed managing reconciliations rather than other closing tasks for which they are better suited. The lack of direct contact between reporting units results in a bottleneck at corporate headquarters that creates an inefficient vertical flow of information between headquarters and the reporting units. Extensive procedures and forms need to be created to manage the process as well.

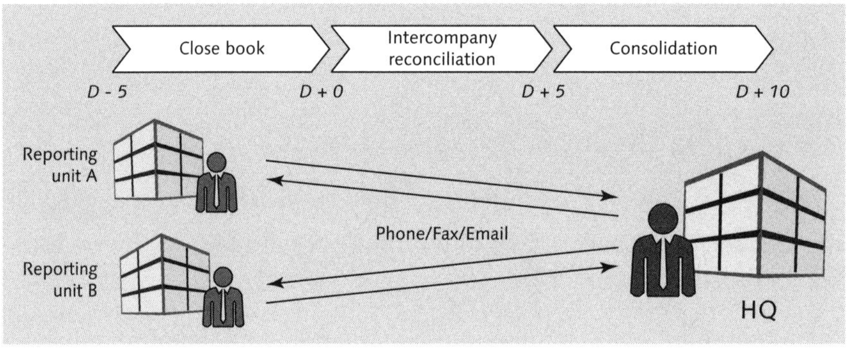

Figure 8.2 Traditional Intercompany Process

8.3.2 Peer-to-Peer Intercompany Reconciliation Process

A peer-to-peer reconciliation process pulls the intercompany reconciliation process out of the critical path of the close process. Reporting units in this process deal directly with one another in a peer-to-peer fashion rather than using corporate as an intermediary (see Figure 8.3).

By distributing the responsibility out to the reporting units, it frees central finance staff from time spent on non-value-added tasks and allows them more time to analyze data and determine *why* things happened rather than just being able to account for *what* happened.

Effective collaboration is key when reconciling intercompany balances. The typical reconciliation process involves emails and phone calls that cannot be easily traced or documented. The collaboration features in SAP Intercompany enable users to attach comments and other documents to facilitate more efficient communication.

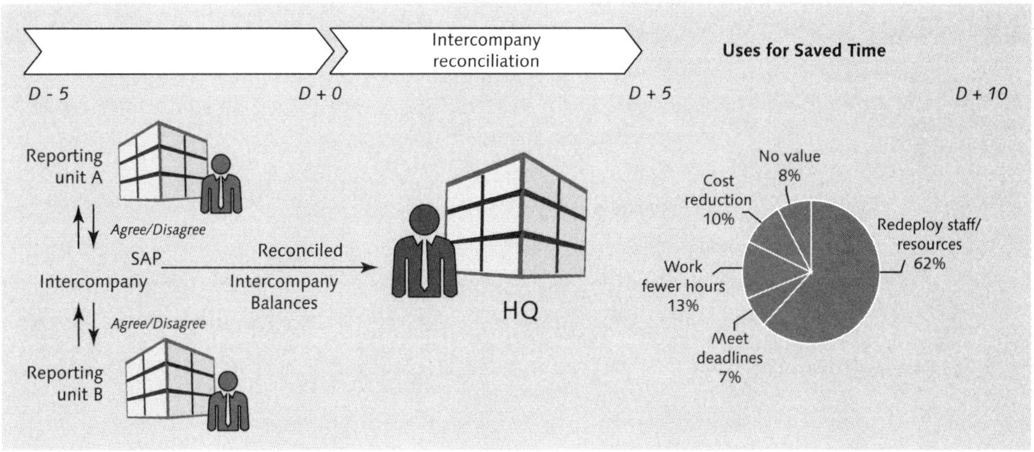

Figure 8.3 Peer-to-Peer Intercompany Process

8.4 Faster, Collaborative Intercompany Reconciliation with SAP Intercompany

SAP Intercompany enables your reporting units to reconcile intercompany balances in real time and allows your corporation to close its books faster. The first intercompany application to work independently of a consolidation system, SAP Intercompany provides the tools for your business units to debate and reconcile account balances and transaction-level detail directly with one another. That means it eliminates extra work and delays at the corporate and divisional levels. The application also helps improve your close process by removing intercompany reconciliation from the critical path, increasing both speed and accuracy.

8.4.1 Web-Based, Peer-to-Peer Communication

SAP Intercompany introduces a web-based, peer-to-peer communication channel between your reporting units that post intercompany balances and transactions against each other. This lateral flow of information and automatic matching helps ensure faster agreements—easing the burden on corporate finance and eliminating days from the time-consuming closing process (see Figure 8.4).

When users log on, they instantly get a clear view of which entities are out of balance and where they need to drill down further, shown in Figure 8.4.

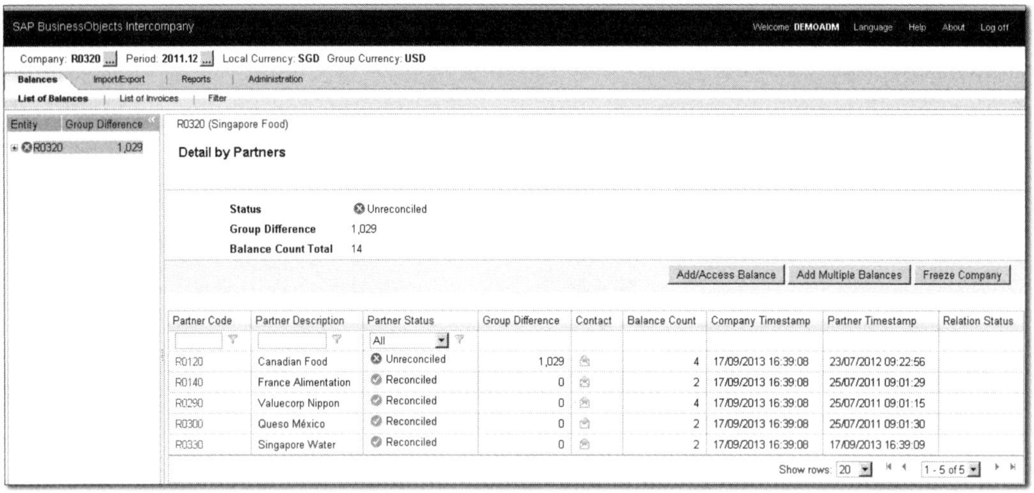

Figure 8.4 SAP Intercompany Reconciliation Screen

8.4.2 Collaboration, Monitoring, and Approval

SAP Intercompany offers sophisticated status tracking, email summaries, alerts on significant events, and a complete audit trail. Users can have threaded conversations within the application so counterparts can easily communicate in a central place back and forth. This is a major benefit because this type of communication would otherwise be done via email or over the phone, neither of which is easily traced. The collaborative nature of the tool makes it easy for multiple people to have access to the information. If someone is out on vacation or sick, or there is turnover in a position, all users with access can see the conversations related to the reconciliation.

In addition to added comments during the reconciliation process, users can also attach documents. Scanned or digitally printed invoices can be loaded to the system for reference, saving the users from having to save them offline somewhere.

You can also leverage a comprehensive set of reconciliation reports that enable individual reporting units as well as corporate headquarters to fully automate and follow their global intercompany process.

Corporate Visibility into the Reconciliation Process

SAP Intercompany allows your corporate or divisional headquarters to monitor the collaborative matching process continuously, using standardized exchange rates, material levels, and dedicated reconciliation views. This enables at-a-glance status checks of the global reconciliation process. Corporate can still maintain control and visibility of the process without having to be the main drivers.

A "freezing" feature prevents users from making additional changes after a cycle has ended. This provides further control for corporate to ensure that changes aren't made after a certain point in time.

Now that we have reviewed the benefits and functions of SAP Intercompany, let's review the different deployment options available.

8.5 SAP Intercompany Deployment Options

SAP Intercompany can be integrated into both SAP and non-SAP software environments and can load source data from any GL or consolidation application. SAP Intercompany is fully supported by the SAP Financial Information Management application discussed in Chapter 3, letting you manage the process of accessing, mapping, and loading information from multiple source systems. SAP Intercompany can be accessed directly from the SAP Financial Consolidation application.

Landscape Scenarios

The flow of data in and out of SAP Intercompany is contingent on your particular landscape and preferences. The flexibility exists to create different types of environments based on different requirements.

In any scenario, reporting units can import intercompany data at either the account balance or invoice level into SAP Intercompany. Once loaded, they can see real-time visibility into other reporting units with which they are out of balance. It is clearly indicated if a corresponding entity has not yet loaded its balances, creating an out of balance.

There are many ways to set up a landscape that includes SAP Intercompany; the following subsections describe a couple of examples.

8.5.1 Data Entry and Adjustments in SAP Intercompany

In this scenario, users are granted the ability to make adjustments and enter data manually into the SAP Intercompany application. The application tracks between what was loaded versus what was entered manually. As such, adjustment data can easily be exported back to the source systems (see Figure 8.5).

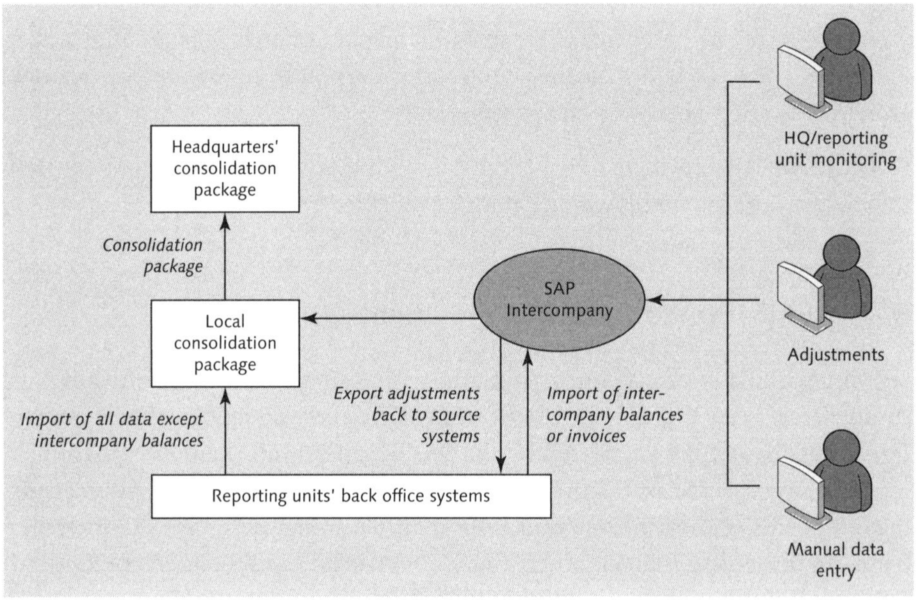

Figure 8.5 Data Entry and Adjustments in SAP Intercompany

Data can then be imported into the consolidation package from both SAP Intercompany and back-office reporting units. Reconciliation reports between the systems are usually used in this scenario to ensure consistency of data across the systems.

8.5.2 No Data Entry or Adjustments in SAP Intercompany

In this scenario, data is loaded to SAP Intercompany, and users use it for collaboration and to share information. Users are prohibited from making any changes to the data within the SAP Intercompany application. All adjustments must be made in the reporting units back-office systems, and then data is reloaded to SAP Intercompany (see Figure 8.6).

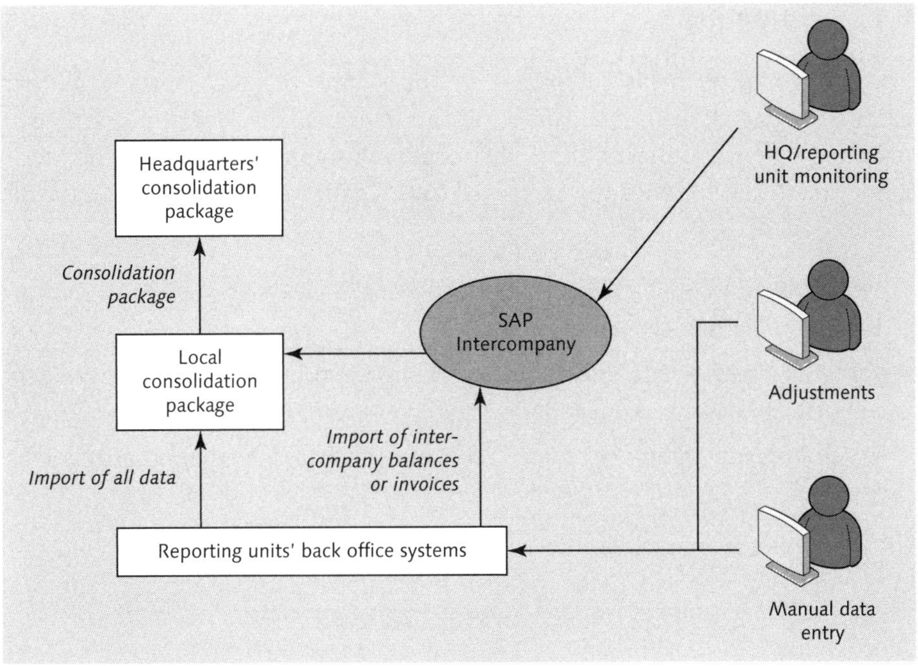

Figure 8.6 No Data Entry or Adjustments in SAP Intercompany

This scenario is commonly used when organizations have one or just a few instances of their GL system. Many organizations consider their GL to be their book of record and want to ensure all changes are made inside those systems. It is also commonly used when there is no separate consolidation package, and the consolidation is performed fully in the GL.

8.6 Security and Configuration

To enhance security, SAP Intercompany provides centrally managed and easily configured access rights and is compatible with existing security infrastructure investments such as firewalls, public key infrastructures, Secure Sockets Layer (SSL), and virtual private networks. Audit reports are available that provide visibility into who logged on to the system and when, as well as what data was loaded.

8.7 Summary

SAP Intercompany helps companies reconcile intercompany balances without extra work and delays at the corporate and divisional levels. According to data provided by our customers, those that deploy this application on an open technology platform alongside their financial consolidation system experience the following benefits:

- Improved accuracy of intercompany transactions
- Reduced length of reporting cycles
- Freed up finance staff and resources, giving them more time to analyze data, not just gather and reconcile it
- Quick implementation (in some cases, in as little as two weeks) at relatively low cost

In this chapter, we learned how it's possible to complement your consolidation engine and finance staff with the SAP Intercompany application. In our next chapter, we will review financial consolidation tools.

Financial consolidation involves collecting data from each subsidiary and reporting entity within an organization and adding it together. Where it begins to get interesting is when you get beyond aggregation to other calculations, including currency, ownership, and eliminations. Streamlining and automating these process eliminates errors and provides information faster enabling more time for analysis and better decision making. This chapter discusses challenges surrounding consolidation and how to manage them.

9 Financial Consolidation

The following three-step general formula was first discussed in Chapter 3. Software in its simplest form is put stuff in, do stuff and get stuff out, as outlined in Figure 9.1. The financial consolidation process is the middle "do stuff" step.

Figure 9.1 Financial Consolidation Simplified to "Do Stuff"

In more detailed terms, financial consolidation is the process organizations must go through to create consolidated financial statements. Companies have operations, divisions, and subsidiaries in different locations. Financial data needs to be collected, processed, and reported to create a top-level set of consolidated reports. These reports are required for many reasons, both external and internal. Externally, governments and industries have reporting requirements for regulatory and tax purposes. Internally, management requires not only consolidated statements but also the detail that supports the totals. While the basic concept of consolidation is all about aggregation, the real value comes from the analysis of disaggregation. Being able to understand where the totals come from enables leaders to make decisions that affect the future of the organization.

Organizations consolidate on the basis of customer-defined consolidation units. Consolidation units are typically legal entities or reporting units that are sometimes geographically based. Consolidation units can also represent, for example, companies, plants, business areas, profit centers, and cost centers.

Chapter 3 covered the basics of "putting data in." In this chapter, we will discuss loading data to a consolidation application and then "doing stuff," such as consolidations and calculations, including percent of ownership calculations. (Chapter 11 will cover the last element of Figure 9.1 which is "getting stuff out.")

Figure 9.2 provides a simplified look at consolidation applications. In this chapter, we will of course build upon this simplified approach and look first at data collection, then processing the data, and finally the consolidation solutions that can best serve finance organizations.

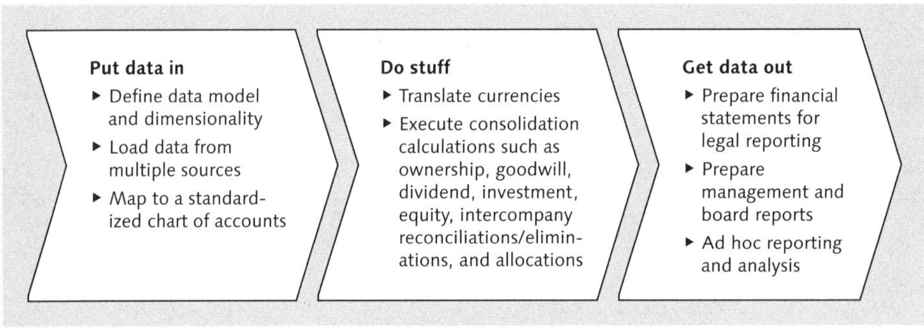

Figure 9.2 Consolidation Applications Simplified

Since consolidation requirements are not one size fits all, SAP has several consolidation solutions.

SAP Enterprise Performance Management (EPM) solutions:

- SAP Business Planning and Consolidation, version for Netweaver
- SAP Business Planning and Consolidation, version for Microsoft
- SAP Financial Consolidation

Classic Solutions part of the SAP Business Suite:

- Strategic Enterprise Management – Business Consolidation (SEM-BCS)
- Enterprise Controlling – Consolidation System (EC-CS)

SAP EPM solutions provide usability, little dependence on IT, more flexibility and enhanced reporting capabilities. Section 9.3 will discuss the differences in the differences between the solutions in more detail.

The following sections will discuss the different requirements and considerations for a financial consolidation and how software solutions can automate and standardize as many processes.

9.1 Data Collection

Before you can effectively work on your financial consolidation, you need to look towards the data collection process. In this section, we will look at the various steps of the data collection process and considerations for your workflow and business process. Data collection can be broken out into several different steps. Along this process, you will look at what level of detail to collect, how to manage your approvals process for data and currency considerations. In this section, we will look at:

- Loading Data.
- Data Mapping.
- Identifying what level of detail to collect, referred to as Dimensionality.
- Data validation and control.
- Managing commentary associated with data.
- Identifying your workflow and the necessary approvals for data.
- Identifying the periodicity of your data.
- Currency considerations.

Chapter 3 discussed more of the technical collecting of data. This section gets more into the business requirements that need to be addressed as opposed to the more technical aspects of the earlier chapters.

Before you can collect data, you need to decide what you want to collect as shown in Figure 9.2. To define what to collect, you need to start by looking at what you want to create. What do the reports look like that will be the result of this consolidation process? Organizations often take reports they have used in the past as a start and then mock up additional reports they would like to have.

After the reports are defined, then they need to be analyzed as to where the data comes from. The majority of data for a consolidation system comes from the General Ledger (GL) system(s). In certain organizations, supporting systems contain additional details. Consolidation applications usually have a more summarized level of data than transactional systems. How summarized the level should be needs to be defined. A cash account, for example, is made up of various bank accounts, but only the total is needed in a consolidation system.

If a company needs to analyze sales accounts by region, for example, it needs to figure out how to detail the sales accounts by region. If this type of detail is not available in the GL, it may be captured in a sales system.

In addition to identifying account balances, how accounts are calculated needs to be analyzed. If your organization allocates IT costs to different entities based on headcount, then you need to make sure headcounts are collected, perhaps from a human resources (HR) system.

As an example let's understand how Altron implemented SAP Business Planning and Consolidation to bring more standardization and automation to their consolidation and financial reporting processes.

9.1.1 Customer Story: Altron Consolidates Financial Data to Better Manage Assets and Risk

Johannesburg-based Allied Electronics Corporation Limited, (Altron), has globally dispersed subsidiaries specializing in telecommunications, power electronics, multimedia and IT. Each subsidiary functions separately which makes financial consolidation particularly challenging. The company was using a DOS-based consolidation tool without a drill-down capability which resulted in a large number of manual queries between head office and the subsidiaries during year-end that could take many weeks to resolve.

Altron recognized the need to deploy software to enable efficient consolidation of group-wide information with better security, standardized data sets and easier ways to aggregate and disseminate information. After reviewing various vendor solutions, Altron selected the SAP Business Planning and Consolidation application and SAP Xcelsius Enterprise business intelligence software and worked with an implementation partner to install the software, train users and roll out the solution across the globe.

Today there are around 300 enterprise-wide users, all securely connected via the Internet, who can instantly find the information they need and quickly generate a report. This has helped reduce the time needed to resolve queries by 50% and has saved an annual US$200,000 previous spent on hiring external consultants needed to support the year end close. The time that the sub–holding companies need to close their year-end books has been reduced by a third; easier access to data needed for tax reports has saved 280 employee days and acquisitions can now be integrated in 1 or 2 days rather than 2-3 weeks.

Deeper insight has also changed the company's practices in many ways such as enabling the more consistent interpretation and reporting of non-financial information to support government hiring regulations. It has also helped Altron consolidate spend with key suppliers group-wide as well as providing more reliable information that helps the company identify its top customers across the globe so they we can invest in growing these key relationships.

Altron says the investment has already paid for itself many times over and is now looking to use the solution to enhance planning and to manage its assets and risks more proactively.

9.1.2 Loading Data

After the required data is identified for your consolidation system, you then need to identify where the data comes from, i.e. identify your source system. Is the source data in another software system or maintained offline, manually? If it is in another source system, it needs to be extracted, transformed, and loaded (ETL) into your consolidation system. There are dedicated ETL tools such as SAP Financial Information Management for this purpose as discussed in Chapter 3.

This automation of the data load is crucial to the project. The more areas you can eliminate manual processes from the more risk of human error you can remove. The automation of data load should not be taken lightly, and you should always budget enough time in your project to sufficiently address this topic. It is often under budgeted even though it is extremely critical to the success of any implementation.

In a perfect world, all data in a consolidation system would be automated. As mentioned, manual work introduces more chances for errors. But in certain situations, it can't be avoided. Sometimes certain subsidiaries may have source ledger systems that aren't easily extracted from. Or sometimes all of the data need for a consolidation isn't captured in a source system. Consolidation software should have the capabilities to accommodate entering data manually to deal with these situations. The control and validation of manual data is mandatory and discussed in the following sections.

9.1.3 Data Mapping/Central Chart of Accounts

Before data is consolidated, it must be standardized. It is critical that you are adding like data to like data. All source systems don't always have the same chart of accounts. Therefore, a central chart of accounts needs to be defined for running a consolidation solution. A central chart of accounts is also known as a standard or uniform chart of accounts. An organization reviews its reporting requirements, as discussed in the introduction to this section, and then identifies a chart of accounts to use in the consolidation system.

Source systems may use a different chart of accounts. GL systems will be at a more granular level. Certain subsidiaries may use different systems with different charts that need to be mapped. The mapping process involves laying each chart side by side and reviewing, account by account, how they match up to each other.

This process can be very time-consuming the first time, but after an initial mapping process is completed, ongoing maintenance typically includes ensuring that new accounts that are added to source systems are mapped appropriately. Figure 9.3 shows the mapping screen from SAP Financial Information Management. You can see the GL account (GL_ACCT) as the source which maps to the target account.

A key step in the mapping process is to clearly document and communicate what is intended to be captured in each account. For example, an account called "Fixtures and fittings" needs to be clearly differentiated from "Office equipment." "Accounts payables" must be clearly differentiated from "Intercompany accounts payables" or "Intercompany notes payable." Creating this standardization is crucial to ensuring consistencies across subsidiaries. The standardization creates integrity in your data as well as providing a standard basis for your calculations.

The challenge in this area is further complicated by international operations and multiple languages. It is extremely helpful to have a system that allows you to translate your chart of account into multiple languages.

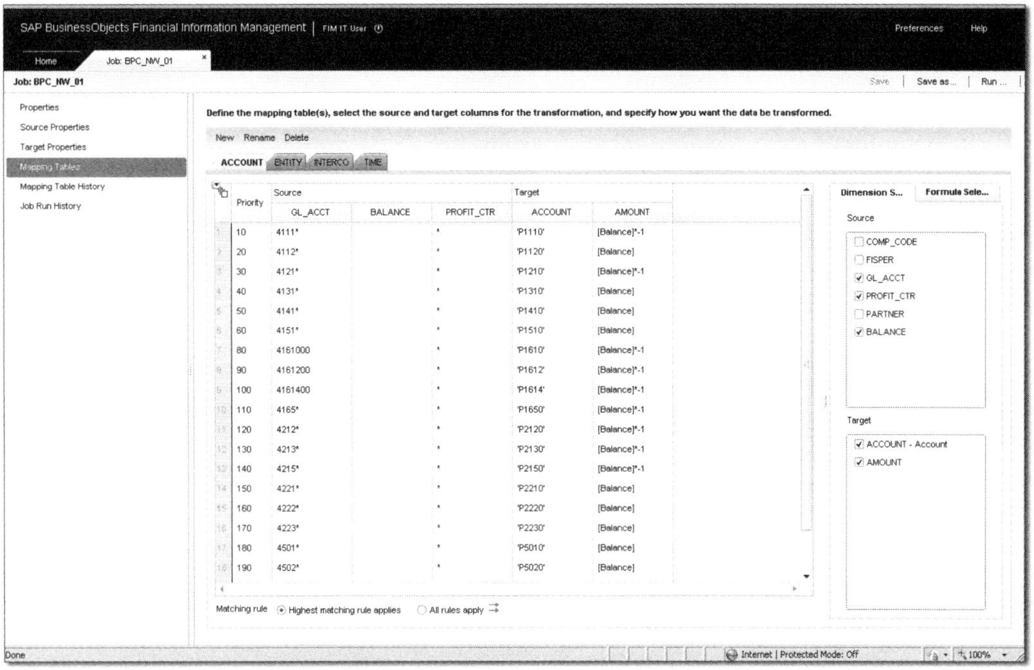

Figure 9.3 SAP Financial Information Management Data Mapping Screen

9.1.4 Dimensionality: Identifying the Level of Detail to Collect

As mentioned earlier, identifying what data to collect for a consolidation system is critical. Not only do you need to analyze consolidated financial reports, but you also need to identify how you need to break that data down. In more specific terms, you need to not only aggregate and consolidate data but also disaggregate and break down the information. For example, every company needs to provide a consolidated income statement, which is an aggregation of all revenues and expenses from each of its reporting entities. (Aggregation is being used as a simplified term here; there are accounting rules which indicate that financial consolidation is a bit more than just adding data together, as discussed later in Section 9.2. But for the sake of simplicity, let's stick with aggregation for the moment.) So the first step is to aggregate the data, and then comes the interesting part—disaggregating the data. Management sees the total numbers, but then wants to know how the data breaks out by country, by product, and by customer segment. Being able to provide that detail quickly and accurately is where a great accounting and financial close system comes into play.

You need to think through all of the supporting reports and ad hoc analysis you'll need to perform. You then start to identify how you need to break down information, for example, by segment, region, or department. Within a consolidation system, these are called dimensions, which help you create your data model.

Figure 9.4 shows an example of dimensions used in an SAP Financial Consolidation solution. Note the dimensions that come standard with the application are indicated by an orange icon (❶) and the configurable (user-defined) dimensions are blue (❷).

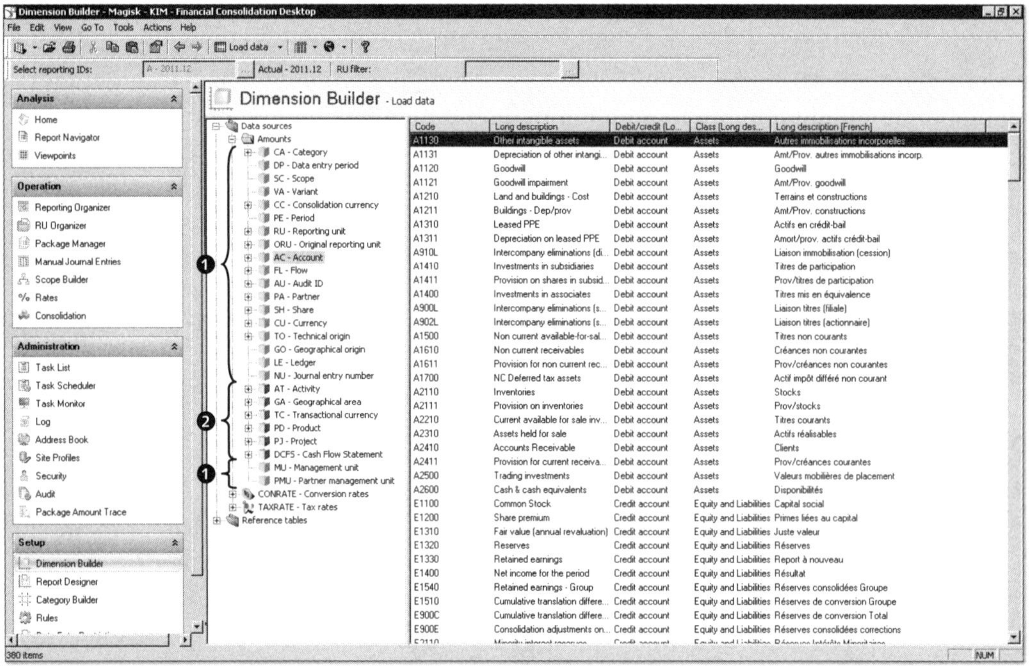

Figure 9.4 SAP Financial Consolidation Dimension Examples

One way to think about dimensions is as the axes needed for analysis. Imagine a financial report and think about the X and Y axis of that report. Think about what would be across the columns and down the rows. For example, one axis, could be accounts down the rows and then periods across the columns. Account and period are dimensions.

GLs systems often manage dimensionality with their account structure, as you can see in Figure 9.5.

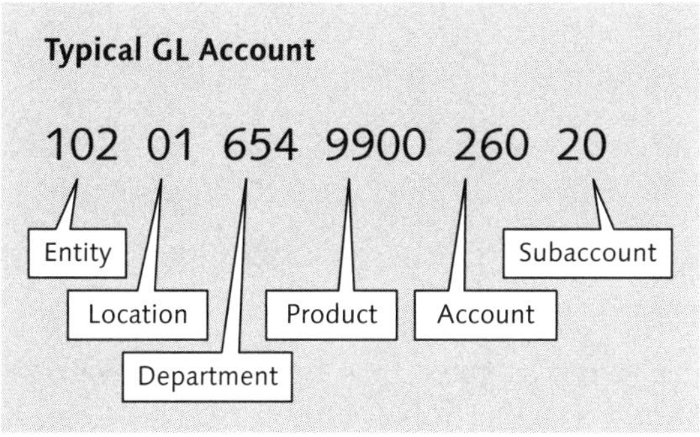

Figure 9.5 General Ledger Account Broken Down by Dimensions

Flow Dimension

A key dimension that is typically used in EPM solutions is the *flow* dimension. Sometimes referred to as the *movement dimension*, this dimension is used to track the flow of an account through the year. Typical flows include opening balance, increases, decreases, and ending balance. Flows can be different from one account to the next; for example, the columns across the top of an equity roll forward report are flows, and they are different from those flows on the balance sheet One of the advantages of the flow dimension is that it enables you to automate the cash flow statement.

Flow Example

Following are some examples of the flows used in the SAP IFRS starter kit described in Section 9.4:

- F00 Opening
- F01 Incoming units
- F06 Dividends
- F09 Change in accounting policies
- F10 Net profit (loss) for the period
- F15 Net variation
- F20 Increase/Purchase
- F30 Decrease/Disposal
- F40 Capital increase/decrease
- F50 Reclassification
- F55 Fair value
- F70 Internal mergers

- F80 Currency translation adjustment
- F92 Change in interest rate
- F98 Outgoing units
- F99 Closing
- Y99 Year to date

To be able to calculate the Statement of Cash Flow items and to produce the Statement of Changes in Equity, changes in the balance sheet items need to be captured or calculated as follows:

- For current assets and liabilities (gross value), the net variation can be calculated and displayed in input forms.
- For other balance sheet accounts, a detailed analysis of movements is required.
- Specific operations are identified separately for all balance sheet accounts: reclassification, changes in accounting policies, internal mergers (transfer of balance sheet accounts from the acquired to the acquiring company in case of an internal merger).
- Opening balances are automatically calculated from the closing balance of the previous year.

To capture data at this level, it either needs to be loaded from a source system or entered manually. If only an opening and ending balance are available, input schedules can be created to collect the additional detail. Figure 9.6 shows an example of a data input schedule for collecting flow data for property, plant, and equipment.

	F00 Opening	F99 Closing	F20 Increase/ Purchase	F25 Increase in depreciation	F30 Decrease/ Disposal	F35 Decrease in depreciation	F50 Reclassification	F55 Fair value	Control
A1110 Lands and buildings	571,000	721,000	250,000		-100,000				OK
A1120 Tangible exploration and evaluation assets									OK
A1130 Fixtures and fittings	16,000	25,000	9,000						OK
A1140 Construction in progress	21,000	30,000	9,000						OK
A1150 Office equipment	3,600	3,600							OK
A1160 Vehicles	13,000	15,000	2,000						OK
A1170 Machinery	8,900	9,000	100						OK
A1180 Other property, plant and equipment	114,000	116,000	2,000						OK
Property, plant and equipment - Gross value	**747,500**	**919,600**	**272,100**		**-100,000**				**OK**

Figure 9.6 Property Plant and Equipment Flow Analysis

9.1.5 Data Validation and Control

Data coming into a consolidation application must be intelligently checked and filtered based on the reporting framework and rules defined by the central finance team. International Financial Reporting Standards (IFRS) and Generally Accepted Accounting Principles (GAAP) presentation, required information breakdowns, starting dates, and ending dates can serve as automatic checkpoints to ensure data quality at every level of a corporate reporting cycle. This way, the incoming information respects the timing and expected format. Data must be consistent, complete, and commented appropriately, and go through the right auditable approval process.

Certain accounting principles must be checked, such as assets equaling liabilities plus equity. You may be collecting certain details from one system such as a sales system and totals from another, so you need to check that the totals equal the detail. SAP EPM consolidation solutions allow you to automate these types of controls.

Another aspect of control is managed through security. Different users are provided with different types of access to a system (see Figure 9.7).

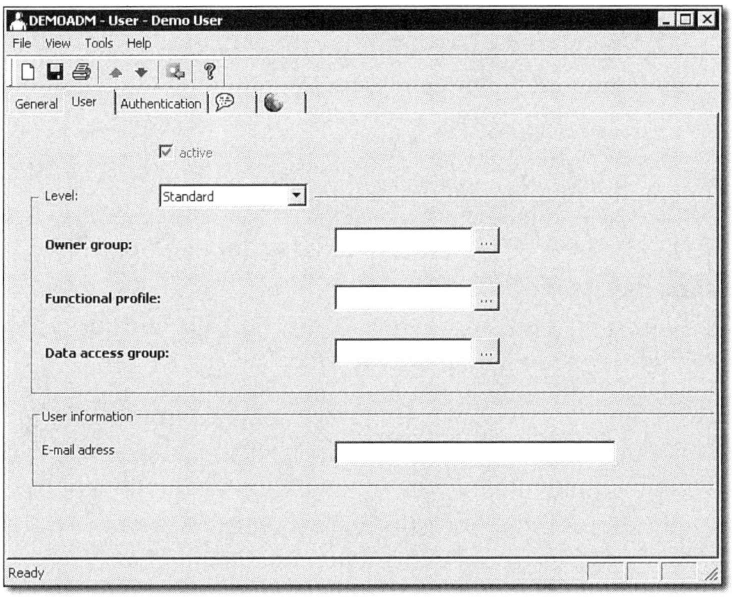

Figure 9.7 User Access

SAP EPM solutions allow you to assign functional profiles and data access profiles to each user. A functional profile defines what they have access to do (e.g., post a journal entry, change a report, run a consolidation); a data access profile defines what level of data they have access to (e.g. only local entity data, all of North America data, all XYZ Division data). This type of security helps you maintain control over the consolidation process.

9.1.6 Collecting Commentary with Data

You may also want to control the amount of commentary that is provided with your data. For example, if there is a more than 10% increase over last year, you may want your subsidiaries to provide comments as to why that information is relevant.

Part of creating financial reports is including a management discussion and analysis (MD&A) section. Here the management of an organization discusses the financial results that have been reported. Corporate therefore needs to collect this detail from its subsidiaries.

SAP EPM consolidation solutions enable you to collect text as well as numerical data. Combining financial data with comments into a publishable report can be accomplished with SAP Disclosure Management, discussed in Chapter 10.

9.1.7 Workflow and Approval of Data

After data has been checked, consolidation software solutions help provide accountability. Often a local accountant is responsible for providing the data to be collected and then a local controller or CFO is responsible for reviewing the data that was compiled and then signing off on that data electronically. SAP EPM consolidation solutions not only track the electronic sign-off but also provide a detailed audit trail of who signed off on it and on what date at what time.

SAP EPM consolidation applications enable you to monitor and record the performance of the various contributors to the close process. It's long been said that what gets measured, gets managed—and that is just as true for the close process as for any other activity. By publishing statistics on the best and worst performers in the close process and by coaching and training in areas identified as weak, you make the process a managed one, increase discipline, and carry out significant improvements to the close time.

Consolidation monitors are available to provide corporate a view of the status for each reporting entity and how they roll up. Figure 9.8 shows the BPC CONSOLIDATION MONITOR. You can see each business unit listed along with its CONTROL STATUS (as discussed in Section 9.1.5), WORK STATUS, CURRENCY TRANSLATION, and CONSOLIDATION. Notice that the statuses roll up into each SUB SCOPE and the total so the user can get a clear view of the status for groups of entities.

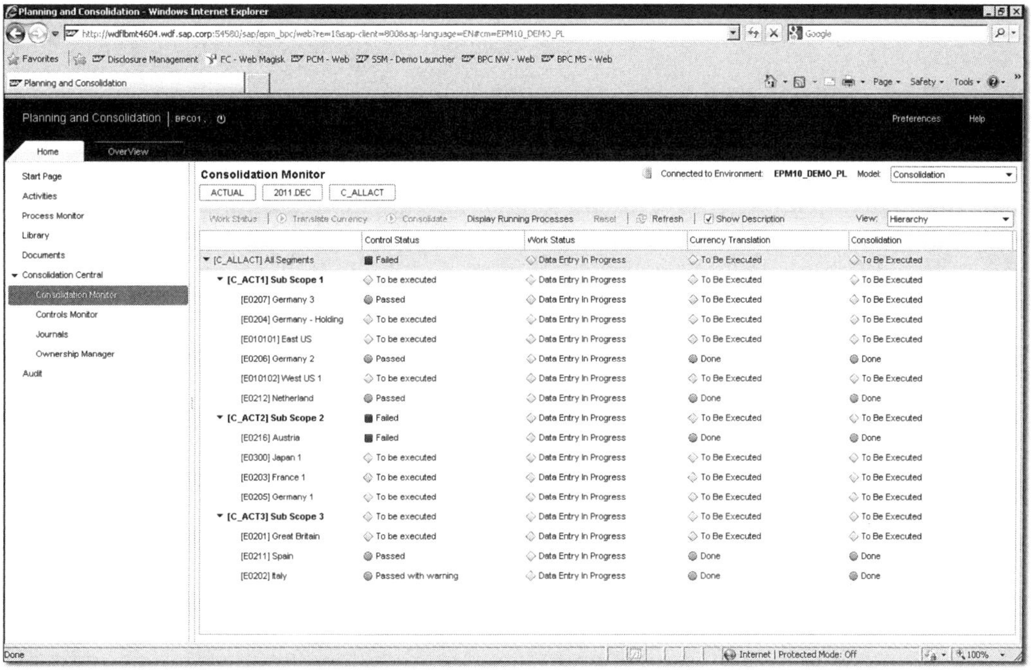

Figure 9.8 SAP Business Planning and Consolidation: Consolidation Monitor

9.1.8 Periodicity of Data (Collecting Year to Date versus Periodic)

Financial reports are a snapshot in time of the financial position of an organization. The balances of each account, on the day of the snapshot, are reported. Different companies have different requirements or processes that they follow in this area. EPM consolidation solutions have the flexibility to accommodate different requirements that also vary based on the type of report or financial statement. Typically, all companies want visibility to month-to-date, quarter-to-date, and year-to-date amounts. This is referred to as the periodicity of data.

A consolidation system needs to capture the ending balance of all accounts on the balance sheet and the year-to-date amount on the P&L statements. This can be accomplished in many ways. Let's discuss two options most widely used by organizations: loading ending balances and calculating ending balances.

- **Loading ending balances**
  In a consolidation system, typically the ending balance is loaded for accounts on the balance sheet/statement of financial position. The opening balance is rolled forward in the consolidation system, and the ending balance is loaded from the GL system. Any activity between the opening and ending is recorded using the flow dimension discussed in Section 9.1.4.
- **Calculating ending balances**
  The accounts on the P&L statement are typically loaded as month-to-date values, and then all months are added together to get the year-to-date value.

9.1.9 Currency (Local, Transaction, Group)

For consolidation purposes, data is typically collected in the local currency of each entity, (e.g., French subsidiaries report euros, United States in US dollars, and Japan in yen.) The local currency is typically calculated into a group reporting currency for standardization purposes. Sometimes, organizations have more than one group currency if they have regulatory or management reporting requirements in multiple regions.

Transaction currency refers to the specific currency used during an individual transaction. For example, a British company has two subsidiaries: one in Paris (subsidiary A) and one in Miami (subsidiary B). The Paris entity sends the Miami entity an invoice in euros for goods provided.

The currencies for these two subsidiaries are represented in Table 9.1.

Subsidiary	Transaction Currency	Local Currency	Group Currency
A	EUR	EUR	GBP
B	EUR	USD	GBP

Table 9.1 Currency Types

Consolidation systems may capture transaction data for purposes of intercompany reconciliation, but typically they capture local and group currency for all accounts.

As such, different currency exchange rates need to be collected, and different types of rates are required to be collected. Figure 9.9 shows an example of a currency rate table from SAP Financial Consolidation.

Actual rates 2011.12		Closing Rate	Average Rate	Average Rate N-1	Opening Rate	Quarter Aver.
US Dollar	USD	1	1	1	1	1
Australian Dollar	AUD	1.638002	1.633720	1.638807	1.629726	1.639344
Canadian Dollar	CAD	1.470588	1.478197	1.446550	1.497791	1.449275
Euro	EUR	0.935664	1.013654	1.113958	1.061327	1.114827
Pound Sterling	GBP	0.618888	0.638802	0.661594	0.669478	0.662252
Hong Kong Dollar	HKD	7.799947	7.805000	7.812500	7.799095	7.969398
Yen	JPY	119.990401	118.595825	103.626943	114.416476	105.820106
Mexican Peso	MXP	0.087033	0.090580	0.098814	0.095429	0.088576
Singapore Dollar	SGD	1.646091	1.642109	1.642036	1.641767	1.639344

Figure 9.9 Example of a Currency Rate Table

The currency conversion calculation is discussed in Section 9.2.6.

Now that we have discussed all of the options for data collection and how to optimize this process, we'll shift focus and review how to process the data collected, including managing organizational structures and making consolidation adjustments—both manual and automatic. From the three-step process discussed at the beginning of this chapter, in Figure 9.1, let's move from the "Put stuff in" to the "Do stuff" Step with a discussion of processing the data that we have now collected.

9.2 Processing Data

Because the industrialization of the close process is key to a successful fast close, the ability to automate as many processes as possible is extremely advantageous. Built-in financial intelligence can further speed the close cycle. Built-in rules logic can automate consolidation entries. Currency translation adjustments, minority interest and equity calculations, intercompany reconciliations, and automatic cash flows can be set up through a standard user interface and intuitive wizards. SAP EPM consolidation solutions have dedicated modules to manage business rules, calculations, and ownership structures.

The ability to automate and standardize as many processes as possible is extremely advantageous to the financial close process. SAP EPM consolidation solutions speed the close cycle by using built-in rules logic to automate consolidation entries. They can handle multiple reporting channels with different charts of accounts and different account flows or analysis dimensions over time. They can also manage the retention of past reporting frameworks so finance professionals can safely adapt to ever-changing financial needs without having to copy and paste, rebuild, or destroy their previous reporting scenarios. In the following sections, we will look at how to manage organizational structures, make consolidation adjustments, and handle intercompany eliminations.

9.2.1 Customer Story: HMY Group Enables More Comprehensive and Up-to-Date Reporting with SAP Financial Consolidation

Headquartered at Monétau in the Burgundy region of France, the HMY Group provides design and shop-fitting services for retailers across the globe, helping them create efficient and attractive shopping experiences for their customers.

Through the know-how and experiences of a number of different companies that have been acquired over the years, the company has a presence in over 50 countries and needed to improve the way it consolidated financial data collected from multiple global sources more efficiently as it sought to further expand into new markets. Previously the company was only able to produce balance sheets every quarter and providing better monthly reporting to management so they had better insight into the financial performance of the group was paramount. So too was improving the traceability of financial information that resulted from intercompany trading between the growing number of subsidiaries that make up the group.

Attracted by its simplicity and proven market credentials, HMY Group deployed the SAP Financial Consolidation application, actively involving various business users across the globe to help define solution requirements with the emphasis being on delivering a standardized accounting and financial reporting processes that could be automated as much as possible.

Once rolled out the new solution quickly delivered tangible benefits. The time taken to consolidate month end data was increased by a factor of four and overall the time spent on the monthly financial consolidation cycle was cut by 25%. Automating and speeding up the month end processes enabled more detailed and frequent balance sheets to be produced, something that was not feasible with the previous solution. And as many reports, such as cash flow statements, were now automatically generated, the finance team can provide the business with more reliable and comprehensive financial reporting.

Overall, reporting is faster and more efficient; the group has greater transparency across the various subsidiaries and managers have more comprehensive information to support their business decisions.

9.2.2 Managing Organizational Structures

Organizational structures refer to how different entities roll up within an organization. It is important to have a tool that meets the requirements associated with organizational structure. The organizational structure refers not only to the legal reporting unit roll up, but in some cases, there are reporting units under a legal entity. SAP Business Planning and Consolidation has an ownership manager whereas SAP Financial Consolidation manages ownership structures in the Scope module.

In a situation in which most entities are owned 100%, and there is little merger, acquisition, and disposal activity, a consolidation system is not necessarily required to manage the ownership structure. Changes in organizational structure can be easily accommodated with manual journal entries.

However, when there is much merger, acquisition, and disposition activity, as well as internal reorganizations, a sophisticated consolidation solution is required. All SAP consolidation solutions can handle complex organization structures.

This book is not meant to be a comprehensive accounting guide, so specific accounting detail is light, but rather we address the high-level principles, including which entities to consolidate and at what percentage, the cost method, the equity method, and majority-owned approaches.

Which Entities to Consolidate at What Percentages

Part of the consolidation process involves identifying which entities to consolidate at what percentages. Direct and indirect ownership need to be taken into consideration. Consider the organizational structure shown in Figure 9.10.

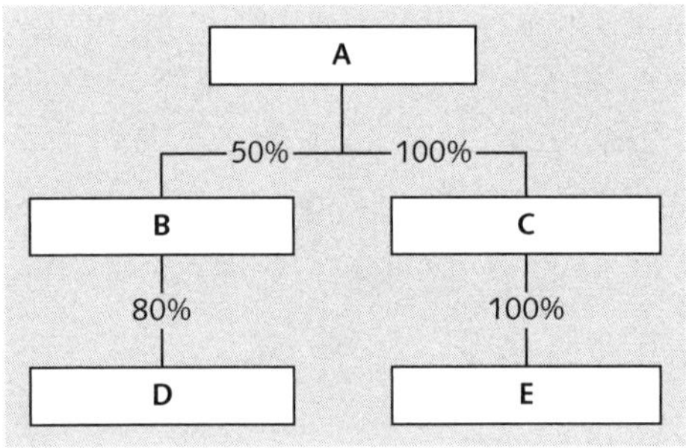

Figure 9.10 Example Organizational Structure

In Figure 9.10, you can see that A directly owns 50% of B, and B owns 80% of D. A therefore has a 40% indirect ownership in D. This is a simple example, but you can imagine the complexity in which entities own a percentage of other entities as is possible in some countries.

The percentage at which entities are consolidated determines the method for consolidation. Standard thresholds along with consolidation methods are listed in Table 9.2.

Threshold	Consolidation Method
0 – 20%	Cost method.
20 – 50%	Equity method.
> 50%	Cost/equity method can be used, but equity is most common.
100%	Wholly owned (global) method.

Table 9.2 Consolidation Methods and the Standard Thresholds

As we have mentioned, different countries have different regulatory requirements. These requirements may cause foreign entities to make adjustments to comply with local GAAP. Companies have the option with consolidation systems to run different consolidation versions based on different regulations or make either automated or manuals adjustment to manage the different reporting requirements. Let's look at the different consolidation methods shown in Table 9.2 in further detail.

Cost Method

The cost method is used when the investor holds too small a share of the entity's equity (usually < 20%) to have any influence or control over the company. Investment is recorded at cost at the time of purchase. There is typically no need for adjustments to the investment except for extenuating circumstances:

- Dividends declared exceed earnings of the company.
- Permanent decline in the value of the company.

Typically, the GL data for an entity that is < 20% owned is not required or used as part of the consolidation.

Equity Method

The equity method is used whenever the investor has significant influence over the investee, such as the following:

- Typically 20–50% owned.
- Can make exceptions for < 20% or > 50%.

The investment is recorded at the original cost. The investment is increased with income and decreased with dividends from the subsidiary. It is also common to have purchase differentials, such as the following:

- Difference in fair market value of assets and cost of the investment (i.e., goodwill).
- Difference between fair market value of assets and book value.

A company may or may not require/use GL data from entities that are less than 50% owned.

Majority Owned

Majority owned is used when the investor owns > 50% of an entity. Majority-owned entities must be consolidated into the parent company's consolidated financial results. The part of the subsidiary's income/balances not owned by the parent company is booked to minority interest:

- Minority interest is typically an expense (right before net income) that reduces net income on the income statement (assuming a profitable subsidiary).
- Minority interest is typically a liability that increases the liabilities of the consolidated company on the balance sheet.

SAP EPM consolidation solutions make automatic calculations based on how the organizational hierarchy is defined within the system. Figure 9.11 shows the ownership manager in SAP Business Planning and Consolidation. This built-in financial intelligence helps to streamline the whole consolidation process.

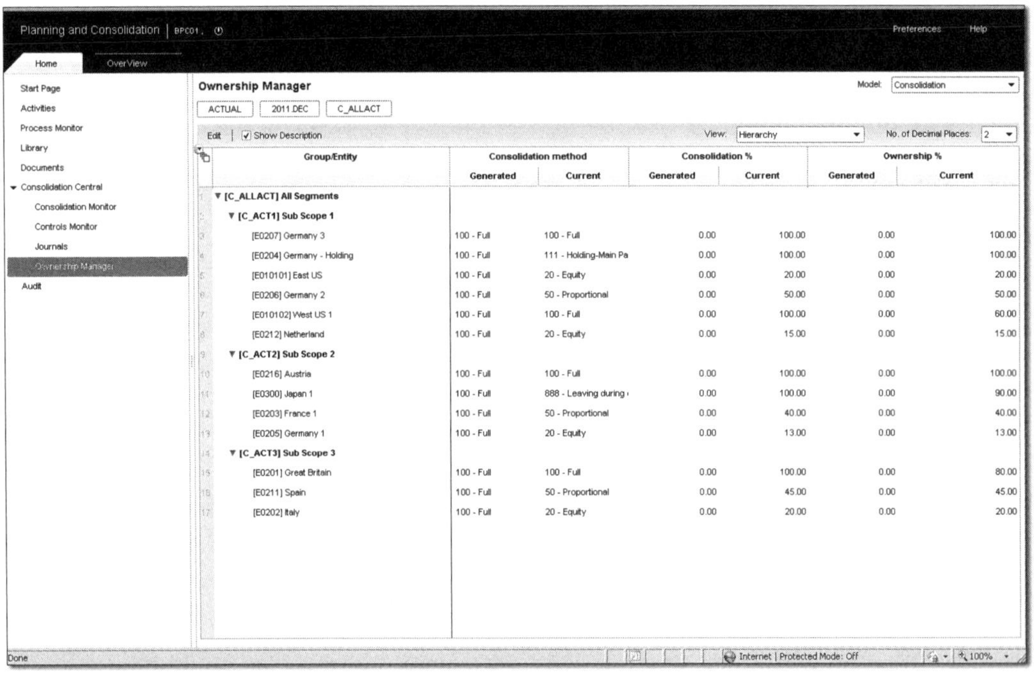

Figure 9.11 SAP Business Planning and Consolidation: Ownership Manager

9.2.3 Consolidation Adjustments

The previous section discussed consolidation calculations that are impacted by an organization's ownership structure. The basis of the consolidation is how it rolls up. There are, however, many other calculations that occur during the financial consolidation process. Let's continue to discuss those here. Consolidation adjustments are made during the consolidation process. Within a consolidation system, there is an electronic record of everything that happens to a piece of data from the time it is collected to the time it is disclosed. SAP EPM consolidation solutions typically have a dedicated dimension called AUDIT ID or DATA SOURCE to track all adjustments to any account. (See Section 9.1.3 where we discussed dimensionality.) Having this dimension makes it extremely easy to report how a number changes though the course of consolidation. There are two types of adjustments—manual adjustments and automatic adjustments—which are covered in the following subsections.

Manual Adjustments

Often called top-side adjustments, manual adjustments are journal entries that are posted to the consolidation system directly. As discussed, data flows from the GL to the consolidation system. Corporate may want to make adjustments to the data manually for various reasons. They may realize one of their subsidiaries misclassified an amount, and in the interest of time, it is easier to book a manual adjustment than to re-collect data from that entity. That entity would book the adjustment in the next period, and the manual journal entry would be reversed in the next period. Manual entries can also be permanent such as differences between local and corporate reporting standards.

The IT landscape sometimes dictates the management of manual journals within a consolidation system. If companies have one instance of a GL system, they may make manual adjustments within the consolidation system. In that case, they need to post the adjustment in the GL system and then reload the data from the source system.

If journal entries are allowed, there is often security limiting who can create journals and who can post them within the consolidation system. Figure 9.12 shows a screenshot of the manual journal entry screen.

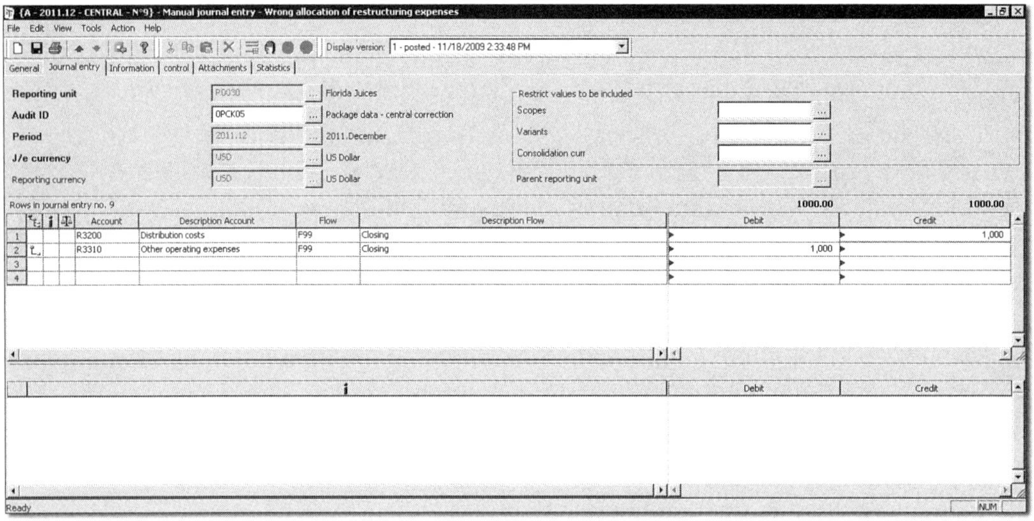

Figure 9.12 SAP Financial Consolidation: Manual Journal Entry Screen

Automatic Adjustments

Automatic adjustments are calculations that are defined within a consolidation application. SAP EPM consolidation applications use business rules to allow users to define what calculations need to automated during the consolidation process.

Any time there is a pattern, logic, or a constant formula to a specific adjustment, there is the opportunity to automate an adjustment. As discussed, any opportunity to automate helps speed the close process. Additionally there will be an electronic trail of the adjustment, including why it was made and the logic behind it. Remember, less manual intervention leads to fewer errors.

Figure 9.13 shows the list of rules used in the IFRS starter kit discussed in Section 9.4. Some of those are discussed in more detail in the following sections.

9.2.4 Intercompany Eliminations

Chapter 8 explains how intercompany reconciliation is a key element in the consolidation process. Many organizations leverage consolidation systems to reconcile intercompany balances. Corporate first collects all of the intercompany information from its subsidiaries and then identifies where the accounts are out of balance. For example, entity A says its accounts receivables amount from B is

100, but entity B says its accounts payable amount to A is 150. SAP consolidation systems provide reconciliation reports that call out these out of balances. But to find out why there is a difference (an accounting mistake, timing differences, etc.), you need to go back to the entities. The entities then look at the transactional detail (which isn't normally captured in a consolidation system) and correct the errors.

After intercompany data has been reconciled, it then needs to be eliminated. In the preceding example, let's assume they finally agreed that the account balance should be 100. These amounts need to be eliminated on the consolidated financial statements. If these amounts are not eliminated, the accounts payable and accounts receivable amounts will be overstated by 100 each.

Elimination of intercompany activity can be automated with all SAP EPM consolidation solutions.

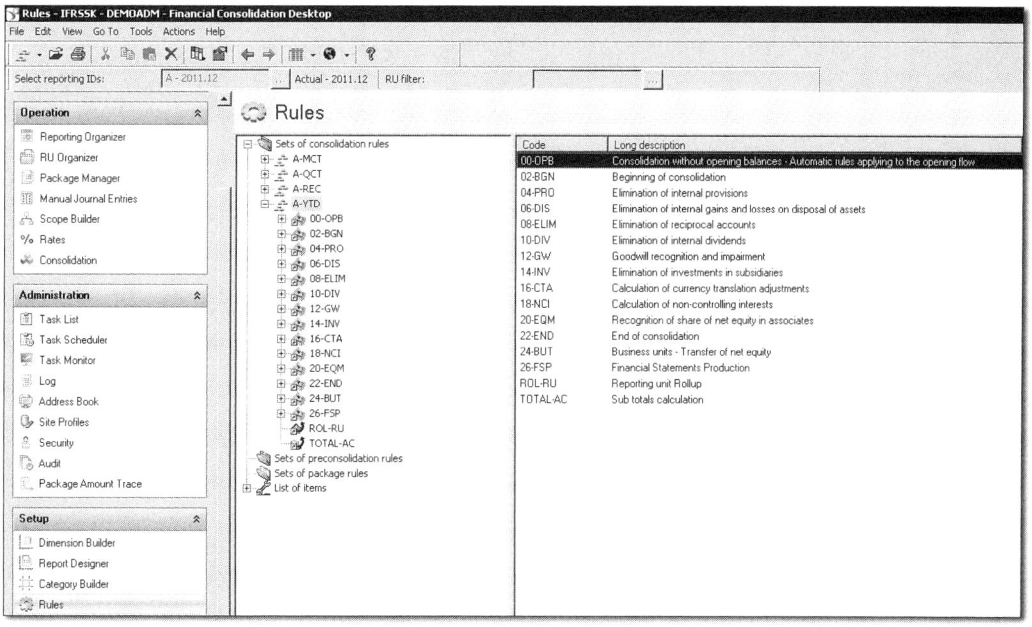

Figure 9.13 SAP Financial Consolidation: List of Rules in the IFRS Starter Kit

See Section 9.4 for more details on the starter kits, including SAP EPM consolidation kits, SAP Disclosure Management consolidation kits and SAP Rapid Deployment Solutions (RDS).

9.2.5 Elimination of Investments

Similar to the elimination of intercompany discussed in the previous section, investments in subsidiaries need to be eliminated so as not to double count them in the consolidated financial statements.

The different consolidation methods each require a different adjustment. Many organizations calculate these adjustments offline in a spreadsheet and then book a manual journal entry to account for the adjustments. SAP EPM consolidation software has functionality called *business rules,* which can help automate and streamline these types of calculations and reduce the amount of manual interaction.

9.2.6 Foreign Currency Conversion and Currency Translation Adjustments

There are several currency conversion rules that you should consider when handling intercompany eliminations and foreign currencies. Best practices configured in the starter kits discussed in Section 9.4 include:

- The income statement accounts are converted using the average rate of the reporting period.
- Accounts in the statement of financial position are converted using the period-end rate, except for investments and equity accounts, which are maintained at their historical acquisition value.
- Balance sheet movements are translated using the average rate. For equity accounts, the currency translation differences are recorded in a dedicated account in the reserves.
- Because some transaction values need to be converted at a specific rate, such as dividends distribution and the balance sheet position of incoming units, the definition of currency rate per company is required.
- All values are translated cumulated, meaning that the year-to-date value for the closing period is translated using the rate of the same closing period.

The currency conversion rules in the preceding list also apply to accounts for additional analyses.

As explained previously, equity accounts are translated using the historical value method. When running the consolidation for one given consolidation scope for the first time, the historical values of these accounts must be recorded as well as the cumulated amount of the conversion reserves as part of the preparatory tasks. This can be done in one of two ways:

- By importing the converted opening balance on the opening flow directly at the converted level on a technical prior year-end time period used for opening data, and defining entity-specific exchange rates for this technical consolidation. The opening rate, the average rate, and the closing rate should be identical so that no currency conversion difference is computed on this time period.
- By posting a journal entry to return to the historical translation amount.

9.2.7 Rounding

Rounding may be one of the most annoying things about financial accounting. What sounds like a very small detail can sometimes create a lot of work. Let's start by giving an example as listed in Table 9.3.

Balance	Balance Rounded
100,456,890	100,457
100,250,367	100,250
100,243,430	100,243
Total Sum 300,950,687	**300,951**
Actual Sum	**300,950**

Table 9.3 Rounding Example

When the numbers that need to be reported are in millions or billions of a currency, the numbers are rounded for presentation purposes. As you can see in the example in Table 9.3, if you simply round all of the balances in the left column, the sum is rounded to 300,951, where the actual sum of the rounded balance is actually 300,950.

Financial statements are a reflection of an organization; as such, it is important not to have errors in your financials. So by simply rounding all of the balances on a report can create an error.

SAP EPM consolidation solutions ease the challenges of rounding. You can easily divide consolidated data by 1,000 and then run reports that calculate totals based on the rounded data.

9.2.8 Workflow and Approval of Adjustments

As discussed in Section 9.1.8 for data collection, work flow and approval of adjustments is important. The beauty of using software is that it automates calculations for you, tracing all of the steps along the way. Manual entries, however, need to be controlled. Often organizations put a policy in place where the person who creates a journal doesn't have the authority to post a journal entry. This ensures that there at least two sets of eyes on a manual journal entry to eliminate mistakes.

SAP EPM consolidation software allows for this type of security and eases approvals by making them an electronic signature.

9.2.9 Consolidation Versions

Different versions of consolidated data are often necessary. The next sections describe some requirements that call for different consolidation versions. SAP EPM consolidation solutions allows for multiple versions for different purposes to address multiple GAAPs, IFRS, currency impacts, modeling scenarios, and reporting requirements.

Multiple GAAPs

GAAPs vary geographically and can be specific to a specific industry. As globalization becomes the norm, organizations are required to report financial information to comply with more than one GAAP.

International Financial Reporting Standards (IFRS)

IFRS is being adopted by more and more countries. In the map shown in Figure 9.14, you can see which countries have adopted the new standards. Because standardization within an organization can help speed the close process, standardizing reporting requirements makes financial reporting easier for multinational companies and facilitates the global economy.

The broad reach of IFRS touches many corporate systems, including Enterprise Resource Planning (ERP) and Enterprise Performance Management (EPM) solutions. The impact of the change is often most significant on financial systems, especially on group financial reporting practices.

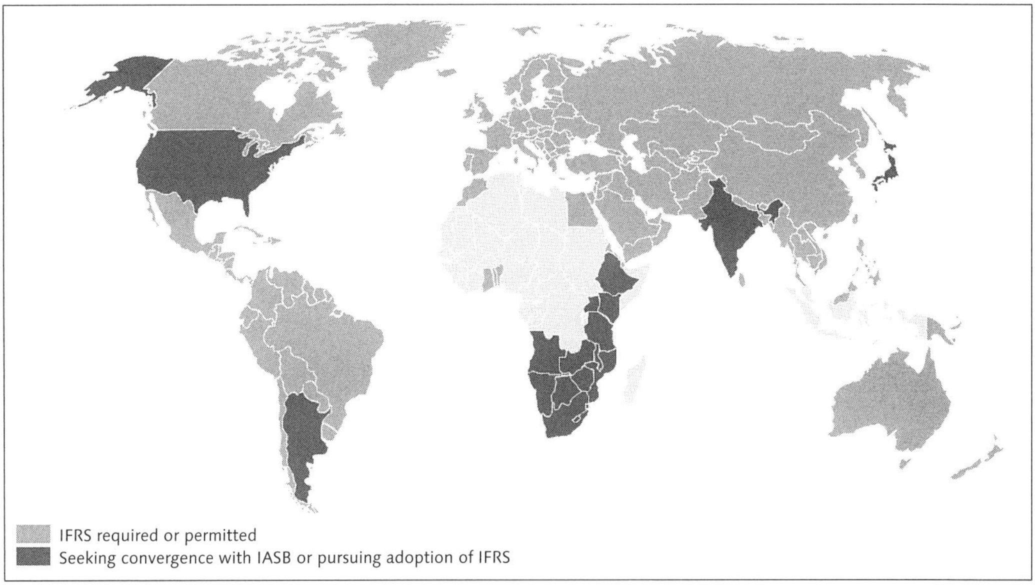

Figure 9.14 IFRS Map

Isolating Currency Impacts

Having the ability to isolate the impacts due to changes in exchange rates versus organic change can be challenging. Being able to run different versions of a consolidation based on different rates allows you to easily calculate the variances.

Consider comparing this year's actual numbers to those of last year. If you run this year's actuals at this year's rates, and then run another consolidation version at last year's rates, you can then take the difference between the versions to isolate the difference. An example of the resulting report is shown in Figure 9.15.

Modeling What-if Scenarios for Mergers and Acquisitions

Organizational structures change often as companies are merged or acquisitions occur. For example, for year-over-year reporting, you will want to see what growth happened from acquisitions and what organic growth occurred. Consolidation software that can support that type of reporting is essential.

Profit and Loss - Growth analysis

Amounts in Euro	Current rate & structure	Last year rate and structure	analysis				Constant rate N-1	Last year rate and structure
	2011.12	2010.12	Total	Organic growth	External growth	Impact of Currency Rate Change	2011.12	2011.12
Sales	9,352,777	7,522,568	1,830,209	1,574,851	745,636	-490,278	9,843,055	9,097,419
Cost of sales	-3,384,792	**-2,373,047**	-1,011,745	**-709,960**	**-516,766**	**214,981**	**-3,599,773**	**-3,083,007**
Gross margin	**5,967,985**	5,149,521	**818,464**	864,891	228,870	-275,297	6,243,282	6,014,412
Selling, General and Administrative Expenses	-1,070,434	-947,627	-122,807	-27,623	-192,096	96,912	-1,167,346	-975,250
Other operating income and expenses	-4,456,862	1,722,386	-6,179,249	-3,956,012	-2,423,408	200,171	-4,657,034	-2,233,626
Operating profit	**440,688**	**5,924,279**	**-5,483,591**	**-3,118,744**	**-2,386,634**	**21,787**	**418,902**	**2,805,536**
Other financial income and expenses	3,597,163	2,351,301	1,245,862	1,491,373	60,312	-305,823	3,902,985	3,842,673
Net results from equity method	35,774	41,609	-5,834	-3,473	0	-2,361	38,135	38,135
Financial result	**3,632,937**	2,392,909	**1,240,028**	1,487,899	60,312	-308,183	3,941,121	3,880,809
Profit before tax	**4,073,625**	**8,317,189**	**-4,243,563**	**-1,630,844**	**-2,326,322**	**-286,397**	**4,360,022**	**6,686,344**
Tax	-163,527	-148,534	-14,992	-12,393	-17,045	14,446	-177,973	-160,928
Profit from ordinary activities	**3,910,099**	8,168,654	**-4,258,556**	-1,643,238	-2,343,367	-271,951	4,182,049	6,525,417
Extraordinary items	172,234	**189,128**	-16,894	**3,771**	**0**	**-20,665**	**192,898**	**192,898**
Group profit before minority interests	**4,082,333**	**8,357,782**	**-4,275,450**	**-1,639,467**	**-2,343,367**	**-292,615**	**4,374,948**	**6,718,315**
Minority interest income	-663,650	-845,368	181,717	175,997	0	5,720	-669,370	-669,370
Net profit	**3,418,682**	**7,512,414**	**-4,093,732**	**-1,463,469**	**-2,343,367**	**-286,895**	**3,705,578**	**6,048,945**

Figure 9.15 Profit and Loss Growth Analysis

In addition to comparing this year to last year, you may also want to do what-if scenarios and various modeling to see the potential impact on your financials if a merger or acquisition occurred.

Management versus Legal Reporting Requirements

By combining legal and management reporting structures, SAP EPM consolidation solutions let you consolidate and directly compare all possible views in one fully integrated data model. This helps ensure a single version of the truth—without tedious, low-value reconciliations—and helps you focus on activities that add value to your business. The software also provides side-by-side what-if simulations for key growth initiatives, such as organizational changes, mergers, or acquisitions.

9.3 Differentiation between Consolidation Solutions

As we have discussed, SAP has several consolidation solutions. All of these solutions are now supported by SAP development. At the time of printing, all SAP consolidation solutions will be supported until 2020. Each solution has many customers, small and large, who perform complex multinational, multi-GAAP consolidations. The available solutions are:

- **SAP Enterprise Performance Management (EPM) solutions:**
  - SAP Business Planning and Consolidation, version for Netweaver
  - SAP Business Planning and Consolidation, version for Microsoft
  - SAP Financial Consolidation
- **Classic Solutions (part of the SAP Business Suite):**
  - Strategic Enterprise Management – Business Consolidation (SEM-BCS)
  - Enterprise Controlling – Consolidation System (EC-CS)

Because financial consolidation requirements differ greatly from one organization to the next, SAP has more than one solution to meet varied types of requirements. SAP acquired Outlooksoft (and BPC) in 2007 to help the office of the CFO innovate in the area of enterprise performance management (EPM). In 2008 SAP acquired SAP Financial Consolidation through the Business Objects acquisition. SAP developed Strategic Enterprise Management—Business Consolidation (SEM-BCS) as part of the SAP Business Suite. Each of these solutions is discussed in more detail in the following sections and the differences between them.

9.3.1 Business Suite Solutions

SAP Enterprise Controlling-Consolidation (EC-CS) is Consolidation and Simulation in ECC 6.0. Strategic Enterprise Management Business Consolidation (SEM-BCS) is the technological successor of EC-CS. EC-CS is based on R/3 where as SEM BCS is based on BW. Both these solutions perform financial consolidations. Consolidation logic is developed, delivered, and maintained by SAP. SAP will only address product issues and legal changes in EC-CS. There are no plans to add functional enhancements to EC-CS.

There are very few new BCS and EC-CS implementations since the EPM solutions provide better usability, little dependence on IT, more flexibility, and enhanced reporting capabilities. That being said, there are many BCS customer who are happy and the product continues to be enhanced.

Differences between Business Suite and EPM solutions

Business Suite and EPM solutions have different "philosophies." As illustrated in Figure 9.16, SAP EPM solutions use a "rules based" approach versus the preconfigured approach for the BCS & EC-CS. With the preconfigured approach, SAP develops and maintains the consolidation logic in the system. In the event that customers have requirements that go beyond what is delivered ABAP programing and technical intervention is required.

SAP EPM solutions on the other hand have "business rule modules" which allow finance or business users to create new calculations by creating business rules which require simpler configuration rather than programming. This brings more flexibility and autonomy: customers depend less on SAP delivering new functionality when wanting to extend the business logic. Customers can cover their requirements by adding or changing consolidation rules. Customers can react more quickly to changes in accounting rules where with the pre-defined logic approach it is necessary to often wait on support or even potentially new enhancement packages before the changes can be delivered.

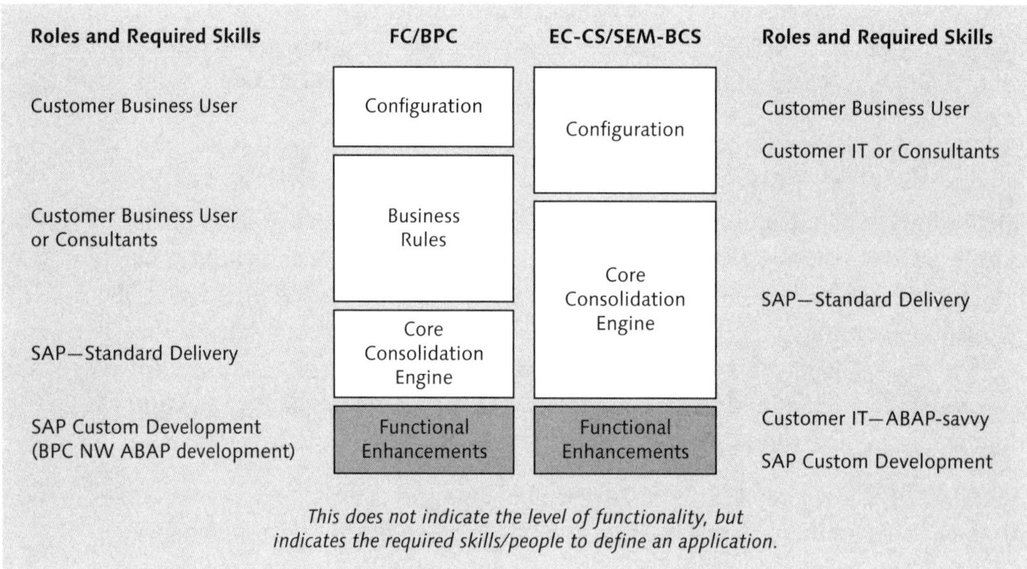

Figure 9.16 Consolidation Philosophies

9.3.2 SAP Business Planning and Consolidation (BPC)

SAP Business Planning and Consolidation (BPC), as stated previously, is part of the EPM suite of products by SAP. BPC accelerates planning and consolidated financial reporting processes. It supports planning, budgeting, and forecasting capabilities with management and legal consolidation functionality in a single application. You can quickly adjust plans and forecasts, shorten budget cycle time, close the books more quickly, help ensure compliance with regulatory and financial standards, and get the information you need to make more confident decisions. The BPC application has had several naming changes, and to clarify the BPC solution, let's look at its history:

- 1999 Foundation of Outlooksoft and Launch Everest.
- 2007 SAP acquires Outlooksoft.
- 2007 Launch SAP Business Planning and Consolidation.
- 2008 Launch SAP Business Planning and Consolidation 7.0, version for NetWeaver & SAP Business Planning and Consolidation 7.0, version for Microsoft.
- 2011 Launch EPM 10.0, including SAP Business Planning and Consolidation 10.0, version for SAP NetWeaver and SAP Business Planning and Consolidation 10.0, version for Microsoft.

Outlooksoft was created by former Hyperion employees. BPC was the result of the desire to create an innovative, easy to use performance management solution to cover both planning and consolidation. Figure 9.17 shows the Start page of BPC 10.0. What differentiates BPC from other consolidation applications is its unified planning and consolidation capabilities. It has a Microsoft Excel interface that is easy to use and familiar for finance professionals and includes business process flows which allow customers a guided approach to different finance processes.

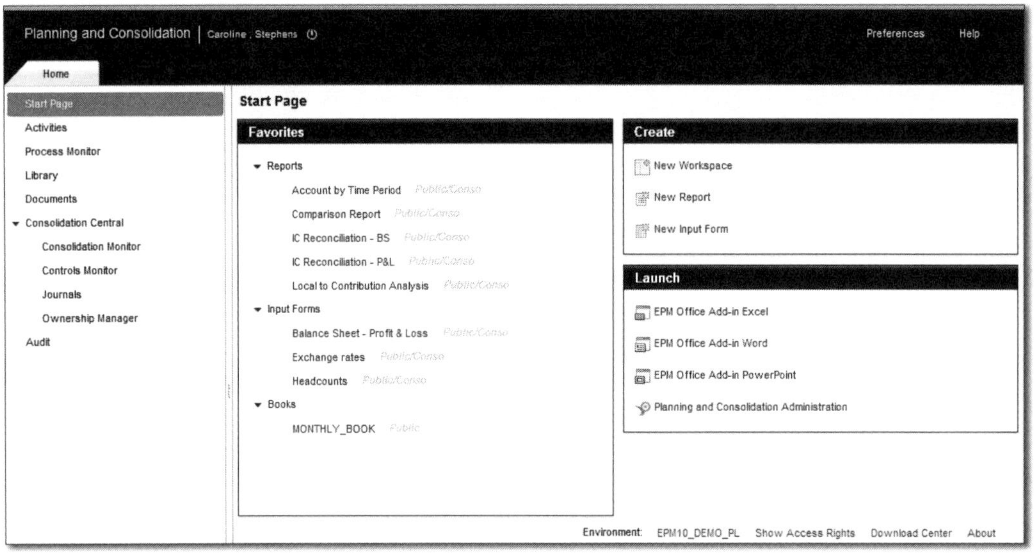

Figure 9.17 SAP Business Planning and Consolidation Landing Page

As an example of a BPC implementation, let's look at Russian Railways who implemented BPC for both planning and consolidation.

9.3.3 Customer Story: Russian Railways Gets On the Right Track with Planning and Consolidation

Carrying just short of one trillion passengers a year and with nearly a million employees, Russian Railways (RZD) is one of the largest transport companies in the world moving people and freight across two continents from Beijing to Berlin along 85,500 kilometers of track.

Born out of the loss making Ministry of Railways of the Russian Federation in 2003, new management instilled a culture of commercial accountability and brought the company into profit. To continue this transformation, management recognized the need to standardize planning and budgeting systems across the various subsidiaries, shortening planning and re-forecasting cycles as they were not able to keep in step with operational changes and speeding up consolidation processes to provide quicker and more reliable information to support decision making.

After choosing the SAP Business Planning and Consolidation application, RZD joined the SAP Ramp-Up program, which provides dedicated expertise for the implementation of new versions of SAP software, as this would accelerate the time to value in what was to be a mammoth implementation. Given the diversity of businesses within the group, RZD chose to implement several instances of the software in order to support different methods of planning and budgeting, all the time ensuring that data automation projects were in place to unify the data at the highest levels.

The central finance team joke that the implementation of SAP Business Planning and Consolidation was a *'smooth ride'*. It has certain delivered important benefits and thanks to the software, RZD can now run their once-slow processes much faster, much easier and with much greater flexibility. The time taken to complete a planning and budgeting cycle has been halved and productivity in the accounting and finance team increased by 30%, while automation has meant that there are now 60% fewer errors in routine financial processes. Given that there is still a considerable amount of manual data entry from remote contributors—another reason why the user-friendly and familiar Microsoft Excel like interface of SAP Planning and Consolidation appealed to RZD—this is considered a remarkable improvement.

9.3.4 SAP Financial Consolidation

To meet strict regulatory consolidation and reporting requirements, organizations need an application that gives control to the finance office yet is flexible enough for subsidiaries. The SAP Financial Consolidation application provides you with the power, agility, and confidence to close your books quickly.

Similiar to that of BPC, SAP Financial Consolidation has had a varied history. The SAP Financial Consolidation application came to SAP through the following history:

- 1990 Foundation of Cartesis
- 1991 Launch Unification (see version naming note for more detail)
- 1995 Launch Cartesis Carat (see version naming note for more detail)
- 1999 PricewaterhouseCoopers acquires Cartesis
- 2000 Launch ES Magnitude (see version naming note for more detail)
- 2003 A consortium led by Apax Partners acquires Cartesis

- 2007 Business Objects acquires Cartesis
- 2008 SAP acquires Business Objects
- 2008 Launch SAP Financial Consolidation 7.0 (see version naming note for more detail)
- 2011 Launch EPM 10.0, including SAP Financial Consolidation 10.0

Version Naming Note

Each of these products are legal successors to each other. They are just different names for the same basic product, which has been further developed and improved over time.

Figure 9.18 shows the home page of SAP Financial Consolidation. This application is a powerful consolidation engine. It provides a very structured approach to financial consolidation. It provides an extremely detailed audit trail of where all information comes from.

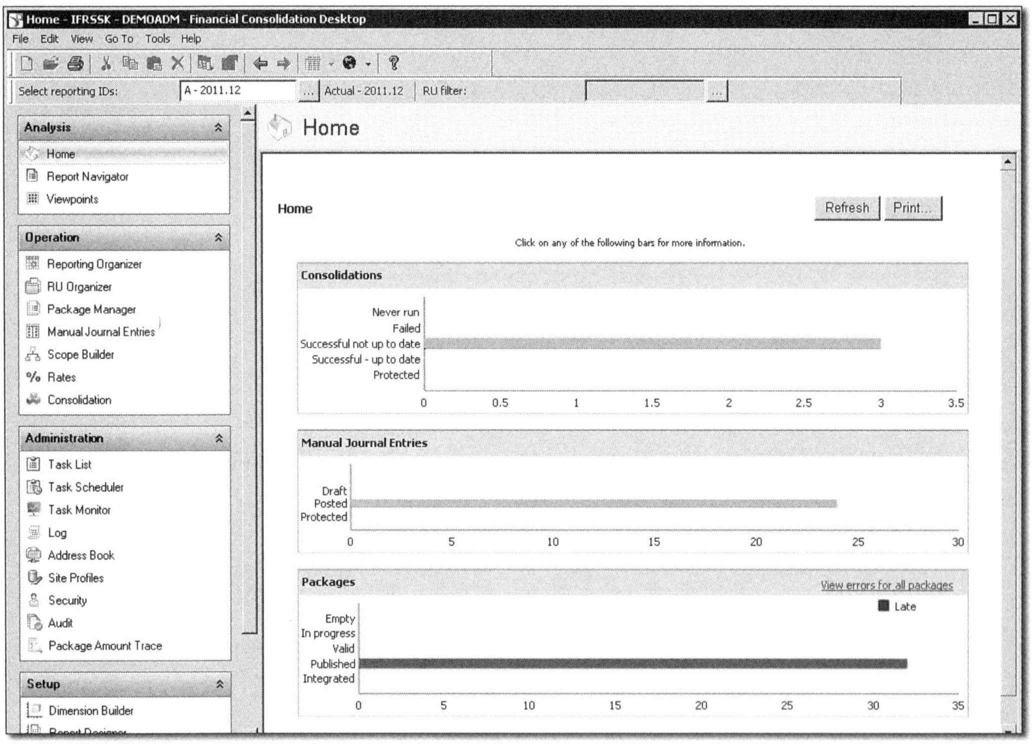

Figure 9.18 SAP Financial Consolidation

The following customer story explains how Belgian company Bekaert leverage SAP Financial Consolidation to increase automation, reducing manual processes throughout their organization.

9.3.5 Customer Story: Bekaert Standardizes Global Financial Reporting

Belgium's Bekaert is a market leader in drawn steel wire products and metal technologies. The company conducts business on a global basis and must adhere to the evolving International Financial Reporting Standards. In recent years, a growing number of Bekaert business units have been running on SAP software platforms. However this was not in a globally standardized way and the company's transactional systems and financial reporting solution were not fully integrated which meant that the finance team had to manually manage fragmented financial information from different parts of the world.

To optimize its financial reporting processes, Bekaert turned to the SAP Financial Consolidation application, which besides offering the functionality and level of integration the company demanded, was the logical choice as it fitted in with Bekaert's "SAP unless" IT strategy. To drive the implementation effort, Bekaert built a strong project team made up from representatives from across the company supported by IT partner Tata Consultancy Services and SAP solutions consultants.

During the project, the team focused on migrating historical data and on the crucial task of training 170 local users scattered around the globe. Bekaert also took the opportunity to enhance the company's existing SAP ERP application platform to optimize integration with the financial consolidation software. Then, prior to the full-scale rollout, the team conducted test runs for local users and at the central location in Bekaert's Group Control.

Today, Bekaert is running the same financial reporting software at all its worldwide locations and joint ventures and can collect its far-flung data more efficiently with greater transparency, accuracy, and speed. Improved efficiency has enabled Bekaert to reduce the time taken for a quarterly financial consolidation by 30% which has given financial controllers across the company time to perform broader and more value-added analysis.

The solution's high degree of automation also means no more manual data entry errors, more accurate data, and less time spent on manual processes. In fact, up to 80% of the financial input is now automatically uploaded. Further time savings have been realized as a result of tight integration between the company's transactional systems and financial reporting software. This has enabled Bekaert to report its full-year results a month earlier than usual, even though much data had to be restated to comply with new reporting requirements.

9.3.6 Engaging with SAP experts

The first step in deciding which consolidation solution is a best fit for your organization is to engage SAP experts. There is not simple decision tree to help you decide. There are many aspects that need to be considered including but not limited to:

- Will the application be owned and maintained by IT or Finance? What are the skill sets of your IT and Finance department?
- Is the organization on one SAP ERP, multiple SAP ERP instances, or are there non-SAP ERPs involved in the landscape?
- Is there a desire to have unified planning an consolidation?
- Is there much merger and acquisition activities?
- Is the organizational hierarchy very complex? Is there a requirement for many different organizational hierarchies?

All these questions need to be considered and discussed both internally within your business and with SAP experts to select the appropriate consolidation solution.

9.4 Starter Kits

Now that you understand the different consolidation solutions from SAP and the processes that they help streamline, let's discuss content. SAP provides preconfigured content for its EPM consolidation solutions called *starter kits*. The content includes data entry schedules, output reports, preconfigured business rules, controls, and validations.

At the time of publication, the following starter kits are available:

Application	Starter kit
SAP Business Planning and Consolidation, version for SAP NetWeaver	IFRS and US GAAP
SAP Business Planning and Consolidation, version for the Microsoft platform	IFRS
SAP Financial Consolidation	IFRS and US GAAP
SAP Disclosure Management	IFRS and US GAAP

A starter kit is available for IFRS. The globalization of capital markets calls for the convergence of accounting standards around the world. Today, more than 120 countries allow the use of IFRS in one form or another.

Countries who have not yet adopted IFRS, such as China, are working to converge accounting standards. The United States will continue to converge US GAAP for existing projects, moving the world toward a global use of a single set of accounting and consolidation rules.

SAP has a regulatory task force comprised of members of the SAP Business Suite and EPM organizations, which monitor financial standards. Its mission is to deliver analysis notes describing foreseen impacts on the products. The task force's focus areas vary according to the International Accounting Standards Board (IASB) work plan; for example, topics such as revenue recognition, financial statements, consolidation, financial instruments, leases, or fair value measurement are at the top of the agenda. Analysis papers and notes are publicly available on the SAP Community Network (SCN).

The starter kit provides a design documentation you can use during the project implementation. It also contains process guidance for business users to achieve IFRS-compliant consolidation and minimize the effort needed to address complex requirements, such as those involving incoming entities, additional acquisition of shares, financial interest, or comprehensive income. Using the documentation provided with the starter kit can help you reduce your total cost of ownership for the SAP application. Because your users can immediately use these documents, you can eliminate the effort needed to document processes and software functionality.

Also available is a series of how to guides dedicated to help you deal with the most frequent merger and acquisition requirements when using the starter kits for IFRS. These guides are available on SCN.

The SAP EPM consolidation starter kits are developed based on extensive product expertise as well as the experiences of helping hundreds of customers deploy and configure solutions. Starter kits can help you perform, validate, and publish a statutory consolidation in accordance with IFRS or US GAAP. The starter kit relies on a generic and IFRS/US GAAP-oriented chart of accounts, using characteristics that enable you to update automatically all configuration elements related to the accounts. The starter kits contain prebuilt data entry schedules and associated controls. The consolidation engine handles full, proportionate, and equity methods, and addresses scope changes. A comprehensive set of consolidation rules enables you to produce consistent consolidated data. Finally, the starter kit provides a complete audit trail and formatted financial statements. Your deployment team can then enhance the foundation to meet your individual requirements, such as accounting policies, business processes, or company structure.

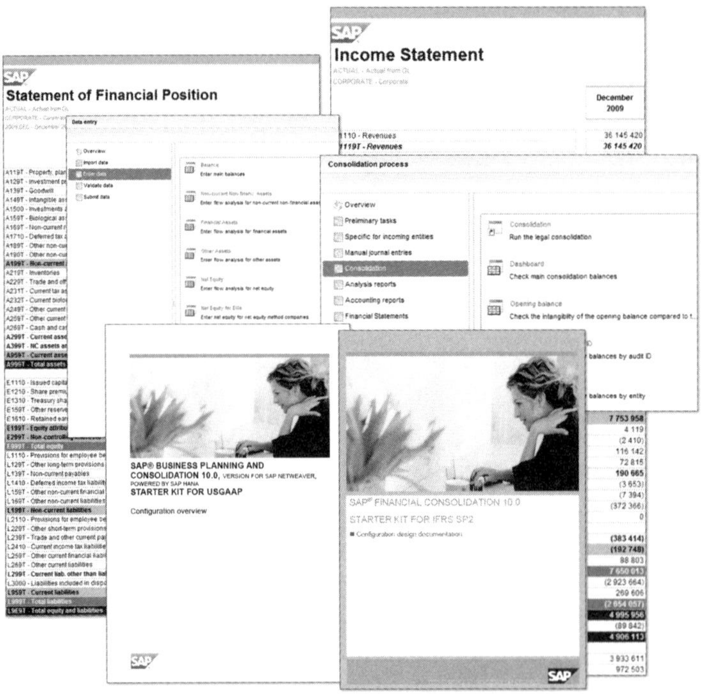

Figure 9.19 Starter Kit Reports

Now that we understand what is included in a starter kit, let see how Bank of Cyprus leveraged the SAP Financial Consolidation starter kit for IFRS to improve their consolidation process.

9.4.1 Customer Story: Bank of Cyprus Group Achieves Clear Audits with SAP Solutions

Bank of Cyprus Group, the leading provider of financial services in Cyprus, operates nearly 600 branches in Cyprus, Greece, Russia, Ukraine, Romania, the Channel Islands, and the United Kingdom. Over recent years, the bank has expanded through organic growth and acquisition. This, plus a changing corporate structure, created a highly complex system for consolidated financial reporting. The complexity increased over time as more demanding reporting requirements were introduced by the International Financial Reporting Standards (IFRS) and other industry-relevant regulators.

Previously consolidated reporting was managed with hundreds of Microsoft Excel spreadsheets that were shared across the bank by e-mail. This increased the risk of error, slowed down the process, and also cost a considerable amount of time and money as the bank's finance team had to work long hours to meet its quarterly and year-end consolidation deadlines. Individual units from various countries would send spreadsheets to corporate headquarters in Cyprus, where data would be checked, but as many units were in different time zones, whole days would be lost waiting for updated data.

Recognizing the need to automate its financial consolidation process, the bank chose SAP Financial Consolidation based on the experience that SAP experts had with other European banks with accounting procedures similar to those in Cyprus. The bank was also attracted by a starter kit for the application that would help them quickly comply with the IFRS reporting requirements.

The implementation of SAP® Financial Consolidation—the first by a bank in the region—involved 70 users, 15 sites, 46 reporting units, and 9 countries. With the centralized software in place, the bank can finalize its intercompany consolidations faster than before and the financial-close has been shortened from 5 to 6 weeks down to 2 to 3 weeks.

The finance team is now freed up to analyze results, which are more accurate and easier for auditors and managers to review. The solution has also provided managers with faster access to reports which gives them a head start on identifying potential challenges and opportunities, as well as giving them access to details that was previously too time-consuming to produce, such as an in-depth analysis by region and type of business. Looking ahead, the bank hopes to give managers self-service dashboards to create their own reports.

9.4.2 SAP Disclosure Management Consolidation Starter Kits

SAP provides preconfigured content for SAP Disclosure Management to support IFRS and US GAAP. In the 2012 "Magic Quadrant for Corporate Performance Management Suites" report, Gartner emphasized that disclosure management capabilities "should support specific generally accepted accounting principles (GAAP) presentation rules to enable the preparation of statutory financial statements with appropriate commentary and supplementary notes. Increasingly, financial-reporting solutions incorporate business rules, workflow, and audit trails to better meet regulatory, compliance and governance programs. In addition, they should support financial-reporting technologies, such as eXtensible Business Reporting Language (XBRL), as regulators increasingly require the submission of financial statements in XBRL format." SAP Disclosure Management starter kits for IFRS and US GAAP leverage SAP's core competency in solving business problems to improve people's lives addressing the world's most pressing challenges of regulatory complexity.

The starter kit's preconfigured sample reports include primary financial statements that comply with accounting requirements related to the presentation of financial statements, such as IAS1 and IAS7. Many formatting templates are delivered and ready to be adapted to your corporate policy. The statements are linked to the data repository, which is designed according to best practices in terms of table organization, data validation, dynamic formatting, and rounding management.

From a product support perspective, SAP Disclosure Management starter kits are enhanced once or twice a year according to changes in regulations and made available on the SAP Help Portal.

SAP Disclosure Management starter kits will help you to rapidly implement your disclosure management application. Designing your application from the starter kits will provide insight on how you can leverage the powerful features of SAP

Disclosure Management for gathering, structuring, formatting, validating, tagging, and eventually filing the publication data.

More specifically, US domestic filers as well as foreign private issuers will efficiently comply with the US SEC mandate. Not only do the starter kits accelerate the creation of the mandatory reports, such as 10-Q and 20-F in HTML format, but the predelivered XBRL taxonomies as well as pretagged documents also help companies comply with the four XBRL tagging levels.

In this respect, the starter kits significantly reduce implementation times of your disclosure application while guiding you on your way to compliance.

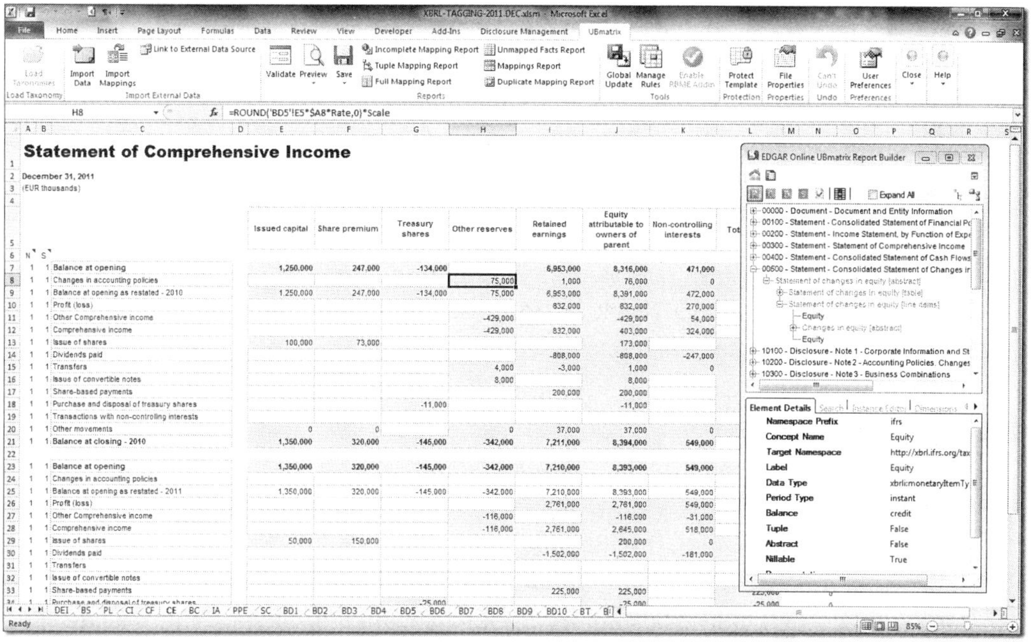

Figure 9.20 SAP Disclosure Management Starter Kit

The starter kits illustrate how you can pull data out of your financial reporting system directly into the data repository to streamline the data flow. The data-extraction scenarios are based on SAP consolidation starter kits and can be easily adapted to your reporting application.

The starter kits also include custom XBRL taxonomies designed per US SEC requirements and based on the public IFRS and US GAAP taxonomies as published by the IFRS Foundation and the FASB, respectively. The financial statements are pretagged against these taxonomies to accelerate the implementation of your XBRL filings.

9.4.3 SAP Financial Close and Disclosure Management Rapid Deployment Solution (RDS)

The SAP Rapid Deployment Solution (RDS) provides a ready-to-consume combination of SAP predefined services, preconfigured content, and enablement content to accelerate the implementation and lower risk. The RDS takes the preconfigured content of the starter kits described in the previous section and couples them with implementation services.

Implementation is supported by standardized methodology and best practices, honed over decades. An optimized mix of global resources, remote support, and onsite consulting gives you access to experts who can help you implement your solution on time and on budget.

The RDS includes educational material and training scripts for the functionalities that matter most—users start right away, without the delays associated with customized training. The RDS brings it all together—preconfigured software, fixed-scope implementation services, and the materials you need for a successful implementation.

The SAP Financial Close and Disclosure Management RDS streamlines the implementation process, bringing together software, best practices, and services that can help you quickly close the books, mitigate risk, and comply with IFRS and GAAP regulations. Start with what you need today, and expand your solution as your business requirements grow and change. SAP's RDSs are delivered with a step-by-step guide that outlines the implementation process and includes SAP Business Planning and Consolidation, SAP Financial Consolidation, SAP Disclosure Management, the related starter kits for IFRS and US GAAP, and a fixed-scope service offering.

9.5 Summary

The financial consolidation process is one of the most involved parts of the financial close. There are complex accounting requirements combined with many technology options that are available to streamline the process. The next chapter discusses SAP Disclosure Management. After all of the data is consolidated and calculated properly, the next question is how you present it properly to your stakeholders. SAP consolidation solutions have reporting tools that come with them, but combining that data with comments and descriptions is where SAP Disclosure Management comes into play.

After a company has completed the close, the financial results then need to be disclosed to internal and external stakeholders. This step is often called the "last mile of finance," which refers to the publication of financial statements and regulatory disclosures. This chapter will explore disclosure management and XBRL filings.

10 Disclosure Management and XBRL Filings

After your company completes the financial close, the final step is to disclose the results to various stakeholders, including regulatory agencies, financial analysts and investors, and corporate executives. Examples of these disclosures include the publication of an annual report, quarterly results in electronic format (such as the 10Q form), annual results (such as the 20F form), tax disclosures (currently mandated in the United Kingdom), sustainability disclosures, and executive board packages.

For these disclosures, financial figures are supplemented with descriptive information, which is usually in an unstructured, or free-form, format. The SAP Annual Report, as shown in Figure 10.1, illustrates this combination of financial key figures with additional narrative and graphical content.

Although many companies have automated the financial close for both the entity and group close, many do not have an automated way to combine their financial results with such narrative and other descriptive information required for financial footnotes. Instead, they rely on manual processes that involve cutting and pasting from various data sources and descriptions into one document, and then emailing the results to multiple approvers. These approvers may make contradictory edits. Consequently, additional manual validations often need to be made to ensure the correct edits are incorporated. This increases risk because the edits and the audit trail are spread throughout various email inboxes.

Figure 10.1 Financial Figures, Narrative Information, and Graphics Elements of the SAP Annual Report

In addition, many companies have separate work streams for creating an annual report and for creating electronic filings. These separate processes and data streams increase the risk of inconsistencies when a last-minute adjustment is required, for example, a final elimination entry that is made late in the consolidation process. Please refer to the "Key Performance Indicators Affecting the Production of Financial Disclosures" box for a discussion of some of the influencing factors of the speed and accuracy of your disclosures.

SAP Disclosure Management automates the process of managing the collection, editing, and validation of information required for the reports, as well as the production, publication, and filing of financial statements and reports, including eXtensible Business Reporting Language (XBRL) electronic filings.

All data needed for disclosures is collected within the application, making it the single source of the truth; this information then feeds all disclosures and reports in various output formats. By introducing automation into the disclosure management process, you can reduce the time and cost associated with manual processes. In addition, you can decrease risk by implementing a comprehensive audit trail and ensuring the consistency of your data in different reports.

Key Performance Indicators Affecting the Production of Financial Disclosures

The process—and speed—of collecting both structured and unstructured information to produce financial statements depends on the size and scope of a company's activities. Some key factors include the following:

- **The number of subsidiaries or legal entities**
  Financial statements and electronic filings must be generated for each legal entity, as well as at the group and corporate levels.
- **The number of financial statements and disclosures that must be filed**
  Financial statements must be filed for each country and jurisdiction in which a legal entity does business. An added factor is that most local jurisdictions have unique rules for the information that is required for disclosure, which may differ significantly from a standard annual report. Finally, certain industries, such as insurance, have additional filing requirements.
- **The number of sources for financial information**
  Many companies have multiple accounting and consolidation systems. In addition to the financial key figures, much of the unstructured information and explanatory notes are captured in local spreadsheets, word processing documents, and email, which is difficult to track.
- **The number of languages required for narrative descriptions**
  Even though the financial figures are the same, the narrative information must often be translated to local languages for regulatory disclosures.

The following measurements are often employed to determine the effectiveness of collecting and validating financial statements and footnotes:

- **The number of days for a financial close**
  The information required for financial disclosures is collected during the standard closing processes.
- **The number of days to generate financial statements after the close**
  After the books are closed, financial statements can be generated, which takes additional time for validation and publication.
- **The cost of finance as a percentage of revenue**
  Streamlining the process of collecting financial statement data reduces the cost of finance as a function and frees up the time of financial analysts to do more value-added work.

The flow of information in the SAP Disclosure Management application includes three stages, as shown in the columns of Figure 10.2:

- **Collect input** (left column)
  Gathering information from source systems.
- **Assemble and manage disclosures** (center column)
  Using workflow to assemble information from the data repository; creating forms and reports; and managing the revisions, validations, and approvals of the disclosures in preparation for publication.
- **Generate output** (right column)
  Generating reports in various formats, including XBRL electronic filings.

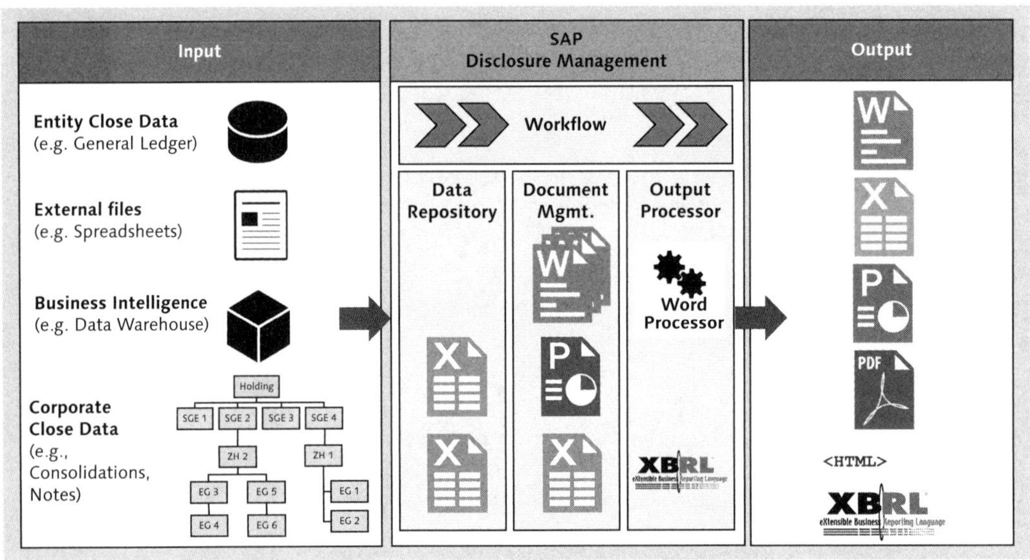

Figure 10.2 Managing the Collection, Assembly, and Publication of Financial Disclosures with SAP Disclosure Management

In most companies, various team roles are involved in the different stages of working with disclosures:

- Financial analysts and consolidations accountants are responsible for collecting the source data and ensuring it is up to date for the disclosure processes.
- Corporate reporting and investor relations teams create and validate the reports for both regulatory disclosures and management reports.

- Marketing teams and product experts are often responsible for the content describing the products that are sold by a company.
- Corporate reporting managers and finance executives are responsible for the final approval of financial statements and reports.
- Accountants who specialize in XBRL filings are responsible for the electronic filing of the financial statements to regulatory agencies.

Using Microsoft Office with SAP Disclosure Management

SAP Disclosure Management provides a lean, web-based user interface to access all of the information collected in the application. You can see examples of these screens later in this chapter in Figure 10.6 for monitoring the disclosure process, and Figure 10.7 for accessing individual data sources, forms, and report chapters.

At the same time, finance teams can still use the tools with which they are most familiar: Microsoft Office applications. As part of the SAP Disclosure Management solution, financial team members install a SAP Disclosure Management client on their local computers, which is an add-in for Microsoft Office. The add-in creates a new menu (or ribbon, as of Microsoft Office 2007) within the Microsoft Office applications, including Microsoft Word (as shown later in Figure 10.8), Microsoft Excel (as shown later in Figure 10.4), and Microsoft PowerPoint. The minimum required release is Microsoft Office 2003.

Using this add-in, you can trigger data refreshes and updates in the Microsoft Office documents, for example, if a key figure has changed in the source data. You can also compare report versions, and update SAP Disclosure Management with any changes that you made to your disclosure reports and forms.

Now, let's take a look at the processes and details found in the left column of Figure 10.2, specifically collecting input in the disclosure process, and how you can collect both financial figures and unstructured data from various source systems.

10.1 Collect Information from Source Systems

As you prepare to gather the information for your financial disclosures, you need to identify the sources of the data and where they reside. This information will likely come from other systems—SAP systems or non-SAP systems—and will include both financial key figures as well as additional descriptive and narrative information. All of this data is stored within SAP Disclosure Management, which becomes your data repository for all disclosures. We will now take a look at obtaining both the structured (financial key figures) and unstructured information.

10.1.1 Financial Figures for Disclosure Reports

Key figures such as financial account balances can be brought in directly from multiple sources. Most commonly, this information comes from consolidation systems such as SAP Business Planning and Consolidation, SAP Financial Consolidation, and SAP Strategic Enterprise Management (SAP SEM) (for additional information about these solutions, please refer to Chapter 9). Other data sources include business intelligence systems, such as SAP BusinessObjects Business Intelligence (BI) solutions and SAP NetWeaver Business Warehouse (SAP NetWeaver BW), and core financial systems such as SAP ERP Financials. You can also bring in data from non-SAP systems and even spreadsheets. In the initial implementation, you create a link from SAP Disclosure Management to each of the data sources. The system administrator uses a wizard during the installation of SAP Disclosure Management to create the links between the source data and the disclosure management database. This typically means providing the location of the source files and systems within a company network. SAP NetWeaver BW is a special case; for this connection, a SAP Disclosure Management BW connector is delivered with the application and is configured with the appropriate server information.

After the key figures are updated within the SAP Disclosure Management application, you can access them from the REPORT tab, using the GENERAL subtab. When you select a data source, it is opened with Microsoft Excel. From within Microsoft Excel, you use the add-in ribbon to use the SAP Disclosure Management capabilities; for more information, please refer to the "Using Microsoft Office with SAP Disclosure Management" box. Still, all standard spreadsheet capabilities that are normally found in Microsoft Excel are available, including formatting and graphs, the use of formulas, and rounding.

When you maintain a link to a source system, you can update the SAP Disclosure Management data repository if information in a source system changes, for example, when additional elimination entries are posted in a consolidation system. This allows you to begin working on your financial disclosures even before the entire financial close is complete, accelerating the overall process. You can access the data sources from the Microsoft add-in, as shown in Figure 10.3.

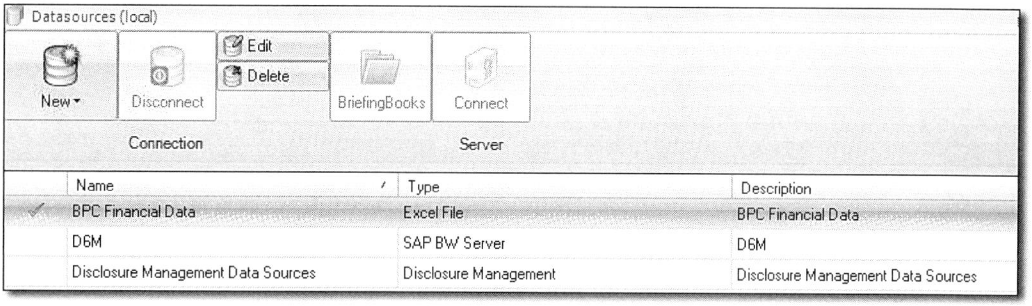

Figure 10.3 Three Data Sources Available for Updates

After the updates, you can see the changes that were made in a particular worksheet by using the COMPARE functionality from the add-in ribbon. You can compare the current data with any of the prior versions. The results of the comparison are shown in a new document, which you can save. Each cell that was changed is highlighted in a different color, for example, in cells R7 and U10 in Figure 10.4.

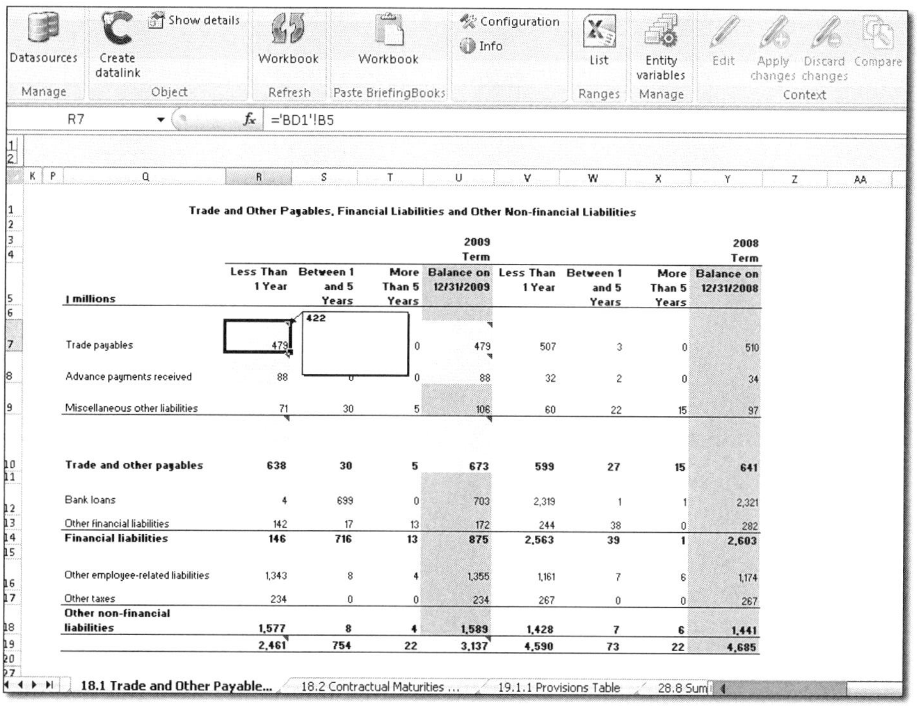

Figure 10.4 Using the SAP Disclosure Management Add-In to Work with Financial Key Figures within Microsoft Excel

In addition, the prior value in the cell, in the version you are comparing against, is captured as a comment to the cell, as shown in cell R7. This capability allows you to easily see changes without having to run multiple reports and perform manual comparisons.

If you have chosen multiple data sources, for example, from multiple consolidation systems, each data source is opened in its own tab, as shown at the bottom of Figure 10.4.

The information in the data repository is used in all of the reports that require this information. Ensuring that the reports and disclosure statements refer to the data repository maintains the consistency of the information across all reports.

10.1.2 Unstructured Information in Financial Statements

While the figures in a financial statement reveal the financial health of a company, this numeric, quantitative data does not tell the entire story. Explanations of those results are found in the fine print—in the narrative and the financial footnotes of annual reports and financial statements. These footnotes contain primarily qualitative, unstructured information, and are required for compliant financial statements. Over half of all enterprise data—as much as 80%—is in an unstructured format.

This qualitative information required can take multiple forms:

- **Breaking down account-level detail**
  Some financial figures disclosed in an annual report or financial statement must be broken down to further levels of detail, for example, deprecation figures for fixed assets based on different depreciation methods. The level of detail required can also change from year to year, so the supplementary information is often maintained as unstructured information so that it does not interfere with the core accounting and consolidations processes, and avoids restructuring the chart of accounts on a regular basis.
- **Explaining the financial results**
  Narrative information is required to explain assumptions and company policies to allow investors and external stakeholders to properly evaluate the company's financial position. Examples include providing details behind the pension plan and assumptions behind goodwill. Narrative is also used to

explain changes in year-over-year results, for example, if there was a significant increase or decrease in a particular financial figure such as revenue, or changes in operating margin which may be due to an acquisition.

In external disclosures such as the annual report, the qualitative information is provided alongside tables and financial statements. In addition, the qualitative information is also required when disclosing financial statements to regulatory bodies. There are several ways you can collect unstructured information:

- **Manual entry**
  Using a system to collect the unstructured information is not necessary; you can enter it directly into SAP Disclosure Management by using Microsoft Office applications.
- **Upload of Microsoft Office documents**
  If you already have existing material, including executive statements, descriptions of your products, or graphics, you can upload these directly into SAP Disclosure Management.
- **Consolidation solutions**
  Both the SAP Business Planning and Consolidation and SAP Financial Consolidation applications allow you to capture financial notes in text fields as part of the consolidation process. It's basically a text field within the BPC and FC solutions. The mapping goes back to identifying the source system (by the sysadmin). For further details, please refer to Chapter 9.
- **SAP Notes Management**
  This application allows you to collect, validate, and report on descriptive and other supplementary data for both the entity close and the group close. For further details, please refer to the "SAP Notes Management" box.

If you are using a consolidation, data warehouse, or notes management system to manage your unstructured information, you can bring this information into SAP Disclosure Management in the same way that you bring in consolidation key figures by creating a mapping to the source systems and documents, as described in Section 10.1.1.

SAP Notes Management

The SAP Notes Management application is a separate application built on top of SAP NetWeaver BW, which allows you to collect and reuse unstructured descriptive data. As shown in Figure 10.5, you can leverage your existing chart of accounts and link directly to consolidation figures using a form that allows you to break down account-level information. You can also create other forms that allow you to enter textual information that is also linked to the consolidation figures.

To ensure data consistency and reliability, you can define validation rules that include calculations of key figures, for example, to ensure that any account breakdowns sum up to the consolidation values. This information can also be exported to Microsoft Excel, including any calculations that are defined in the forms. For narrative information, rules can also ensure that textual descriptions are not missing. A report is available as an Adobe PDF (Portable Document Format) document to allow finance teams to ensure that the descriptions are complete and do not contradict each other.

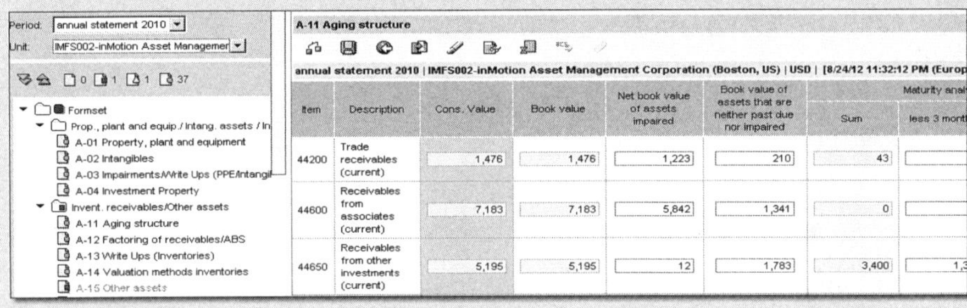

Figure 10.5 Linking to Consolidation Figures and Breaking Down Account-Level Information in SAP Notes Management

You can monitor the progress of collecting all data source information in a cockpit view, in the same way that you can monitor the progress of the completion of reports and forms; for more information, please refer to Section 10.2.1.

Now that we have seen how to use source data from different systems, let's look at a customer story. Metcalf was able to include data from SAP and non-SAP source systems into its disclosure management process for better control of its regulatory reporting processes.

10.1.3 Customer Story: Metcash Delivers the Goods in Corporate Governance

Sydney-based Metcash Ltd. is a wholesaler and distributor that works with independent Australasian retailers in the grocery, liquor, automotive, and hardware sectors, providing them with the scale necessary to create competitive buying power together with marketing, distribution, and financial expertise and support.

Founded as a family business in 1927, Metcash listed on the Australian stock exchange in 2005, which took the company into a business environment with an increasing number of regulatory and compliance challenges. Recognizing that trying to tackle regulatory reporting without automation was highly inefficient, Metcash initiated a project to introduce software tools that would deliver an end-to-end process for the financial close and provide a robust platform for compliance with corporate governance requirements.

When it came to automating the management of external reporting, Metcash needed a solution that was easy to integrate with both its SAP landscape and non-SAP solutions and was scalable to meet reporting needs that the company may face in the future. The SAP Disclosure Management application satisfied these requirements, and the company partnered with Innogence Ltd., a recognized leader in supporting SAP solutions that is known for delivering successful enterprise projects. Critically the company also had personnel who were already fully familiar with the chosen solution, which ensured a rapid implementation and roll out.

From struggling with manual processes, the introduction of SAP Disclosure Management means that Metcash now enjoys a very high level of monitoring and control throughout the financial close process, with managers able to collaborate to identify and address issues before they result in delays. As finance staff can map and audit the flow of data from core financial systems through to final reports and disclosures, Metcash has greater confidence in the accuracy of the information displayed in its published reports, and the company can more easily satisfy all of its corporate governance responsibilities. The workflow management functionality at the heart of the solution also expedites the process with faster processing so that reports are completed on schedule.

Having satisfied the needs of the regulators, the next step for Metcash is to expand the use of the application to produce its annual and board reports.

Now that we understand how data sources are linked to SAP Disclosure Management, let's take a look at the center column in Figure 10.2, assembling and managing the various disclosure reports and forms.

10.2 Manage Financial Statements and Reports

Within SAP Disclosure Management, you define the structure of various financial reports, forms, and disclosures. Let's look at how you can keep track of the progress of each report, and then we'll review how to manage individual report documents.

10.2.1 Tracking the Progress of the Disclosure Process

You can create multiple reports and break them down by chapter and subchapter. Examples are an annual report and forms such as the 10Q and 20F. You can reuse a single chapter in more than one report and form, so that you do not need to duplicate the information. You define these reports on the ADMINISTRATION tab, using the MANAGE REPORTS link. In addition to the report structure, you also define which Microsoft Office application is used for editing. Finally, a report is created for a particular period; periods are defined on the SETTINGS tab, using the PERIODS link. Once created, a report can be copied for subsequent periods.

At any time, you can see an overview of the progress of the disclosure report or form from the cockpit of each report within SAP Disclosure Management, from the REPORT tab on the COCKPIT subtab. Note that this status view is also available for the import of data that was discussed in Section 10.1.1.

In Figure 10.6, you can see the status of the annual report using traffic light symbols; that is, when you are past the due date (in the DUE DATE column) for a particular chapter or section, the status (in the STEP column) automatically turns red, and completed chapters are green. Other information that is available includes the number of times the chapter has been revised (REVISION column), whether it is currently being edited (CHECKED OUT BY column), the file size (SIZE column) the document type used for editing (TYPE column), and the last date (LAST MODIFIED ON column) and person (LAST MODIFIED BY column) to make a change. A more comprehensive audit trail of all versions and changes is also available in the detailed view of the chapter, shown in Figure 10.7 in the next section, from the HISTORY subtab.

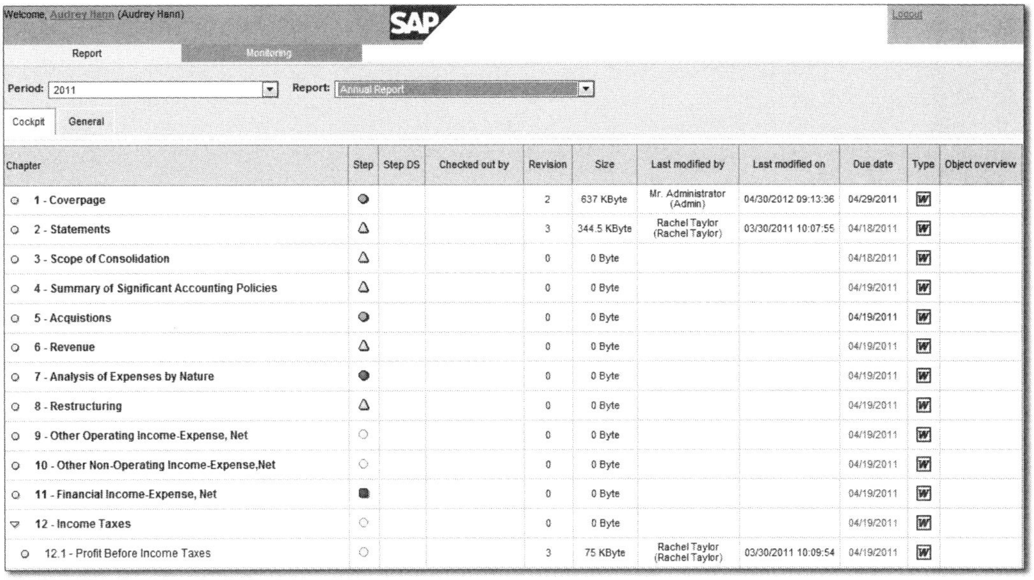

Figure 10.6 The Overall Status of the Disclosure Process in the Cockpit within SAP Disclosure Management

10.2.2 Manage Report Documents

After you have defined the structure of each report and form, you can assign the responsibility for updating the document at the chapter and the subchapter levels (for additional information, please refer to Section 10.3.1). In addition, when a team member accesses a chapter, it is considered "checked out" and is therefore locked for changes by other team members. This capability allows multiple team members to work on the overall annual report at the same time without overwriting each other's sections, ensuring one version of the truth.

As shown in Figure 10.7, selecting either the entire document at the highest level, or an individual chapter within the report structure, will bring you to the GENERAL subtab, changing the view to show the report structure on the left and the header information about the chapter you selected on the right. This detailed information includes the status of the document and the associated possible actions, the last time it was checked out, and any comments that summarize the most recent changes. From this detail screen, you can either edit (choose the EDIT button) or view (choose the VIEW button) the document.

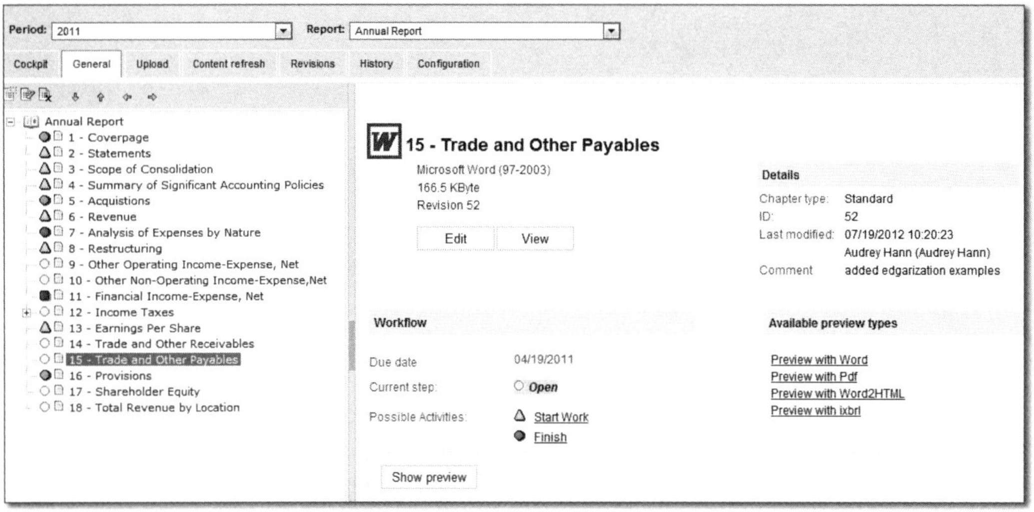

Figure 10.7 Edit or Preview a Document on the Detail Screen for the Entire Report or an Individual Chapter

When you edit a document, you can work on it directly within Microsoft Word, again leveraging the add-in to Microsoft Office (please refer to the "Using Microsoft Office with SAP Disclosure Management" box). Microsoft Word is the primary application in which you combine information of financial key figures, unstructured information, charts from either Microsoft Excel or Microsoft PowerPoint, and other graphical elements for financial statements and forms. For board packages, Microsoft PowerPoint is often used to combine structured and unstructured information for executive presentations.

The link to the financial key figures is especially valuable because you can refresh the information from the data repository of SAP Disclosure Management in case of changes. Examples of incorporating financial figures into the narrative include the following:

- **Tables**
  You can insert entire statements or statement sections of your financial reports; to do so, you must define them as named ranges in Microsoft Excel.
- **Individual key figures and text fields**
  This is especially valuable if you are referring to a number within your descriptive text, for example, by calling out a revenue number for a particular product line.

- **Formulas**
  In addition to standard formulas, you can also define logic that will change wording within descriptive text. For example, if you are making a statement about a year-over-year comparison based on a calculation, you can change the wording "increased" to "decreased" when describing the result, ensuring that your text is always in sync with your figures.

Changes are tracked within Microsoft Word using the standard Track Changes review functionality, as shown in Figure 10.8. This applies to changes that are made when refreshing the key figures from the data repository, as well as any changes to the narrative or graphical information. Similar to the comparison functionality described in Section 10.1.1, you can compare the current Microsoft Word document against any prior version; the results are shown in a new document, which you can save.

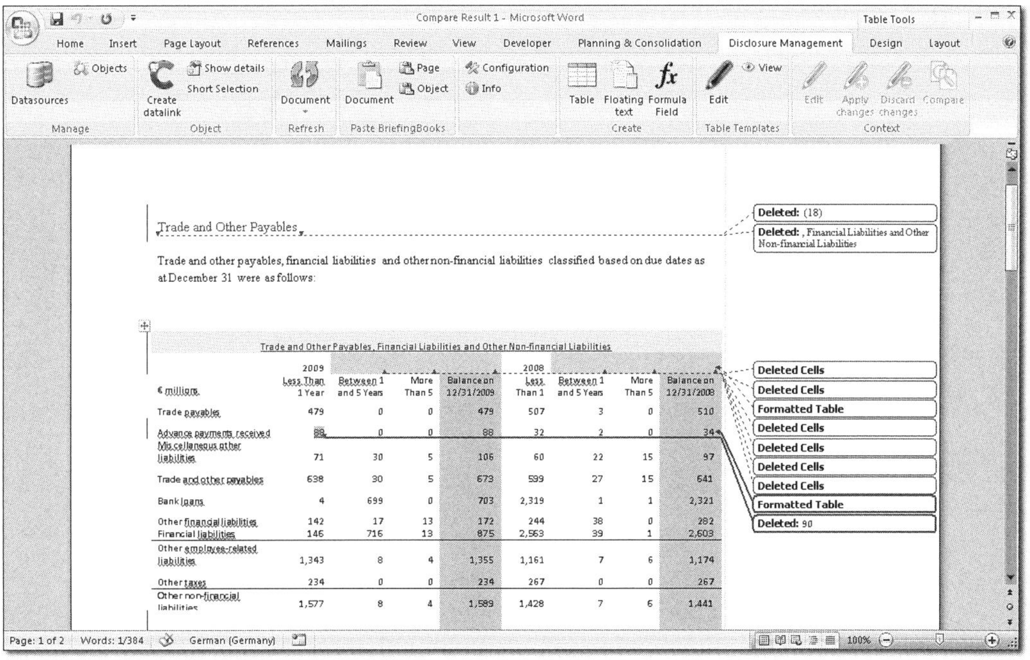

Figure 10.8 Tracked Changes between Document Versions in Microsoft Word

When working with documents, you can use SAP Disclosure Management to facilitate communication, to guard against conflicting edits, and to ensure that the disclosure reports are generated in a timely fashion. Let's look at the collaboration and workflow features available to facilitate this speed and consistency.

10.3 Collaboration and Workflow

At each step of the disclosure management process, you can use collaboration to enable better communication between team members to accelerate the completion of the financial and regulatory statements, as well as to ensure that there are no conflicting edits to the chapters and reports.

SAP Disclosure Management enables communication and workflow between team members who are responsible for creating financial statements and reports. The collaboration features can apply to the management of the data repository, to the individual chapters within a financial statement, and to the summary level of each complete financial statement and regulatory report. In this section, we will look at the elements of creating the collaborative environment, including role definitions, document control, workflow and status management, and approvals.

10.3.1 Role Definitions and Configuration of Workflow

Various roles are delivered standard within SAP Disclosure Management, and new roles can be configured under the ADMINISTRATION tab by using the ROLES link. The permissions that are available to be assigned to each role are shown in Figure 10.9. Typical roles include the following:

- **Editor**
  You can define whether an editor has access to only a specific chapter; for example, a receivables manager may only have access to the accounts receivable chapter. At the same time, you should still define an editor that has access to the overall report, for example if a global change needs to be made.
- **Manager/Approver**
  Similar to the role of an editor, you can define whether a manager can approve only certain chapters or the entire report. From a process standpoint, after all chapters and subchapters are approved, one or more executives should still be named to approve the financial statement or form as a whole.

- **Administrator**
  The system administrator has access to create mappings to data sources, create report structures, create users and roles, and configure the workflow. After SAP Disclosure Management has been set up, the administrator also has the capability to unlock a chapter or report that was finally approved; in most companies, this capability is not given to business users, but to administrators or power users. For additional information about approvals, please refer to Section 10.3.4.

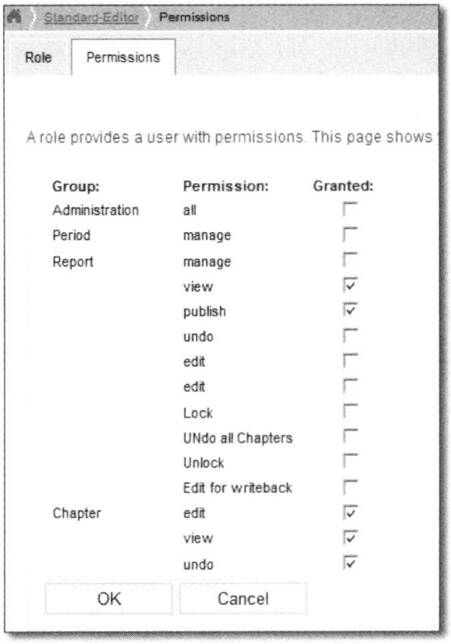

Figure 10.9 The Roles Assigned to Users Contain Specific Permissions for the Activities They are Allowed to Perform

It is possible to assign multiple roles to the same user, which allows you to standardize the role definitions, yet still provides you with the flexibility to give users additional authorizations within the disclosure management process.

10.3.2 Document Control

As mentioned, your finance team members have the ability to check out a portion of the data repository and the financial reports and forms. Either an individual chapter, or the entire financial statement, can be checked out for editing. When a team member checks out a chapter, it is locked so that no other team members can make changes; this guards against a proliferation of versions and conflicting edits. Checking out documents at a chapter level also allows multiple team members to work on the same overall document without blocking each other.

The check-out occurs automatically when you access a chapter in edit mode. When the document is checked back in using the add-in ribbon functionality (please refer to the "Using Microsoft Office with SAP Disclosure Management" box), all changes are tracked, and an audit trail is created to record each check-out, cancellation of check-out, and check-in of a document. Team members also have the ability to enter a comment that summarizes the types of changes they made.

When a chapter is checked back in after editing, workflow can help with collaboration by sending a notification to the next person who needs to work on the chapter, either for further edits or for an approval. In the next section, we will discuss the elements of workflow and how it enables status management for disclosures.

10.3.3 Workflow and Status Management

Workflow capabilities are embedded within SAP Disclosure Management to define each step that is required in producing chapters and financial statements. For each step that is part of the workflow, you can define the following options:

- **The next possible activities, or steps, that you want to allow a financial user to carry out**
  For example, if a chapter is open, it cannot be approved without being completed or finished. For a chapter that is finished, the possible subsequent activities are an approval or rejection, but not editing.
- **The definition of the status that is active for each step**
  This option allows you to simplify monitoring of the progress of a financial statement on overview screens in the cockpit, using meaningful statuses and the traffic light symbols.
- **Conditions that further refine the possible actions**
  The most common type of condition allows you to assign specific user roles to individual steps, such as editor roles to the processing of documents, and managerial roles to the step that controls document approval.

A standard workflow is delivered, but you can change it or create new workflows. You can access the workflows from the ADMINISTRATION tab, using the WORKFLOW link. Figure 10.10 shows a graphical view of the delivered workflow. You can see that the workflow does not need to be linear, and you may have multiple options for each step. For example, from the initial Open status, you can set the status to be either In Progress or Finished, but you cannot approve directly from the Open status. By using these workflow statuses, you can define the appropriate controls for each chapter which results in a documented audit trail.

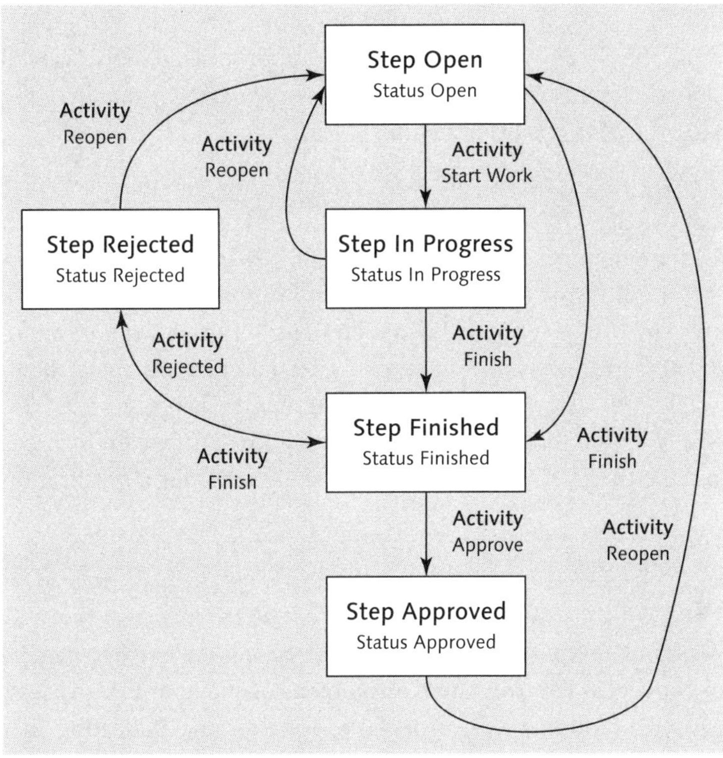

Figure 10.10 The Workflow and Associated Next Activities Displayed Graphically

As part of the workflow setup, you can also determine the status that is displayed for each chapter, based on the activities that have taken place through the workflow. Figure 10.11, accessed from the STEPS subtab of the workflow configuration, shows the status (in the LINKED STATUS column), the next possible steps that can be taken for each status (in the NEXT STEP column), and the role associated with that step (in the CONDITION VALUE column).

Step	Linked status	Next step	Condition-Step	Condition value	Activities	Condition-Activities	Condition value
Open	○ Open	In Progress Finished			Start Work Finish	UserHasRole UserHasRole	Standard-Editor Standard-Editor
In Progress	△ In progress	Finished Open			Finish Reset	UserHasRole UserHasRole	Standard-Editor Standard-Editor
Finished	Finished	Rejected Approved			Reject Approve	UserHasRole UserHasRole	Standard-Manager Standard-Manager
Approved	Approved	Open			Reopen	UserHasRole UserHasRole	Standard-Manager Standard-Admin
Rejected	Rejected	Open Open			Reset Finish	UserHasRole UserHasRole	Standard-Editor Standard-Editor

Figure 10.11 Customizing How the Status Is Shown in the Workflow Configuration

You can define different workflows for different types of reports and forms using the parameters that we just covered. Each report can only be linked to a single workflow. However, you can use the same workflow for more than one report. The workflow then applies to all chapters within that report or statement, as well as to the overall report. The link between a report and a workflow is made in the SETTINGS tab by using the MANAGE REPORTS link.

Finally, you can enable notifications and determine if they are mandatory or optional; if notifications are enabled, an email is sent to team members after a chapter or financial statement has been checked in and is ready for the next step, whether that is further editing or approval. These notifications are activated on a report level and are part of the setup of the assignment between a report and a workflow. If notifications are activated, they apply to the entire financial statement or form, as well as to each chapter within these reports. If notifications are mandatory, an email is sent automatically; if they are optional, the team member will see a popup during the check-in of a chapter, asking whether a notification should be sent.

10.3.4 Approvals

When the editing steps have been completed for a chapter or entire financial statement, the workflow also controls the management of the approval process. The document status configured in the workflow, for example indicating that work on the chapter is finished, determines that the only available activities are approval or rejection. The approval step is typically assigned to managers and executives who have responsibility for corporate financial reporting. Figure 10.12 shows the options of approval and rejection on the detail screen of a chapter in the SAP Disclosure Management application.

Figure 10.12 The Approval Screen for a Chapter after it is Complete

When a chapter is approved, it is locked for further editing. You may choose to give a select group, usually in an administrator or a power user role, the ability to unlock an approved chapter or statement to accommodate additional changes.

Now that we've reviewed the collaborative tools found in SAP Disclosure Management, let's look at a customer story. The GEA Group was able to use the collaboration features of SAP Disclosure Management to accelerate the creation of financial statements.

10.3.5 Customer Story: GEA Group Produces Audit-Compliant Financial Statements Faster

As a publicly listed company with its stock listed on the German MDAX stock index, the food and energy system process provider GEA Group must publish its quarterly, midyear, and year-end financial statements by specific deadlines. Besides the consolidated balance sheet, profit and loss statement, cash-flow statement, statement of stockholders' equity, and notes concerning the consolidated financial statements, these reports include management reporting, a business outlook, and stock information.

With the results of six business divisions to manually update and report on, this used to be a labor-intensive and time-consuming task with an inherent risk of errors. But since GEA Group implemented SAP Disclosure Management, all of the financial data and information needed is in a single data repository, and the integrated workflow management functionality means the company has a closed-loop process from financial consolidation right through to the generation of its financial reports.

Working with SAP partner cundus AG, the accounting department at GEA Group successfully implemented the new solution within eight weeks and went live immediately as the 20 users found the application so user-friendly and straightforward to work with that they needed little training. Working with familiar Microsoft Office tools, the team created more than 40 standard templates, and now everything required for producing the reports—the balance sheet figures, notes, texts, graphics, and tables from the business divisions—flows into the SAP solution at the click of a mouse.

At the same time, all of the steps are documented in an audit-compliant way so both company management and external auditors can track the source of the financial figures and see who changed them and when. Furthermore, reports can now be produced in a variety of formats, including Microsoft Word, Microsoft Excel, Microsoft PowerPoint, and the Adobe PDF files needed by the external graphic design agency responsible for the printed version of the annual report.

Using SAP Disclosure Management, reports can be created up to 20% faster, so GEA Group can meet the increasingly tough legal requirements with timely external reporting, while accounting employees have more time for their core tasks.

Now that we have seen how to complete the process of managing the disclosure documents, let's take a look at the different types of output formats you can generate within SAP Disclosure Management, as shown in the right column in Figure 10.2.

10.4 Publish Disclosure Statements and Reports

Multiple document output formats are available for the disclosure information. For external statements, such as the annual report, the most common format is Microsoft Word or Adobe PDF. Alternately, for executive board packages, Microsoft PowerPoint can incorporate numeric and narrative disclosure information and display it in a graphical presentation format.

At any time in the process of collecting and editing the financial and disclosure statements, you can generate a preview in various formats, either for an individual chapter or the entire document or form, such as the entire annual report. You access the preview in various formats under the AVAILABLE PREVIEW TYPES links in the right side of the detail screen, as shown earlier in Figure 10.7. The types of preview formats that are available for a particular report are defined in the report type definition, which you can access on the ADMINISTRATION tab using the REPORT TYPES link. These previews allow you to see the complete report or a chapter without checking it out.

You can control the formatting of the document in Microsoft Word through the use of templates that are applied to the document. The template contains default style information, such as the font, logos, and table formatting. The templates are associated with a report, by selecting a report from the initial SAP Disclosure Management cockpit, from the TEMPLATES subtab. The temaplate applies to all chapters within a report. Figure 10.13 shows an example of an annual report in Adobe PDF format, including the cover graphic, table of contents, and formatted narrative text and tables.

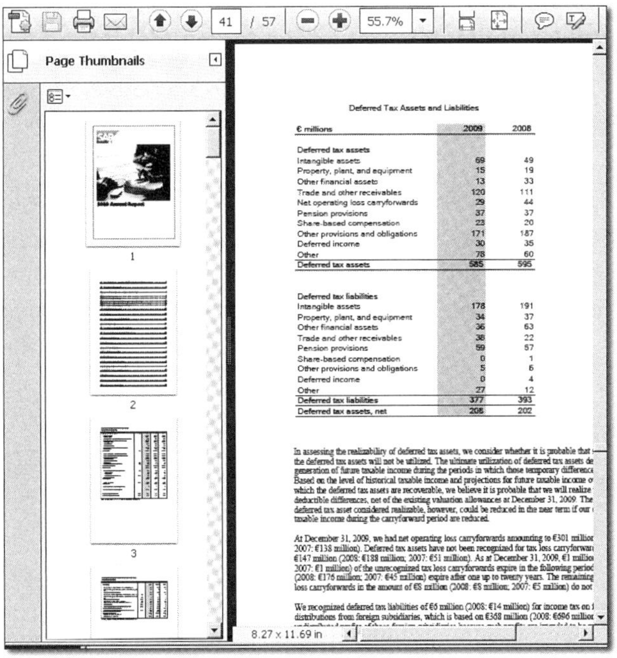

Figure 10.13 A Preview of an Annual Report in Adobe PDF Format

Just as it is possible to compare versions of documents in Microsoft Word and Microsoft Excel, further comparison capabilities are available within SAP Disclosure Management. Select a period and report under the REPORT tab, and go to the REVISIONS subtab. Here you can compare against prior versions (called REVISIONS); you can also select an external file to compare again. The comparison is published as an Adobe PDF document.

A special use case is a comparions of a publication-ready report in Adobe PDF with a version that is returned from an external printer, which is accessed as an external document. In addition to highlighting standard changes—such as key figures and text changes—the comparison feature is able to identify whether whole sections have been moved around within the document, so that it is easier to see the actual changes, not just the reorganization of a statement.

Finally, the disclosure information can also be published in a web format, or HTML. This eases the process of publishing results on a corporate website, which public companies typically make available for their investors.

We will now look at a special case of output in the XBRL instance document, which is necessary for the electronic filing of financial disclosures with various regulatory agencies.

10.5 Create and File XBRL Statements

An increasing number of countries are mandating the electronic filing of financial and other regulatory documents in the XBRL format. To meet these requirements, companies doing business in those countries need to be able to tag source information and create XBRL instance documents. These documents are then filed electronically with various regulatory agencies; a few examples include the United States Securities and Exchange Commission (U.S. SEC), the United Kingdom's Her Majesty's Revenue and Customs (HMRC), Germany's E-Bilanz, and sustainability disclosures for the Global Reporting Initiative (GRI) Sustainability Disclosure Database. Please refer to the "XBRL for Electronic Filings" box for additional information on XBRL. There is a trend to expand the usage of XBRL to other scenarios as well; for additional information, please refer to the "Trends in XBRL" box.

The capability to tag data and create XBRL documents is built directly into SAP Disclosure Management, which leverages UBMatrix applications. You access these capabilities on the XBRL FACTORY tab. The same information in the data repository that is used to create financial statements is also leveraged to create the XBRL instance documents, which are used for electronic filing. This ensures the consistency of information across all reporting formats, regardless of whether the completed regulatory statement information is published in a report or is filed electronically.

While some companies outsource the tagging and generation of the XBRL instance documents, this often takes additional time. After the data has been given to the outsourced service provider, it is very difficult to make changes; if a late financial entry must be made, having separate work streams for publishing the statements and the electronic filings increases the risk of inconsistencies. And after an outsourced service has been provided, your company is still responsible for ensuring that the information in the XBRL instance documents is correct, which adds even more time.

It is important to realize that bringing the process of XBRL submissions in-house requires companies to ensure that their internal teams have the appropriate knowledge of the requirements of jurisdictions; however, for final validations even in an outsourced process, the responsibility was already squrely on the side of the filing company. With SAP Disclosure Management, you can save time and reduce the risk of inconsistencies by making it part of one workstream.

XBRL for Electronic Filings

XBRL is an open standard that is fast becoming the global standard for electronic filing of disclosures. Information in financial and other regulatory disclosures is tagged with a set of standard, computer-readable tags based on the eXtensible Markup Language (XML). These tags identify the components of a statement, such as a footnote or a table, and individual data elements, including a description of individual values, rounding factors (such as identifying whether rounding is to the thousands or millions), and reporting currency. Standard taxonomies have been agreed upon by the XBRL international organization. A taxonomy is a set of tags for a particular regulatory agency or tax jurisdiction. These tags can be extended in certain circumstances. More information is available at *www.xbrl.org*. A company may need to file multiple financial results for different jurisdictions and accounting principles; for example, a company may need to file in U.S. GAAP (Generally Accepted Accounting Principles) and in IFRS (International Financial Reporting Standards).

Several levels of detail are required for tagging. As an example, for the U.S. SEC, there are four levels:

- **Level 1**
  Each complete footnote is tagged as a single block of text.
- **Level 2**
  Each significant accounting policy within the significant accounting policies footnote is tagged.
- **Level 3**
  Each table within each footnote is tagged.
- **Level 4**
  Within each footnote, each amount (e.g., monetary value, percentage, and number) and each description is separately tagged, and each narrative disclosure required to be disclosed by the applicable accounting standard and regulating agency is separately tagged.

Other countries have different regulations regarding formats. For example:

- In the United Kingdom, iXBRL (inline XBRL) tags are used, meaning that the XBRL tags are added to standard business reports. Readers of these reports may not even be aware that there are computer-readable tags embedded in the report.
- In the United States, filing must be done through EDGAR (the Electronic Data Gathering Analysis and Retrieval system), which requires specific HTML tags to be included as part of the electronic filing. The EDGARized file is created from within the Microsoft Word document, using the SAP Disclosure Management add-in, as shown in Figure 10.14. For more information about the add-in itself, please refer to the "Using Microsoft Office with SAP Disclosure Management" box.
- In Germany, the E-Bilanz filings must be performed via the ERiC (Elster Rich Client).
- In India, the the MCA (Ministry of Corporate Affairs) has a validation tool that must be used when filing XBRL instance documents.

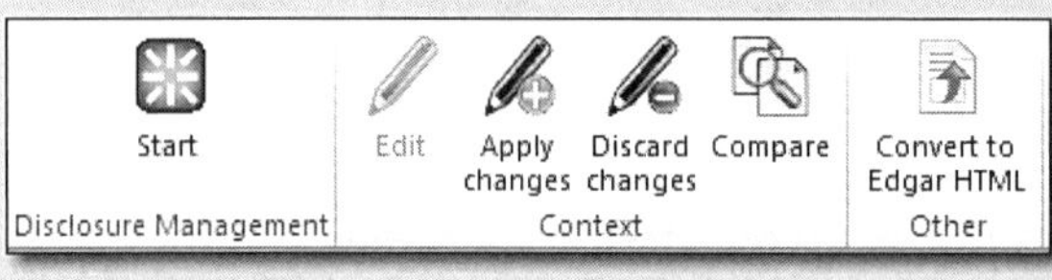

Figure 10.14 EDGARization Option in the SAP Disclosure Management Add-In for Microsoft Word

Let's look at what is involved in tagging the information in preparation for filing, as well as the generation of the XBRL instance document.

10.5.1 Tagging Data for Filing Financial Statement and Forms

Each jurisdiction typically has a standard taxonomy that you can access through the web or download and store locally. Within the SAP Disclosure Management application, all taxonomies are supported.

To work with XBRL capabilities, access the form or report from the REPORT tab from the GENERAL subtab, and edit the document. Team members who work on XBRL tagging and publication must install the REPORT BUILDER add-in similar to the general SAP Disclosure Management add-in. This add-in allows you to choose a taxonomy and also facilitates searches, filters, and the use of business rules so that you can identify the appropriate tag for each data element.

You can then easily tag the information in the Microsoft Excel document through drag and drop as shown in Figure 10.15. After the information is tagged, you can reuse the spreadsheet that contains the tags in future periods with refreshed values. XBRL tagging can also be done in Microsoft Word.

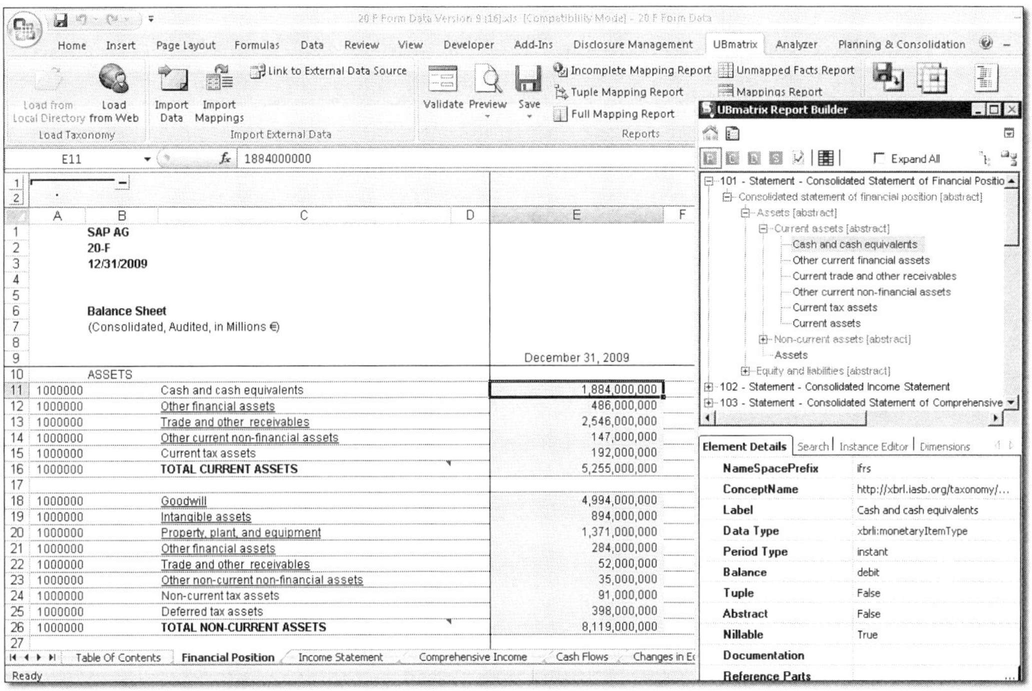

Figure 10.15 Tagged Data Elements and Key Figures in Preparation for the Generation of XBRL Instance Documents.

To assist companies with tagging, starter kits are available with pretagged content (please refer to the "Accelerating Disclosure Management Processes" box). Also, after the tagging has been completed in the initial implementation, the source documents—in Microsoft Excel, Microsoft Word, or an XML editor—can be rolled forward to future years. You can simply update the figures and narrative, but it will only be necessary to update newly introduced tags that may have become a part of the standard taxonomy since the prior year.

Accelerating Disclosure Management Processes

To accelerate the implementation of SAP Disclosure Management, starter kits are available that contain preconfigured content, specifically for pretagging of XBRL content for several different accounting standards, including U.S. GAAP and IFRS. For additional information, please refer to Chapter 9, Section 9.4.1.

In addition to starter kits, a Rapid Deployment Solution (RDS) is available that bundles preconfigured content and SAP services. The SAP Financial Close and Disclosure Management rapid-deployment solution leverages the starter kits and helps you to connect SAP Disclosure Management to the consolidation solutions available within the portfolio of the SAP solutions for enterprise performance management (SAP solutions for EPM). For additional information, please refer to Chapter 9, Section 9.4.2.

In addition to the financial close, several industries have additional disclosure requirements. The SAP Solvency II Regulatory Reporting rapid-deployment solution supports the insurance industry's Solvency II, Pillar III, which includes quantitative reporting templates (QRTs) for the required disclosure reports, such as the Report to Supervisor (RTS) and Solvency and Financial Consolidation (SFCR) reports.

10.5.2 XBRL Instance Documents

After all of the information has been tagged, you can create the XBRL instance document. This is done from the XBRL Factory tab. You select the period, the legal entity for which you want to create the XBRL instance document (which is defined in the Administration tab, using the Entities link), and the tagged report or form.

From this screen, you can run validations in the system for both syntax and semantics to ensure that the data is correct. Examples of validations include finding data elements for which tagging is not complete, and finding errors and inconsistencies, such as whether or not the assets and liabilities are balanced within the balance sheet.

You can also access a preview of the XBRL instance document. Because the syntax of this document is difficult to read, you can use a preview capability to more easily verify that the information in the instance document is correct. Figure 10.16 shows the native XBRL instance document, which is a type of XML, as well as a more user-friendly preview used by finance teams. Once validated, you can then submit the electronic filing.

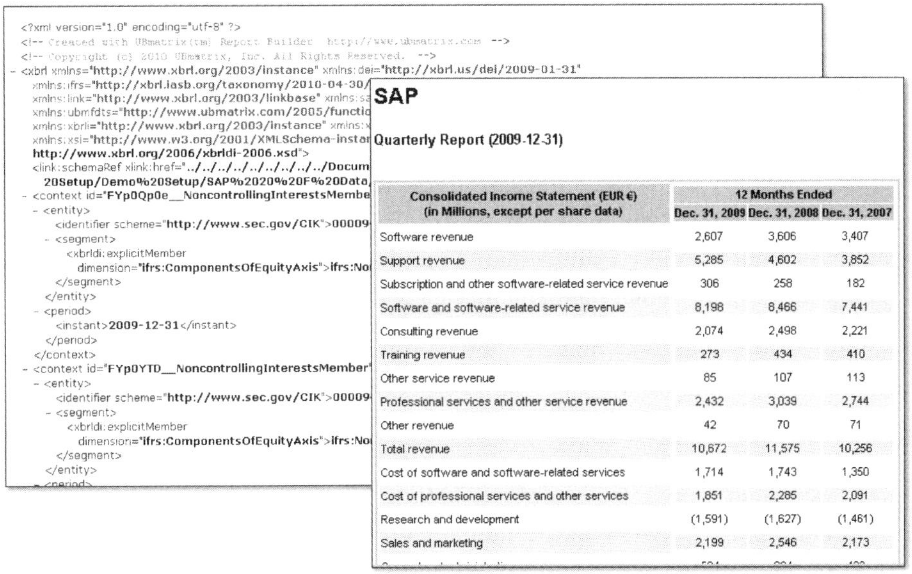
SAP

Quarterly Report (2009-12-31)

Consolidated Income Statement (EUR €) (in Millions, except per share data)	12 Months Ended		
	Dec. 31, 2009	Dec. 31, 2008	Dec. 31, 2007
Software revenue	2,607	3,606	3,407
Support revenue	5,285	4,602	3,852
Subscription and other software-related service revenue	306	258	182
Software and software-related service revenue	8,198	8,466	7,441
Consulting revenue	2,074	2,498	2,221
Training revenue	273	434	410
Other service revenue	85	107	113
Professional services and other service revenue	2,432	3,039	2,744
Other revenue	42	70	71
Total revenue	10,672	11,575	10,256
Cost of software and software-related services	1,714	1,743	1,350
Cost of professional services and other services	1,851	2,285	2,091
Research and development	(1,591)	(1,627)	(1,461)
Sales and marketing	2,199	2,546	2,173

Figure 10.16 The Native XBRL Document (Left) and the More Legible Preview (Right)

The following customer story illustrates how SAP itself has implemented both SAP Disclosure Management and SAP Notes Management to support financial disclosures and XBRL filings.

10.5.3 Customer Story: SAP Speeds Up the Last Mile of Financial Reporting with SAP Disclosure Management

SAP faces exactly the same challenges as its growing list of customers, so it should come as no surprise that it makes extensive use of its own solutions. To gather financial data, such as pension disclosures, that is not available in the company's accounting records from its 235 subsidiaries around the globe, the company uses SAP Notes Management. Corporate finance also uses SAP Disclosure Management to automate the data transfer from the company's accounting and consolidation systems to generate both internal and external reports. The combination of these two applications supports SAP in the preparation and generation of reports in compliance with key regulatory requirements such as the U.S. SEC's Form 20-F and IFRS. An important feature of SAP Disclosure Management is its support of XBRL, which is now mandated by an increasing number of regulatory bodies.

With an intuitive user interface and a collaborative document management tool that allows users to work in their familiar Microsoft Office environment, it only took a one-hour web-based training session to familiarize users with SAP Disclosure Management. The cockpit that comes with the solution shows the current status of the reporting process at a glance and instantly highlights changes so they can be scheduled for review and approval—the entire process being managed with automated workflow to expedite reporting cycles. Another extremely useful feature is the document-locking function that prevents users from simultaneously editing the same document and amending approved documents.

SAP Disclosure Management helps SAP streamline the collection and management of relevant information across the enterprise and generate and publish reliable and auditable financial and regulatory statements. It helped the company cut down the preparation time for the statement of cash flows from three days to three hours and the preparation of the 2011 financial statement took a full week less than it did the previous year, releasing the corporate finance team for other value-adding activities.

Trends in XBRL

Currently, the primary use of XBRL is for external, regulatory disclosures for company financial results. An increasing number of jurisdictions, as well as industries, are requiring disclosures in this format. More countries are also investigating other uses of electronic filings, such as electronic tax filings.

Another potential use is for integrated reporting, which is a periodic report that communicates how a company engages in value creation over time through strategy, governance, performance, and prospects. This report brings together not only financial figures and narrative information but also operational, environmental, social, and brand elements. More information on integrated reporting and the associated standards is available on the website of the International Integrated Reporting Council (IIRC) at *http://www.theiirc.org*.

The use of standard data taxonomies may facilitate internal reporting as well in the long run. One of the most common examples is the idea to bring external market data into a disclosure management system to compare your own company's performance against the market using information in these standard tags. As companies become more versed in the use of XBRL, additional scenarios will likely be developed.

10.6 Summary

SAP Disclosure Management helps you collect both structured and unstructured information from various source systems, and manage the production of financial statements and reports using familiar Microsoft Office tools and collaborative features such as workflow. You can then publish the resulting statements in a variety of formats, including the annual report in a PDF and HTML format, board packages in Microsoft Office formats, and generate XBRL electronic filings.

In the next chapter, we will look at various financial reports that allow you to analyze your financial results and the SAP tools that support sophisticated reporting and analytics.

The culmination of the financial close process is the creation of financial reports. The purpose of financial reporting is to deliver information about an organization so that people can make decisions based on financial performance. In this chapter, we will look at reporting requirements and delivery methods.

11 Financial Reporting

The specific data that is analyzed and reported can be a huge differentiator for a company. Information is extremely powerful, and being able to leverage it accordingly can make or break an organization. Financial reporting is all about "getting stuff out" as shown in Figure 11.1. Once data has been reconciled, translated, eliminated and adjusted, as discussed in our previous chapters, it then needs to be reported.

Figure 11.1 Financial Reporting Simplified to "Getting Stuff Out"

This chapter discusses several different reporting requirements and then discusses some different delivery methods as well. We will address these at a relatively high level because the specific requirements for different organizations vary immensely.

11.1 Reporting Requirements

In this section, we will explore at a high level the following various financial reports as well as the requirements that shape them:

- Balance sheet, P&L, and cash flow reporting
- Management reporting

- Statutory reporting
- Variance reporting
- Periodic comparison
- Budget, plan, and forecasting
- Versioning and what-if statements
- Drill-down vs. drill-through functionality

We will delve into each requirement and explore how this shapes the report outcome. In Section 11.2, we will discuss the different reporting delivery methods, such as report delivery through SAP BusinessObjects Business Intelligence (BI) and mobile reports. First, let's look at the three major reports that are the foundation of financial reporting.

11.1.1 Balance sheet, P&L, and Cash Flow Reporting

Three major reports form the basis of financial reporting. These are the core reports for any financial reporting and are heavily used by SAP financial users to look at the health of their financial portfolios:

- Statement of financial position (i.e., balance sheet)
- Statement of profit & loss (i.e., income statement)
- Cash flow statement

Figure 11.2 shows the SAP 2012 Annual Report table of contents, which lists all of the major financial statements.

155 Consolidated Financial Statements IFRS

Consolidated Income Statements
Consolidated Statements of Comprehensive Income
Consolidated Statements of Financial Position
Consolidated Statements of Changes in Equity
Consolidated Statements of Cash Flows
Notes to the Consolidated Financial Statements
Management's Annual Report on Internal Control over Financial Reporting in the Consolidated Financial Statements

Figure 11.2 SAP 2012 Annual Report: Table of Contents

The major reports provide the big picture, but how those numbers were arrived at really tell the story. For stockholders of SAP, it's not just the high-level reports that are interesting but also the breakdown of that detail. Revenue by region and by industry is also provided in the 2012 SAP Annual Report as shown in Figure 11.3 and Figure 11.4.

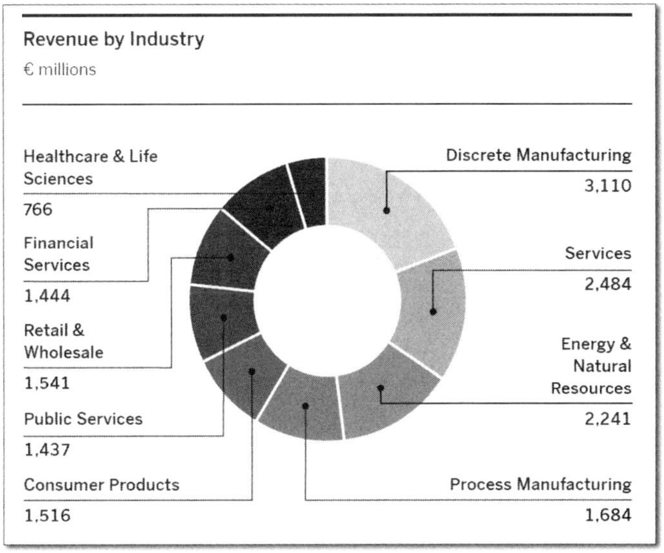

Figure 11.3 SAP 2012 Annual Report: Revenue by Industry

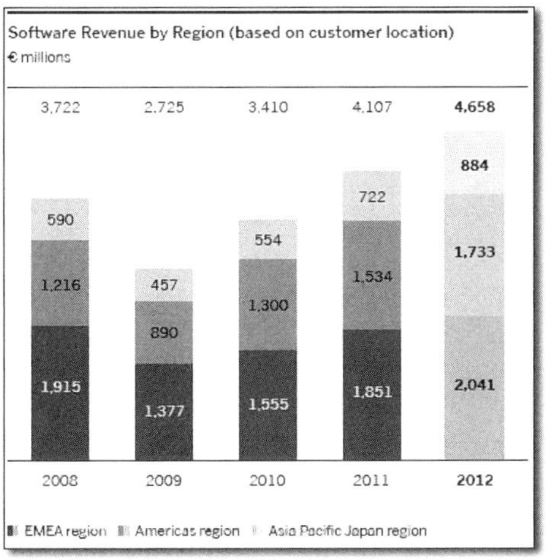

Figure 11.4 SAP 2012 Annual Report: Revenue by Region

They say the devil is in the details, but the question is, how you get the detail. This is where automating the financial reporting process provides most of its value—the ability to get to the detail quickly and accurately. Financial professionals can then in turn make decisions based on the information they receive.

11.1.2 Management versus Statutory Reporting

Statutory reporting is the reporting of financial reports and information to governments and regulatory organizations. There are many different regulations, including International Financial Reporting Standards (IFRS) discussed in Chapter 9, Section 9.2.5. The purpose of such standards is to provide transparency into an organization as well as create consistency, which allows investors and creditors to more easily compare one organization to another.

Where and what industry an organization does business with will mandate which reporting regulations the company needs to comply. But legal and statutory reporting is just the beginning. The purpose of financial reporting is to provide financial information to stakeholders. It is important to note that stakeholders are not just limited to stockholders. There are many different types of stakeholders both internal and external to an organization. Table 11.1 lists examples of both internal and external stakeholders.

Internal Stakeholders	External Stakeholders
▸ Board ▸ Company owner ▸ Decision makers ▸ Chief executive officer ▸ Chief financial officer ▸ Department and division leaders	▸ Industry analysts ▸ Stock exchanges ▸ Governments ▸ Auditors ▸ Investors ▸ Lenders

Table 11.1 Types of Stakeholders

The management team of an organization needs to be provided with financial information in order to make decisions. Financial reports help leaders understand what is working well and what is not. Management reports and board reporting are key to the success of an organization.

11.1.3 Variance Reporting

Everything is relative, including financials. As such financial information becomes more interesting when it is compared with other information. This type of reporting is commonly referred to as variance reporting. Two major comparisons are periodic reports and budget reporting. Figure 11.5 shows an example of both budget and year-over-year reporting.

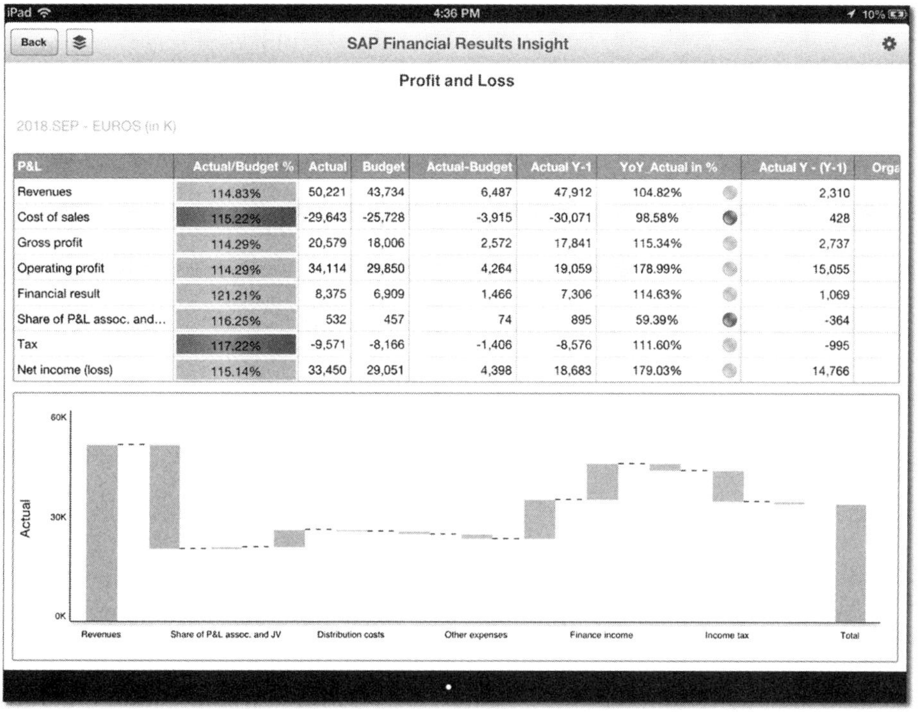

Figure 11.5 Variance Reporting: Profit and Loss Report

11.1.4 Periodic Comparison

When financial data is reviewed period over period, it allows organizations to trend information. Looking at trends of data allows financial professionals to identify patterns and then leverage that information to make decisions that affect the organization. Growth over time is an important indicator of the health of an organization.

11.1.5 Budget, Plan, and Forecast

Creating a budget is a valuable way for organizations to make decisions on what they expect to happen. Typically, a *budget* is a one-year expectation of expenses and revenues. A *plan* typically occurs over more time, such as 5 or 10 years. A *forecast* is a combination of actuals and planned data. For example, a forecast created in May would include the actual January through April numbers and then what is expected to happen for May to December. This provides a more accurate view of expectations for the year.

11.1.6 Versioning and What If Statements

Being able to easily create reports where finance professionals can compare different scenarios or versions that are based on different conditions is an extremely valuable tool. Much analysis and isolation can be done if you can easily and quickly run different versions of reports. Figure 11.6 shows revenue by division (DIVISIONS column), actual versus budget (ACTUAL/BUDGET %), and year over year (ACTUAL Y-1, YOY_ACTUAL IN %, and ACTUAL Y – (Y-1) columns).

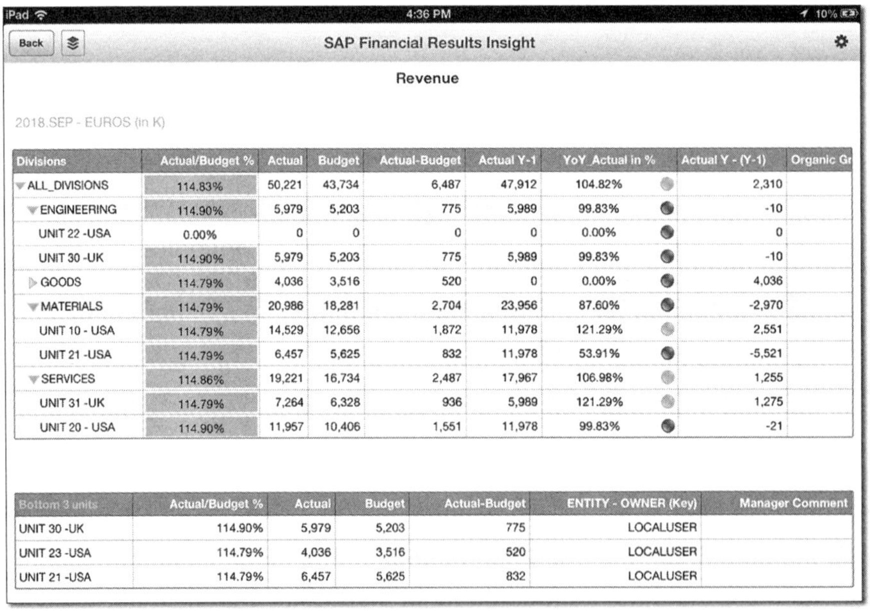

Divisions	Actual/Budget %	Actual	Budget	Actual-Budget	Actual Y-1	YoY_Actual in %	Actual Y - (Y-1)	Organic Gr
ALL_DIVISIONS	114.83%	50,221	43,734	6,487	47,912	104.82%	2,310	
ENGINEERING	114.90%	5,979	5,203	775	5,989	99.83%	-10	
UNIT 22 -USA	0.00%	0	0	0	0	0.00%	0	
UNIT 30 -UK	114.90%	5,979	5,203	775	5,989	99.83%	-10	
GOODS	114.79%	4,036	3,516	520	0	0.00%	4,036	
MATERIALS	114.79%	20,986	18,281	2,704	23,956	87.60%	-2,970	
UNIT 10 - USA	114.79%	14,529	12,656	1,872	11,978	121.29%	2,551	
UNIT 21 -USA	114.79%	6,457	5,625	832	11,978	53.91%	-5,521	
SERVICES	114.86%	19,221	16,734	2,487	17,967	106.98%	1,255	
UNIT 31 -UK	114.79%	7,264	6,328	936	5,989	121.29%	1,275	
UNIT 20 - USA	114.90%	11,957	10,406	1,551	11,978	99.83%	-21	

Bottom 3 units	Actual/Budget %	Actual	Budget	Actual-Budget	ENTITY - OWNER (Key)	Manager Comment
UNIT 30 -UK	114.90%	5,979	5,203	775	LOCALUSER	
UNIT 23 -USA	114.79%	4,036	3,516	520	LOCALUSER	
UNIT 21 -USA	114.79%	6,457	5,625	832	LOCALUSER	

Figure 11.6 Revenue Report: Actual versus Budget and Year over Year

Figure 11.7 features several columns: ORGANIC GROWTH, RATE EFFECT, and SCOPE EFFECT. ORGANIC GROWTH refers to how a company grew organically, meaning not through acquisition. The RATE EFFECT is how much exchange rates affected revenue. Lastly, the SCOPE EFFECT is how changes in scope affected the amounts. In this case, the scope is defined as which entities are to be consolidated at what percentages. If the percentage that a company owns of an entity changes, that will affect the financial statements. The ability to isolate these amounts comes from being able to run different versions of a consolidation.

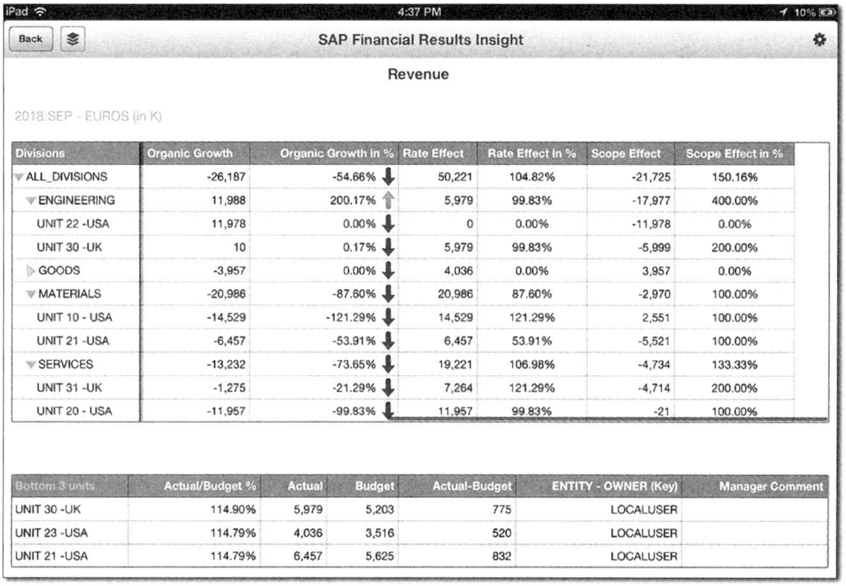

Figure 11.7 Financial Indicators: Organic Growth, Rate Effect, and Scope Effect

Let's discuss a simple example. Let's say revenue for a reporting unit is 100 last year and 110 this year. The exchange rate was 1.3 last year and 1.4 this year. So the year-over-year difference is 24 as listed in Table 11.2.

	Last Year	This Year	Variance
Local currency	100	110	
Exchange rate	1.3	1.4	
Group currency	130	154	24

Table 11.2 Currency Example: Part 1

The translated difference can be split into two parts: the piece that was due to the change in the exchange rate and the piece that was due to actual growth in revenue as listed in Table 11.3.

	A	B	C	D	E	Total Variance
	Last Year at Last Year's Rates	Last Year at This Year's Rates	This Year at This Year's Rates	B – A	C – B	C – A and/or D + E
Local currency	100	100	110			
Exchange rate	1.3	1.4	1.4			
Group currency	130	140	154	10	14	24

Table 11.3 Currency Example: Part 2

As such, the ability to run last year's numbers at this year's rates is extremely valuable in order to isolate why numbers change year over year. SAP's Enterprise Performance Management (EPM) solutions allow customers to do this easily.

11.1.7 Drill Down versus Drill Though

We introduced the concept of dimensionality in Chapter 9, Section 9.1.4. If you recall, dimensionality is the ability to break down a number into its various pieces. Examples of dimensionality include country, division, year, and category (actual, budget, etc.). Dimensionality can also be thought of as an axis of analysis; that is, if you think of a report and think of what is on the X, Y, or Z axis of that report, across the rows or the columns, those are typically dimensions. Figure 11.7, for example, has divisions along the Y axis.

If you want to see further detail of an amount when looking at a report, you want to be able to *drill down* on that report. For example, Figure 11.8 shows a high-level CASH FLOWS statement, but you might be interested in the detail behind the investing activities.

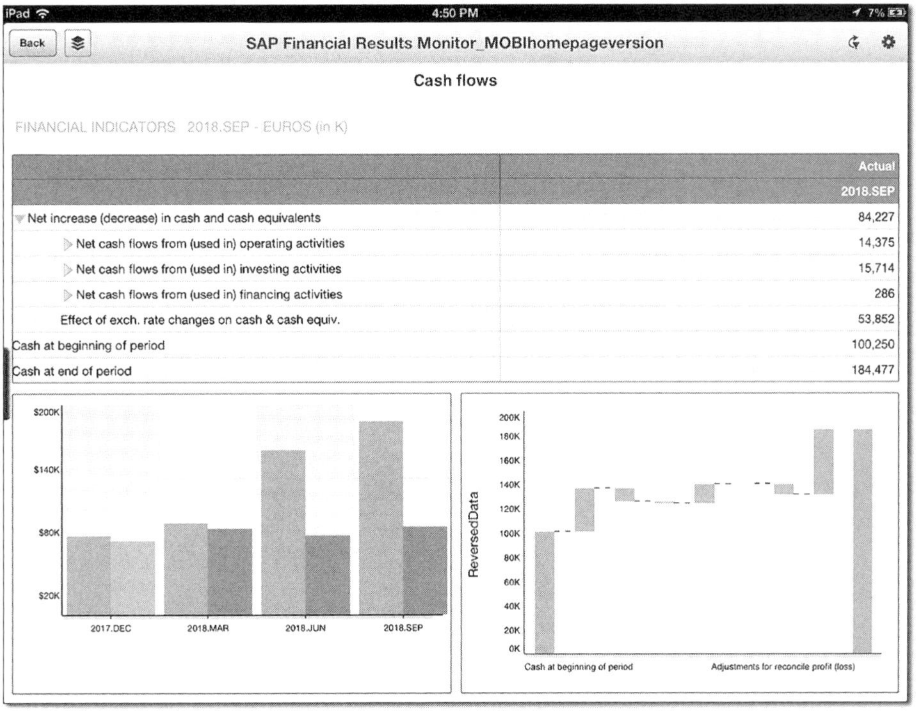

Figure 11.8 Cash Flows Report

In Figure 11.9, you can now drill down on that number to see the detail below it using the arrow options. There is, however, a software limitation on how far you can drill down. In Microsoft Excel, for example, you cannot drill down.

After you drill down to a certain level within a report, you may want additional details. For example, you can drill down through net cash flows from (used in) investing activities and see revenue reporting from other inflows of cash, proceeds from sales of intangible assets, and so on. The transactional details aren't typically contained in consolidation systems, so you can't drill down to the transactional-level data. SAP EPM solutions allows users to drill through to source systems.

Now that we have explored the common reporting requirement for a financial report, let's look at the delivery methods for the various reports available.

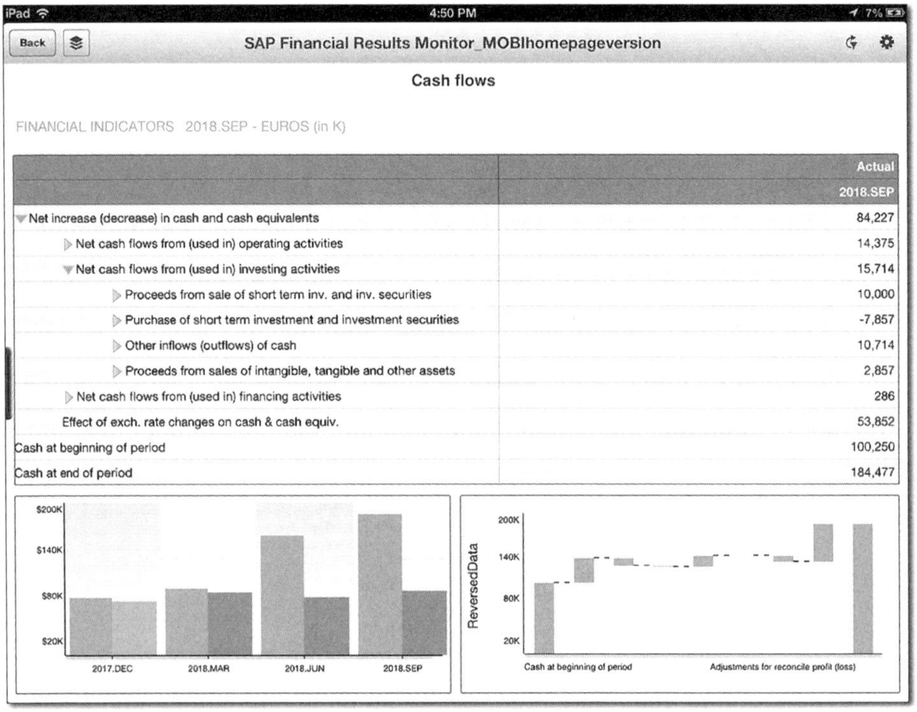

Figure 11.9 Cash Flow Drill Down for More Details

11.2 Reporting Delivery Methods

As mentioned in the previous sections of this chapter, there are many financial reporting requirements. So the question we now need to ask is what tools should you use to create these reports? Each of the previous chapters discusses different software solutions to address different parts of the close process. Each solution has reporting as part of the standard functionality.

In a perfect world, there would be one mega software solution that did everything: financial reporting, budgeting, planning, payroll, accounts receivables and payables, project management, customer relationship management, and the list goes on and on and on. But for many reasons, that does not exist.

Different software is used by different people for different purposes. Different organizations have unique requirements, so there is no one size fits all that will work across all organizations. This is the rationale for not exploring the myriad different reporting options available in SAP in this chapter. In fact, there is already a book on this topic titled *Financial Reporting with SAP* (SAP PRESS, 2012). The financial close action plan discussed in Chapter 2 of this book is a good place to start. For our purposes, we'll explore the delivery methods for reporting: SAP BusinessObjects Business Intelligence (BI) and mobility.

11.2.1 Business Intelligence

SAP BusinessObjects Business Intelligence (BI) solutions simplify data manipulation, allowing users to access, navigate, analyze, format, and share information across a corporate environment. They allow a wide range of processes, from search and navigation to advanced analytics, enterprise query, reporting and analysis, dashboards and visualization, and information infrastructure management.

SAP BusinessObjects BI 4.0 is illustrated in Figure 11.10. There is a full book on the topic as well titled *Reporting and Analysis with SAP BusinessObjects* (SAP PRESS, 2012).

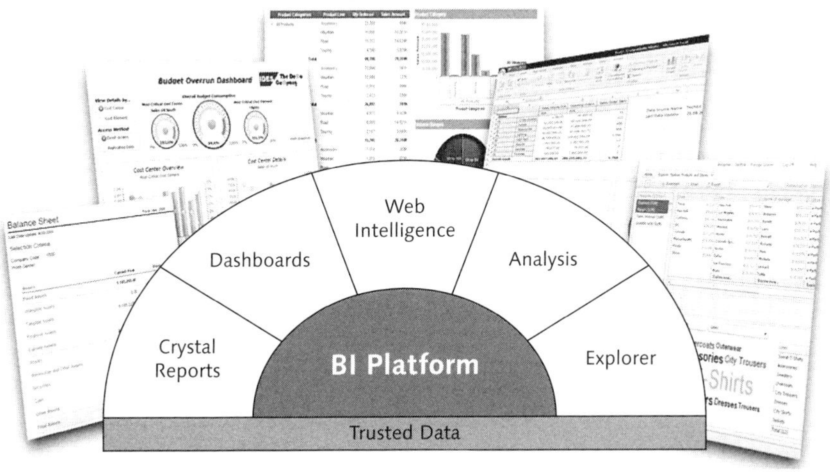

Figure 11.10 SAP BusinessObjects BI 4.0

11.2.2 SAP Crystal Reports

SAP Crystal Reports is the de-facto standard for formatted reporting across the world. It offers business users easy to consume, pixel-perfect reports, giving them the power to make informed decisions quickly and transform the way they run their business. With an easy-to-use, intuitive interface, report authors can access any data spread across disparate systems, and design compelling reports with guided interactivity. They have the option to publish personalized reports to over millions of users securely inside and outside the organization or embed reports in business applications. Organizations can reduce total cost of ownership and accelerate time-to-value by leveraging the collective intelligence and full support from a vibrant community of Crystal reports developers and partners.

11.2.3 SAP BusinessObjects Dashboards

SAP BusinessObjects Dashboards is a drag and drop visualization tool designed to create interactive analytics that can be turned into powerful, personalized dashboards. Drop-down menus and sliders allow you to present complex business data clearly, giving decision makers an easy way to interact with data and test out business scenarios –all with the click of a mouse.

Securely and easily source your dashboards from any live data connection, to any back-end system. Then share insightful visualizations live via Microsoft Office, Adobe PDF, the Web, Crystal Reports, or the SAP BusinessObjects business intelligence (BI) or SAP portal.

11.2.4 SAP BusinessObjects Web Intelligence

SAP BusinessObjects Web Intelligence puts the power of business intelligence into the hands of business users with self-service access, ad hoc reporting and interactive analysis on all types of data represented in everyday business language. With its intuitive, feature rich interface and easy workflows, it will help you turn information into actionable insight and make confident decisions in less time without depending on IT. Web Intelligence offers flexibility to perform online and offline analysis and share those insights with colleagues. With better visibility and transparency of information to business users, it enables organizations to not only manage their business more efficiently, but also respond to changing market conditions rapidly.

11.2.5 SAP BusinessObjects Analysis

SAP BusinessObjects Analysis, OLAP edition, is a next generation business intelligence solution that provides self-service multidimensional analysis workspaces for personal or shared use over the Web. It enables analysis of existing SAP NetWeaver Business Warehouse cubes, SAP Business Explorer queries, and Microsoft SQL Server cubes, to uncover deep business insights. With SAP BusinessObjects Analysis, users of SAP NetWeaver Business Warehouse or Microsoft SQL Server enjoy a modern look-and-feel with a few simple clicks and intuitive drag-and-drop steps to run analyses across multiple multidimensional and hierarchical data sets. SAP BusinessObjects Analysis increases end-user autonomy and self-service usage leading to a broad adoption of business intelligence for more informed decision making across the organization while optimizing the return on investments and minimizing the total cost of ownership.

11.2.6 SAP BusinessObjects Explorer

SAP BusinessObjects Explorer combines the simplicity and speed of internet search and exploration with the trust and analytical power of BI to provide immediate answers to "on the fly" questions, discover relationships, and uncover root causes. Users employ familiar keyword search to find information and explore data directly without needing to understand the data, its location, or structure. Customers can fully leverage existing BI investments like metadata, security, and administration services to have SAP BusinessObjects Explorer up and running in days and reduce IT backlog.

11.2.7 SAP BusinessObjects BI platform

SAP BusinessObjects BI platform is a flexible and scalable solution designed to make it easy to discover and share insight for better decisions. Built on a service-oriented architecture, the software offers a comprehensive BI suite on a single platform. With SAP BusinessObjectsBI platform, IT departments can extend insight through a single, trusted BI infrastructure that integrates with existing applications, information sources, and technology investments, and provides everyone with decision-ready information.

11.2.8 Mobility

Early in 2013, SAP published *SAP IT Market Trends and Predictions* with industry and financial analysts. There were two main lessons learned for accelerating and securing the "last mile of finance" through mobile BI. First, there is a consensus among major analyst firms to rank mobility adoption as one of the most important trends for 2013. They point out the "mobile proliferation" and the significant introduction of iPad tablets in the enterprise. The second, and equally important, trend is that the number of mobile BI users in the enterprise is expected to grow from 20% in 2012 to 54% by the end of 2013.

The financial close to disclose process can be accelerated and streamlined by the use of mobile BI in combination with EPM.

SAP Financial Results Insight

SAP Financial Results Insight is a starter kit that provides mobile financial reports integrated with SAP Business Planning and Consolidation. It is an essential piece of the "last mile of finance" process and brings visibility to financial indicators for CFOs and financial professionals during the critical days before financial statements are made publicly available. It connects EPM data to iOS mobile through BI, ensuring full security on corporate data, and it leverages data from the financial consolidation software part of the EPM suite. Key financial indicators are displayed in current/constant currency and with/without M&A effects to provide CFOs with the complete vision on consolidated data.

SAP Financial Results Insight includes a set of prebuilt indicators—consolidated revenue, profit and loss, income and return on equity, revenue by geographical area, cash flows, financial ratios, and tax impact—that can be easily customized or enriched by business end users according to their enterprise needs.

Figure 11.5 through Figure 11.9 all show images from the SAP Financial Results Insight application.

11.3 Summary

Financial reporting is the main purpose of the financial close process. Different organizations will have many different requirements. Customers must work closely with SAP, their other software vendors, and their implementation partners to develop the best reporting strategy for their company. The financial close action plan in Chapter 2 is a great place to start.

For many people in Finance, the economic crash of 2008 was the first time in their careers that they had experienced a serious recession. It was simply no longer business as usual, and the future looked very uncertain. This chapter looks at how finance will need to evolve and how this might impact reporting.

12 The Future of Finance and Its Impact on the Financial Close

As Chapter 2 describes, the last stage in any financial close project is to establish a foundation for ongoing improvements or, at the very least, the ability to maintain the close times delivered as part of your project. This inherently looks to the future. It would not have been appropriate to close out this book without also looking to how the future role of finance is likely to evolve and understanding its impact on the use of technology and the financial close.

Given the complexity of the finance organization, its breadth, and the internal and external stakeholder community, predicting the future of such an organization is uniquely challenging. This chapter has been structured to look at the future impact and role of finance across four key dimensions that we will deal with in turn, looking at the impact of future changes, how technology impacts this, and what it means for the financial close:

- Economic environment and the role of finance
- Financial operations
- Managing stakeholder expectations
- Ensuring regulatory compliance

12.1 Economic Environment and the Role of Finance

The economic crisis that started in 2008 was, for many, a new experience and was the first time they had experienced a serious recession. It was no longer business as usual, and facing up to it required special resilience. The anxiety and stress involved in realigning their businesses with the new reality and having to let staff go left deep scars that no one wants to suffer again soon—and let's hope that is the case.

In the months immediately after the crisis, what needed to be done was obvious, and many companies took the knife to expenses and discretionary spending with the result that many are sitting on cash reserves that collectively run to trillions of dollars. The finance and controlling department was of course critical to this process. In many respects, this indirectly highlights the importance of a string financial close process, one of the benefits of which is more time for value-added activities, which might well include the time and ability to support the type of stewardship required under such economic circumstances. However, five years later, consumer demand remains febrile with many western economies still struggling to deliver sustainable economic growth and suggesting that it will take another five years to turn the corner. So burdened with burgeoning cash reserves needing to be invested on one hand, but faced with low growth and persistent economic uncertainty on the other, it is no surprise that CFOs and finance professionals are concerned about the future.

As part of SAP's ongoing research into the future role of finance, we commissioned a study published in January 2013 to examine the economic outlook and see how this was impacting finance professionals and their priorities. Conducted by Bloomberg BusinessWeek Research Services, the "Finance as Analytical Partner to the Business" research report surveyed CFOs and finance professionals from around the world and from a range of industries what their expectation was regarding the global economic outlook over the next 18 months. As Figure 12.1 shows, only a quarter were expecting growth of more than 3%, about half expected growth under 3%, and the remaining quarter were looking at some kind of decline.

The same survey asked about the expectation of the economic outlook for the organizations they worked for over the next 18 months, and a similar pattern emerges with only 31% expecting growth greater than 3%. Earlier in this book, we mentioned that the prospect of more regulation was one of the few certainties we could count on, perhaps another is simply that that times were easier a decade ago.

If there is any good to come out of the past five years, it has to be that the crisis has accelerated the transition of the role of finance from custodian and bean counter to business partner. It has been written about in the journals of the accounting profession for decades, but has only been realized in recent years so that today, CFOs and their teams are expected to take a leading role in developing and delivering strategies to create value for investors and other key stakeholders.

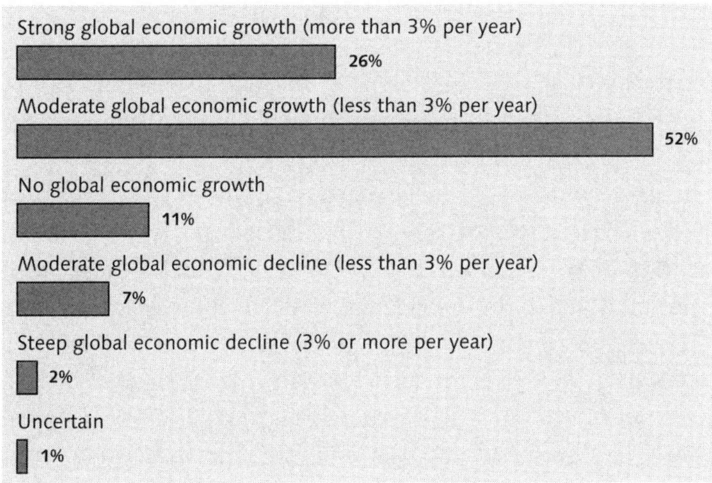

Figure 12.1 CFOs' and Finance Professionals' Expectations for Economic Growth in the Next 18 Months

It is clearly a challenging time to be exalted into such a prominent position, but CFOs and finance professionals are confident with nearly every piece of research suggesting they are armed and ready to exploit the green shoots of any returning economic growth. At the time of writing, the more recent quarterly figures coming from some countries give support to their optimism; in others, the recovery is far from certain, and many will likely experience a long and drawn out climb back to economic health. No matter where you look around the globe, it is clear that the best thing that finance can do is to build a strong, flexible balance sheet and focus on financial performance. Although some companies that were weak prior to 2008 failed spectacularly during the global downturn, many reined in expenses and are in good financial health. As economic uncertainty continues, we can reasonably expect the impact on the role of finance, particularly controlling staff to move more and more in this same strategic direction, making the need for a fast and efficient close process as important as it has ever been.

So from the uncertain position of today, let's examine the priorities for finance for the next decade or so across their three areas of responsibility: to manage financial operations to deliver a superior service and drive down costs; to outperform on the financial objectives their company has promised to stakeholders and to ensure that profitability is sustainable in the future; and finally to ensure that their company has effective governance and risk management processes in place and complies with external regulation—one of the main concerns of this book as it relates to the financial close.

12.2 Financial Operations

Knowing that profitable growth would be hard to come by in the immediate future, many businesses wisely invested some of the cash sitting on the balance sheets to drive process improvements and automation that would protect profit margins in the short term. Much of this investment was driven by chief operating officers (COOs), who many suggest may be eventually responsible for managing core financial processes—an interesting prospect for many managing the financial close process no doubt. But for the moment, that is not the case in most companies, and it was finance that grasped the opportunity to address any remaining weaknesses in core areas, such as the financial close, payables, receivables, and budgeting, that had been tolerated for far too long.

With a dual thrust to improve efficiency and productivity, anything that can be done to reduce departmental costs and ultimately drive down the overall cost of finance as a percentage of revenue has to be welcomed in the current climate. This is good news for those using cost as a key part of their business case for a financial close initiative today and in the immediate future.

As indicated in Chapter 1, with vast amounts of benchmarking data available, organizations can now easily see where they stand across a whole range of detailed criteria to help them focus on cost saving. Traditionally, this was, if anything, restrict to data about the cost of finance, often expressed as a percentage of revenue, but now details such as the proportion of journal entries made manually and the cost of general accounting per journal entry line item are available, which allows a greater level of granularity in cost-saving processes. What's more, because most best-in-class companies have already been through some form of financial process improvement program, such as a financial close program, they are now able to apply the same lessons, better able to quantify the benefits, and yield a time to value, which is often surprisingly quick as our section of financial close quick wins in Chapter 2 indicates. Therefore, it should come as no surprise that despite a fragile economy, spending on core financials—software for billing and collections, and investment in shared services—has remained remarkably buoyant. Such investments are low-hanging fruit, and analysts have repeatedly written that if you cannot justify investment in core financial processes in the current environment, then perhaps you never will.

As a case in point, the SAP survey run by Bloomberg BusinessWeek Research Services also looked at technology investment and best practices, asking finance professionals which technology functions or practices their company plans to use in the next two years to achieve their business goals. While the results for the individual areas themselves are perhaps not surprising, when looking at them as a whole, all of these have applications within the financial close process and the wider evolution of finance as a whole. We'll come back to this several times in this chapter, but as Figure 12.2 illustrates, the first two areas we want to look at in more detail are real-time reporting, and embedding analytical functions into existing financial systems. These come out as the top two priorities, and both are extremely relevant to finance operations. SAP's roadmap for finance delivers on both areas.

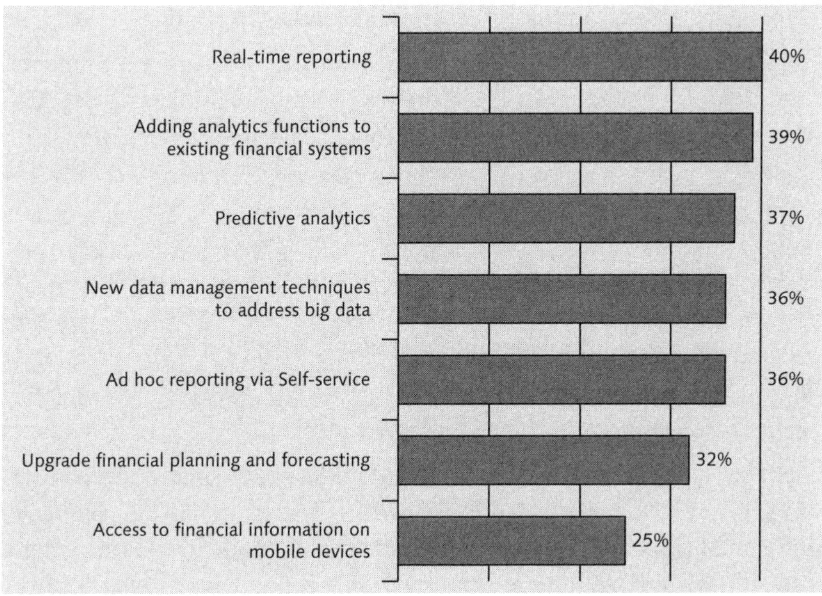

Figure 12.2 The Technology Functions or Best Practices CFOs and Finance Professionals Plan to Use in the Next Two Years to Achieve Their Goals

12.2.1 SAP Business Suite Powered by SAP HANA

SAP announced early in 2013 that SAP Business Suite would run on SAP HANA to deliver numerous innovations for a number of lines of business, including finance. These innovations include those directly impacting the financial close, such as automatic reconciliation with automated real-time matching, a single repository for company and corporate data, and deeper and faster insight down to the lowest level of detail. Other innovations delivered with SAP Business Suite on SAP HANA will impact other parts of finance as well, including the following:

- More efficient payables management processes by providing immediate insights into account payables and days payables outstanding (DPOs), real-time access to comprehensive purchasing reports, and increased transparency about selection criteria, allowing payment of dedicated items
- More efficient receivables management processes by allowing users to investigate drivers of changes in days sales outstanding (DSOs) and therefore working capital, and the provision of real-time insight on credit ratings, disputes, and open invoices to sales teams on any device
- Improved compliance and access control processes, including real-time analysis of role usage, faster identification of similarities between roles, and the ability to combine role data coming from different sources (e.g., HR systems)
- New central treasury exposure management, which includes a central integration platform at the headquarter level, the inclusion of real-time market data, and the flexible aggregation and slice and dice of real-time treasury data

12.2.2 Embedded Analytics

As Section 12.2.1 indicates, the SAP Business Suite innovations, enabled through SAP HANA, are driving toward more analytic functions. However, SAP has and will continue to embed additional content within SAP ERP Financials directly addressing the desire of finance professionals for more analytics functions in existing financial systems.

Enhancement packages 5 and 6 (EhP5 and EhP6) for SAP ERP Financials delivered a broad range of prebuilt reports and dashboards based on the SAP BusinessObjects Business Intelligence (BI) 4.0 release. These reports and dashboards deliver analytics directly within SAP ERP at the point where a user is engaged in a key finance or business process. As a result, they enable greater insight and decision making across a range of financial operations, including cash, collections, credit, and dispute management.

Given such innovations in the area of finance operations and the desire of finance professionals to plan for their future adoption as the Bloomberg BusinessWeek research shows, we believe there is big opportunity for finance to develop an even stronger business case and investment strategy for technologies to support the financial close. In the future, this will also fuel the opportunity for more quick wins or continuous improvement within the close process. So as teams look beyond the immediate financial close objectives they have set, it will become more important to understand how the broader technologies described in this chapter will impact future finance and controlling operations.

However, while this investment in short-term efficiency can and should be taken as a positive in the context of the financial close, the long-term prospect of these types of efficiency savings is somewhat limited. Such process improvements eventually suffer from the law of diminishing returns and will never be sufficient to sustain profitability or alone deliver growth, something every CFO is now anxiously helping their companies to identify and successfully exploit. This is essentially what is accelerating CFOs and finance professionals in their quest to function as a true partner to the business.

12.3 Managing Stakeholder Expectations

As Section 12.1 explains, it has been written about in the journals of the accounting profession for decades that CFOs and their teams are expected to take a leading role in developing and delivering strategies to create value for investors and other key stakeholders. However, as we have just described, it has only started to materialize in recent years. As the office of finance seeks to manage expectations across the business, new challenges will arise. In particular, as finance evolves in the future, it's crucial that key accounting staff and processes evolve to support this move from stewardship to strategy. Fail to do that, and those processes and people run the risk of being marginalized while finance continues to change. As a result, we believe that it's critical for those working in the financial close process to develop a greater understanding of how Enterprise Performance Management (EPM) processes are changing and how supporting technology innovation creates new opportunities to make the financial close more strategic as part of an overall performance management framework.

This is perhaps most easily highlighted by the uncertainty of recent years, which rapidly demonstrated the inadequacy of many planning, budgeting, financial reporting, and cost management systems to support the business, just at the time when finance was being tasked with working alongside their peers to help shape and deliver strategy that produced sustainable growth and profitability.

If finance is really going to deliver in this new role of helping to identify and capitalize on emerging growth opportunities and steering their companies through the challenges that are endemic in the current business climate, many CFOs are coming to realize that they need to invest in business processes and solutions that are not only "up to the job" but also give them the insight and time to act in the new capacity. This means implementing planning and budgeting cycles that can be counted in days rather than weeks or months; having management and financial reports that give insight into the operational variances that underpin the numbers and can lead to better decision making; and having all of this information as fast as possible while there is time to act on it. In the context of this book, we are addressing the core reporting piece, but this highlights the need to then apply the learning to other business processes as Chapter 2 outlines under the guise of continuous improvement.

Somewhat fortuitously, the advent of better performance management solutions, new technologies such as in-memory processing that are fundamental to real-time reporting, and the ability to proactively provide information to managers on their mobile devices no matter where they happen to be, are all available today. These methods are being rapidly adopted as companies seek to bolster their capabilities and ensure they have performance management systems that will help them make better decisions than their competitors.

These new technologies, such as in-memory computing, not only deliver quicker information but also better discernment by providing insight into data that was previously effectively inaccessible. In turn, the role technology plays in enabling better business processes and in leading the CFO and his team to act in this new capacity is critically important.

For example, after you start to analyze profitability across multiple dimensions, (e.g., customer, channel, SKU, day of week, period, version, etc.), the volumes of data result in slow calculating models and tiresome queries. Today, with cost and profitability solutions powered by in-memory calculation engines, the speed of processing is dramatically improved—think seconds rather than hours. There is also no limit to the depth of analysis, so that managers can gain instant reports on the profitability of individual product variants supplied to each one of their customers' outlets through a complex manufacturing and supply chain. At a time when improved profitability depends on the cumulative accretion of small improvements in margins throughout the value chain, being able to effectively mine "big data" is a definite competitive advantage.

Likewise, the need to be agile in order to survive the uncertainty of this persistent economic downturn has made companies realize the need to move to a state of perpetual planning with rolling reforecasts that can be quickly and easily updated.

Example: Professional Services

Let's take professional services as an example in that many people reading this book will probably work in such an organization. The financial plan is typically set at the beginning of the year and—sometimes—updated during the year. In addition to this, there are sales forecasts based on a weighted sales pipeline and a resource forecast based on sold work and nearly sold work, including holidays. In addition, there will be actuals of sales, revenue and resource usage, and absence. The resource managers will want to be able to ask questions, such as the following:

- If we sell these key projects, what will the impact on revenue and recruitment be?
- What are the areas for which I don't have a mid-term pipeline to fill current expected resource demand?
- Where are the areas of resource in which I have least availability?

In this situation, both the revenue and risk profile change very quickly, and changes in demand or supply or even totally unexpected events such as a volcano erupting require a decision to be made immediately. So although a planning and budgeting application may not sound like a typical big-data solution, when you include detailed sales and operations plans, products plans and so on, you can easily be talking about hundreds of thousands of records—especially when a company is dealing with snapshot versions, matrix planning, and reference data. As we see more complexity grow within our business network, we will see an increasing need for solutions built on in-memory calculation engines that enable planning and budgeting to happen in real time with new forecasts being rapidly pushed down into the business so they can quickly realign to the latest changes. More and more, the task of planning will become a big-data problem.

Having the finance team work alongside its business colleagues to drive revenue growth and profitability has also made many CFOs realize the need to extend performance management systems so they span the traditional divide between financial and operational data. This has led to a growing number of companies implementing driver-based planning and budgeting where key inputs (and KPIs), such as productivity ratios, the sales pipeline, the unit cost of inputs, exchange rates, and the like, can be actively monitored and managed on a daily basis with corrective action taken as required. Such an approach can be a much-needed catalyst that will facilitate and accelerate the path for finance to work alongside the business as true partners.

Again technology has become an enabler. Until now, driver-based budgeting models have been somewhat onerous to work with in that recalculating a large multi-dimensional planning model that contains a lot of business rules that span time periods and departments could take considerable time even when models have been partitioned across servers and the ingenious workarounds have been brought into play. Similarly, updating sales and operational drivers relied on waiting until contributors found some quiet time to open their laptop, which is never easy with managers who are out in the field or based in a busy production or distribution unit.

Today, any inputs that are not system generated can be collected using mobile devices with the process automated by workflows so that reminders and templates flash up on the screen ready for the two or three critical bits of data to be entered. And as drivers are typically things that any manager will be routinely monitoring as part of his daily work, it takes seconds to submit the data. Secondly, building planning models that make use of in-memory calculation engines means that that even the biggest driver-based planning and forecasting models will run in real time. That way, everyone in the business from a junior line manager to the CEO can get instant insight into where they stand against their goals and targets. What's more, because the model is based on drivers, automated variance analysis will show them exactly which issues need to be addressed, and they can run scenarios to assess the impact of any changes that need to be made.

Admittedly, finance would need to plan the collection of drivers starting with sales and working through production, distribution, and finally back office, repeatedly calculating the model so that contributors could see what demands the new forecasts of earlier upstream contributors make on their own responsibility center. It may take a couple of elapsed hours to generate a new forecast, but coming from four to six months, surely this is as near real-time planning and budgeting as possible.

As highlighted in Section 12.2, CFOs and finance are now looking to adopt such solutions in the next two to three years, and similarly SAP's innovation strategy and roadmap support this.

12.3.1 In-Memory Powered Planning, Budgeting, and Forecasting

As the previous section clearly demonstrates, planning, budgeting, and forecasting, as well as profitability and cost management are processes that demonstrate compelling use cases for in-memory computing. While the idea is not new, it has not traditionally been enabled on packaged EPM suites. By introducing SAP Business Planning and Consolidation powered by SAP HANA in early 2012, SAP not only delivered a packaged in-memory powered planning and budgeting solution but also one which uniquely in the market is unified with a consolidation and reporting engine. The benefits of this extend much further than mere processing speed, and it allows for a whole new type of planning, budgeting, and reporting that links strategic, financial, and operational planning together on a single platform and manages the associated big-data challenge that comes with it. Such a solution should therefore form part of the future design of EPM implementations and should be intrinsically linked and integrated within financial close projects.

12.3.2 Predictive Analytics and Data Discovery

Moving beyond planning, budgeting, and forecasting, there are other areas that additionally support the ability for finance professionals and those in the close process to become more strategic, and, like the other examples we have described, they too are seen as priority areas for investments according to the Bloomberg BusinessWeek research. The ability to leverage more advanced analytics in the form of predictive capabilities has been around for decades, but today new market forces are changing the landscape and creating new opportunities for its application. With data volumes exploding, organizations need to extract the maximum possible value, whether from transactional financial or sales data typically generated within the enterprise or from unstructured data created by external sources such as social media. The introduction of in-memory technology has dramatically reduced the time and cost of data processing and makes it possible to perform predictive analysis against vast volumes of data in real time. The spectacular growth of the open-source statistical and data mining language "R" has empowered a new breed of data scientists with a vast array of analytical possibilities at their fingertips. To address this need, SAP has introduced a brand new solution, SAP Predictive Analysis to provide users from across the enterprise with an intuitive, productive environment for data modeling and advanced data visualization. Analysts use its drag-and-drop visual interface for data selection, preparation, and processing. They create models by using native, predictive algorithms, and by employing algorithms from R, users can gain deeper knowledge that reveal hidden insights. The solution integrates with SAP HANA to unlock the value of big data and with BI solutions to extend predictive insight to thousands of business users. Such a solution therefore directly addresses the desire of finance professionals to anticipate outcomes rather than just better understand past performance.

At the same time, the evolution in desktop-based data discovery solutions is driving increasing numbers of finance professionals to invest directly, and often outside of centrally managed IT business intelligence initiatives, to obtain solutions they can use to further analyze financial data, visualize it, and share the insight with others. This is particularly sought after as finance uses the financial close to free time to answer ad hoc questions from management. SAP therefore continues to innovate in this area, and in mid-2012, introduced SAP Visual Intelligence, which delivers a simple point-and-click interface that creates graphical visualizations allowing the user to quickly analyze data. It does this in a completely self-service way and accelerates decision making with immediate, fact-based answers to complex business questions. The powerful combination of such predictive analytics and data discovery tools dramatically and most importantly quickly expands the capabilities finance teams can use either directly within the financial close process or as part of a wider EPM initiative.

12.3.3 Mobilizing Finance

The final innovation we want to highlight in this area and which should certainly form a part of all future financial close projects is the role of mobility. The Bloomberg BusinessWeek research showed that a quarter of all respondents wanted to deliver financial information to employees' mobile devices. The case for this requires little explanation as the value of giving key stakeholders and decision makers the ability to review up-to-date and trusted financial information wherever their increasingly strategic role takes them speaks for itself. But it represents significant challenges. First, you must have the technology to display and visualize financial data on a mobile device, but you also have to allow people to interact with it and take action. In addition, we are talking about mission-critical and highly sensitive financial data, so securing the data and the device is essential. As a result, SAP has introduced several solutions to help users achieve their aims of delivering financial information to mobile devices. This includes the combination of the SAP BusinessObjects Mobile App and the SAP BusinessObjects Explorer Mobile App, which both enable users to review and interact with any form of business data, including financials on a mobile device. In addition the forthcoming release of the SAP EPM Unwired solution provides a direct mobile interface for EPM solutions such as SAP Business Planning and Consolidation, exposing key parts of the financial close and planning cycle to a mobile device. Other transactional mobile solutions also support the financial process, including the SAP Payment Approvals application, which speeds the payables management processes, and SAP Customer Financial Fact Sheet, which delivers key financial information about customers to frontline staff. All of these solutions are powered by the SAP Mobile Platform, which secures both data and device.

Clearly these are just examples, but for those involved in the financial close process, they highlight a key trend. First, that CFO and finance responsibilities are changing; second, that technology, much like in the close process, is enabling this change; and, most importantly, that investments in improving the financial close and making it more strategic are a key contributor to achieving the new role. Given the shift is only likely to accelerate, positioning financial close projects in this context seems advantageous.

12.4 Ensuring Regulatory Compliance

The third core responsibility of finance centers on risk management, reporting, and compliance, which are at the very heart of this book. Initially, you might think this is the most mature area of finance, subject to the least change, and one that the CFO can afford to pull back from. However, that is far from the case as we have mentioned throughout this book.

Being able to close books fast, deliver reports on time to support fact-based decisions, and ensure regulatory compliance is critical for every business. But with growing amounts of ledger, cost, and material data held in various ledgers, this is not always possible as running detailed interim reports needed as part of the close process means lots of dead time. In some situations, there is so much data in material and production cost ledgers that it is virtually impossible to run a detailed analysis without severely jeopardizing month-end routines.

Technologies such as in-memory computing means all those issues disappear, which speeds critical steps in period-end routines. At the same time, these technologies also help drive productivity because despite considerable levels of unemployment across western economies, finding suitably qualified staff appears to be the biggest issue for finance functions across the world, and many are resorting to interim professionals to make up the numbers. It might be necessary, but it's likely to drive up the overall cost of the finance function in the long run. Some of these interim professionals are probably helping out with the growing burden of compliance—something many CFOs predict will take up more of their time—and reporting, which in recent years appears to be somewhat stuck in the doldrums.

On average, it is taking businesses longer to produce their annual draft financial statement and to file statements with the respective regulatory agencies. Now while this is perhaps understandable as companies are generally being extra cautious with their external reporting in the current climate, many companies are still reconciling their accounts manually, which compromises both quality and productivity. Similarly, recent research shows that less than a quarter of U.S. companies have started to report in IFRS and less than 1 in 10 have automated XBRL tagging or the disclosure and publication process, both of which are requirements that are essentially in the pipeline already but continue to evolve globally.

What's more concerning is that with so few companies addressing known or imminent challenges to reporting, who knows how well those responsible for financial reporting will cope with new challenges. Two such changes that could be potentially very disruptive are taxation and integrated reporting, which we explain further in the following sections.

12.4.1 Taxation

With many governments pulling back on public spending that is directly impacting many vulnerable groups in society, it's not surprising that people and the press are making noise about the amount of tax paid by the super-rich and some of our global companies. Although they are complying with regulations, most international companies currently minimize their tax exposure by repatriating high royalty fees for using their brands, transferring pricing service fees for IT and the like, and basing their entities in countries with low rates of corporate taxation.

Many governments seem to be pressing for changes such as unitary taxation where companies are taxed according to the genuine economic trading they do in each country coupled with some form of minimum tax payable locally, which would be determined by looking at the global profit of a company and then applying a formula based on where sales are made and where people are employed to allocate a fair share of the taxable profit to each country. Should such regulation come into force, it will mean that every company that trades outside its national borders will need to make an annual submission to the tax authorities of each country where it does business. This submission will combine the consolidated accounts for the whole global group that ignores all internal transfers and shows the group's physical assets, workforce, sales, and the overall profits, which are broken down by country according to the weighting set out in the final formula. Now if you thought getting ready for IFRS or XBRL was a challenge (albeit challenges that continue to evolve on a worldwide basis), step back and reflect on the internal implications of this. Overnight, the number of published reports has gone through the roof as one needs to be submitted in each country where you trade.

12.4.2 Integrated Reporting

Integrated reporting poses similar issues, although it includes a wider opportunity as well. The changes, including the possible introduction of a new *International Integrated Reporting Framework*, are being driven by the Integrated International Reporting Council (IIRC) (*www.theIIRC.org*). The IIRC is a coalition of investors, regulators, companies, standard setters, members of the accounting profession, and non-governmental organizations, which was established to promote the view that communication about businesses' value creation needs to be at the center of the evolution of corporate reporting. The group is leading the development of a global framework for integrated reporting that has potentially profound impacts on the way organizations report and the role of finance in this process.

What Is Integrated Reporting?

Integrated reporting is a process that results in communication, most often in the form of a periodic "integrated report" about value creation over time. An integrated report is a concise communication, an explanation to an interested party, about how an organization's strategy, governance, performance, and prospects lead to the creation of value over the short-, medium-, and long term. An integrated report should be prepared in accordance with the International Integrated Reporting Framework. While the communications that result from integrated reporting will be of benefit to a range of stakeholders, they are principally aimed at providers of financial capital allocation decisions.

This is based on the growing realization that a wide range of factors determine the value of an organization. Some of these are financial or tangible in nature and are easy to account for in financial statements (e.g., property, cash), while many are not (e.g., people, natural resources, intellectual capital, market and regulatory context, competition, energy security). Integrated reporting reflects the broad and longer-term consequences of the decisions organizations make based on a wide range of factors in order to create and sustain value. Integrated reporting enables an organization to communicate in a clear, articulate way how it is drawing on all the resources and relationships to create and preserve value in the short-, medium-, and long term, which helps investors to manage risks and allocate resources most efficiently.

The IIRC believes that the current corporate reporting framework needs to evolve to reflect the wide range of factors that affect corporate performance. The current focus on an organization's financial statements is insufficient to determine the value of the organization. Financial reporting covers both financial performance and risk, and this will remain an important part of the reporting universe; it is, however, insufficient by itself to provide all of the information that users now need for rational and high-quality decision making. In a scenario where the majority of the information available to investors is historic, they are required to navigate a course around the next corner with reference only to a rearview mirror as if there were no road ahead. Integrated reporting is the route map that supports investment decision making, reflective of the integrated thinking and decision making within organizations.

Source: The International Integrated Reporting Council, 2012

More than 80 companies, including SAP, are participating in the pilot program that aims to provide feedback on the key building blocks of such a reporting framework, as well as create and drive business momentum toward its implementation. As the IIRC indicates, to some extent, this is a continuation of numerous previous discussions about the value of non-financial data to key stakeholders, but the work and aspirations of the IIRC go much further. We would certainly lend our support to a framework like this and recognize the value of such an approach. Moreover, we would advocate that even today, companies should be taking steps, perhaps as part of the disclosure management process, to incorporate a broader reporting framework as part of their financial close processes.

Implementing this globally will be not be easy for the IIRC and will be potentially disruptive for companies as well, especially in today's economic conditions. However, the value to stakeholders is clear and further underlines the need for flexible and adaptable reporting processes, so understanding the implications sooner rather than later seems appropriate.

It's clear that the global financial crisis has stepped up the pressure from investors and regulators for accounting and reporting processes that are rock solid with no errors, faster reporting, and agility in dealing with new disclosure requirements, such as these which certainly raise the bar on transparency. But with a scarcity of suitably qualified finance professionals to recruit from and an increasing workload due to compliance and reporting, this will not be easy. Clearly there has to be a change in the level of investment in financial systems to improve productivity and flexibility in financial processes and to allow existing head count to get on with addressing compliance and reporting challenges.

12.5 Summary

In discussing how the role of finance is likely to evolve across its three main areas of responsibility—managing financial operations, helping the business outperform on its financial objectives, and ensuring regulatory compliance—it is apparent that none of these challenges has diminished in recent years. What's more, we can expect all of them to grow in importance in the coming years, placing ever greater demands on CFOs and their teams to be more effective, most likely with fewer resources. They will have to keep all of these plates in the air—and we have not even mentioned other activities such as mergers and acquisitions that are making a comeback as companies use some of their cash piles to acquire new revenue streams.

Thankfully, advances in financial systems and technologies are keeping in step in this endless pursuit for effectiveness and efficiency. So much so that when someone comes to write the history of the IT industry in the first quarter of the twenty-first century, it might well be referred to as a "golden age." They may also write that it came at a very opportune moment! Retrospectively, it may also be the golden age of the CFO and finance, when after years of promises, they finally occupied a more central role working alongside their commercial colleagues to help analyze, quantify, and compare growth opportunities and risks, and ensure that sufficient resources are available so they can effectively and efficiently deliver optimum profitability.

But we should not assume that it's always going to be a harmonious partnership. Finance will always be a custodian of costs, both in driving down the cost of their own department and in critically reviewing the costs and profitability of the resources, products, and customers in individual business units as is discussed in this research. Likewise, finance will have a central role in allocating resources and even rejecting or curtailing someone's cherished business opportunity in favor of another that is able to demonstrate a greater return. Sometimes, they will have to simply say, "No." But ultimately, supported by performance management solutions that provide better insight and timelier decision support, their commercial peers will recognize the undeniable value they bring to the business.

13 Conclusion

The aim of this book was to provide finance and controlling professionals with the insight to understand how existing and future investments in SAP solutions can be leveraged to help organizations run a best-in-class finance close process. By taking a broad view of SAP's portfolio of finance and analytics solutions from SAP ERP Financials through to applications from the market-leading enterprise performance management, business intelligence, and governance, risk and compliance portfolios, we have explained how such solutions could be systematically deployed to break down traditional barriers to a fast, high-quality financial close process.

Through the structure of this book, we have taken you through a series of best-practice steps that will help you and your organization structure and execute a successful, fast high-quality financial close project using these key technologies, but we have also set this in the context of process change and people. There are a number of key takeaways we encourage you to keep central to your own projects and which are articulated with the four-step action plan, starting with a broad understanding and definition of the business problem and ending with an ongoing process of continuous improvement.

The first of these really forms the foundation for everything else, and therefore the definition of your company's vision for a fast close is of critical importance. It should span the benefits you want to achieve, the barriers your organization faces, and the articulation of your objective, which is typically an expression of how quickly you want to close based on benchmark comparisons with your regional or industry peers. Together, these help drive strong sponsorship, which is critical for any successful transformation initiative such as a fast-close project.

The second key takeaway is the need to identify your "quick wins," which are designed to allow you and your teams to make a positive impact on the financial close process with relatively little effort. Resolving data collection errors or problems within the intercompany reconciliation process, for example, can go a long way to helping an organization close its books with the speed and quality it desires.

As we have described, bigger, more time-consuming and complex actions, our so-called "big wins," are needed to help you reach your objective and identifying the right areas is critical and something we encourage you to examine in detail. By definition, "big wins," including the implementation of new financial consolidation or disclosure management solutions, which become platforms on which broader change can be delivered, come with a cost and effort that may require their own business case.

Finally, we cannot emphasize enough the importance of ensuring that all of this needs to be wrapped up in a culture of change management and ongoing continuous improvement that not only looks at the financial close process itself but also looks beyond it to other associated finance processes, including planning, budgeting, and forecasting. Continuous improvement should seek to understand how changes to the financial close process can positively be applied to these associated processes and by the same measure how a change to planning and budgeting may positively or negatively affect the close process itself. Understanding the wider changing regulatory landscape and how technology continues to evolve should all be part of this process.

As we have done in the structure of this book, you should use these four steps as a guide but subsequently look in detail at specific functions. Move beyond the definition of the project framework to demonstrate how specific applications and innovations can deliver both speed and quality to the financial close process and address the barriers you will have identified.

With all of this in mind, we wanted to draw this book to a close with a few final thoughts and observations to help you on your way. First, it's unlikely this book is being read out loud around a table and perhaps more unlikely to be featured on a book club reading list. Instead, it's far more likely that you are an individual either interested in learning a little more about the financial close and how you can make a difference or perhaps you are already charged with speeding the close process at your organization. At this point, it may seem like there is a mountain to climb, and it's difficult to know where to start. In part, the aim of the action plan is to provide such guidance but in all the financial close projects the authors have worked on, they almost all started with a single individual driving a vision for change. This is both the challenge and the opportunity. As you approach this challenge, talk to your peers and seek out other like-minded individuals within your organization and beyond your organizational boundaries. Attend conferences and talk to people at organizations that have already been through such a process. There are plenty of like-minded and experienced people out there, and most will jump at the opportunity (assuming you're not their competitor) to share their experiences. We have included a number of real-life customer case studies in this book, but SAP offers many more either as written case studies or as references, and you should actively seek to engage with as many as you can. Include your auditor and appropriate consulting firms in this dialogue because although we have seen many organizations make incremental improvements on their own, the structure and experience such consulting firms can bring is highly valuable in the larger, more transformative financial close initiatives (note that your own auditor may be restricted from offering certain consulting services due to local independence rules).

Second, look at this book for what it is: a guide, not a prescription. As the book highlights a number of times, particularly early on, there is often no right or wrong answer, especially in terms of how fast your own close process should be. Defining such targets is subjective, and the use of this book is much the same. Absolutely this is designed to support your efforts as part of a formal financial close transformation process, but it can just as easily serve as a guide for how to best maximize the value of your existing SAP landscape further, that is, "sweating the assets" as it is often referred, or to simply help you identify future selection criteria as you consider new technology investments. This flexibility is typical of a financial close process, and often the best financial close projects are the ones designed with your organizational needs and resources at their heart. One size does not fit all, and we have tried to reinforce this message within our structure.

Finally, the success of finance as a whole is something that should be defined, measured, and reported on by a range of KPIs and not just on how fast you close your books. Just as you have identified the areas you need to focus on in your financial close project by benchmarking your performance, the finance organization as a whole needs to establish KPIs that demonstrate how the finance team is creating value. For example, KPIs such as cost of finance as a percentage of revenue or days sales outstanding (DSO) are highly measurable, comparable to peer groups, and demonstrate success. We strongly believe that you should encourage your organization to measure its performance in such a way and that naturally you should build the speed of close into this framework as a key measure of overall finance effectiveness. This focus will create a platform by which you can build new business cases, compete for scarce internal resources, identify new opportunities, and further demonstrate how innovation within financial close processes can add value to finance and the business as a whole.

In closing, the financial close is a business-critical process. They say time and tide will stop for no man, and the same is true of the financial close. Good or bad, fast or slow, it has to be done, but it need not be a painful process, and it certainly should be a process that adds real value to the organization and that helps you become a true strategic partner to the business. Good luck.

Appendices

A Glossary

barriers to a fast close Specific issues or problems that effectively prevent an organization from closing its books quickly, and often with high quality.

benchmarking The process of comparing processes and performance metrics, typically relating to a business, to industry best practices and standards.

big wins In the context of the financial close, big wins represent those actions an organization may choose to take to significantly improve the speed of close, but which may require equally significant effort.

business intelligence (BI) The process by which an organization collects and manages business data and then applies this in the process of decision making.

chart of accounts (COA) The accounting structure of the organization, which lists the accounts used by a business entity to define each class of items for which money or the equivalent is spent or received.

consolidated financial statement The aggregated financial statement of a group of companies, which is designed to provide a true and fair view of the financial and operating conditions of the group.

continuous improvement In the context of a fast close, the process by which an organization always looks to maintain or further optimize its financial close processes, after an initial project has been completed.

cost and profitability management A process in which the cost and profitability of key products, services, and solutions is defined and modeled.

drivers for a fast close The reason—often expressed as business benefits or regulatory pressures—that forces or compels an organization to close its books faster.

Enterprise Performance Management (EPM) The processes, methodologies, and applications used to define strategy, plan, budget and forecast, and report and optimize business performance, both in financial and operational terms.

enterprise resource planning (ERP) Enterprise resource planning (ERP) systems integrate internal and external management information across an entire organization, embracing finance/accounting, manufacturing, sales and service, and customer relationship management.

eXtensible Business Reporting Language (XBRL) An XML-based open source computer language for the electronic transmission of business and financial data.

financial close The process by which a corporation completes its accounting cycles and produces financial statements for internal management and external legal or statutory reporting.

financial consolidation The process by which a corporation collects and aggregates financial statements from a group of companies to produce a consolidated financial statement.

governance, risk, and compliance (GRC) An umbrella term covering an organization's approach most common to corporate governance, enterprise risk management, and corporate compliance with applicable regulations and laws.

integrated reporting A process that results in communication, most often in the form of a periodic "integrated report" about how an organization's strategy, governance, performance, and prospects lead to the creation of value over the short-, medium-, and long term.

intercompany reconciliation A process that compares two sets of intercompany records (either balance on accounts or transactions) to make sure they are in agreement.

International Financial Reporting Standards (IFRS) A common global framework for business affairs so that company accounts are understandable and comparable across international boundaries.

International Integrated Reporting Committee (IIRC) A coalition of investors, regulators, companies, standard setters, members of the accounting profession, and nongovernmental organizations that was established to promote integrated reporting.

key performance indicators (KPIs) A metric commonly used by an organization to evaluate its success or the success of a particular activity.

last mile of finance The last stage in the financial close process in which consolidated financial statements and narrative are combined to produce final company reports and filings. This includes the production of XBRL instance documents.

quick wins In the context of the financial close, quick wins represent those actions an organization may choose to take to significantly improve the speed of close, but which may only require minimal effort.

Rapid Deployment Solution (RDS) Affordable, scalable packages which combine prefigured software and implementation services that reduce implementation time. They include a defined scope and predictable cost.

SAP Access Control An application from SAP's GRC portfolio that supports the process of managing and authorizing user access to key business systems.

SAP Business Planning and Consolidation An EPM application from SAP that provides a unified system for planning, budgeting and forecasting, and financial consolidation processes.

SAP BusinessObjects Explorer Mobile App A BI solution from SAP that combines the speed of in-memory data exploration and interactive views to allow mobile users to search, categorize, and visually explore data directly from an iPad or iPhone.

SAP BusinessObjects Mobile App A BI solution designed for the iPhone and iPad that connects to the SAP BusinessObjects Business Intelligence platform and provides dashboards and visualizations to mobile workers.

SAP Disclosure Management An EPM application from SAP that supports the last mile of finance and XBRL publishing as part of a financial close process.

SAP ERP Financials The SAP ERP module that supports financial processes, including accounts payable, accounts receivable, accounting and financial reporting, risk management, regulatory compliance, cash flow monitoring, and travel management.

SAP Financial Consolidation An EPM application from SAP that supports financial consolidation and reporting as part of a wider financial close process.

SAP Financial Information Management An EPM application from SAP that supports the processes of collecting, mapping, and loading enterprise data from source systems into and between SAP solutions for EPM.

SAP HANA A unique, powerful, in-memory computing platform that delivers a next-generation technology stack to transform business by streamlining applications, analytics, planning, predictive analysis, and sentiment analysis.

SAP Intercompany An EPM application from SAP that supports the process of peer-to-peer intercompany reconciliation as part of a financial close process.

SAP Predictive Analysis A BI solution from SAP that provides an intuitive, easy-to-use environment for designing predictive models, the ability to acquire and manipulate data as well as visualize results and accelerate predictive analytics, leveraging the embedded predictive analysis library in SAP HANA.

SAP Process Control An application from SAP's GRC portfolio that supports the documentation, automated testing, and remediation of internal controls, policies, and procedures.

SAP Visual Intelligence A BI solution from SAP that addresses the data discovery market and allows users to easily visualize and learn from data directly on their desktop.

Sarbanes-Oxley Act A 2002 U.S. federal law that sets out standards for all U.S. public company boards, management, and public accounting firms. Named after sponsors U.S. Senator Paul Sarbanes and U.S. Representative Michael Oxley.

XBRL instance document An XML-based document containing XBRL that represents the financial reports (or similar) of a given organization for a given reporting period and according to a predefined template or standard.

B References

Bloomberg BusinessWeek Research Services. Finance as Analytical Partner to the Business: An Exclusive Research Report for SAP. January 2013. Available from Bloomberg BusinessWeek, accessed December 7, 2012.

Decker, John Van. "Gartner Q&A: Current Issues in Financial Governance." Gartner, Inc. April 2011. Available from Gartner, Inc, accessed August 8, 2012.

Decker, John Van. "Quadrant for Corporate Performance Management Suites." March 2012. Available from Gartner Inc., accessed October 13, 2012.

International Integrated Reporting Council, the. SAP Integrated Report 2012: Financial and Non-Financial Performance. Available from International Integrated Reporting Council, available from *http://www.sapintegratedreport.com/2012/en/*, accessed December 30, 3012.

Meyer, Paul J. *Attitude Is Everything: If You Want to Succeed Above and Beyond*, 1st ed. Texas: Meyer Resource Group, Incorporated, 2003.

SAP AG. SAP IT Market Trends and Predictions. January 2013, available from SAP AG, accessed February 12, 2013.

Ventana Research. Keys to a Fast, Clean Close: Fixing the Lengthening Financial Close. April 2012. Available from Ventana Research, accessed August 8, 2012.

C The Authors

James Fisher is vice president of product marketing for analytics at SAP, where he is a key stakeholder in solution strategy and is responsible for go-to-market strategy, positioning and messaging, demand generation and events, and roadmap communications. He has more than 16 years of experience in the analytics, performance management, and finance industry.

Prior to his current role, James was responsible for solution marketing for SAP's entire portfolio of finance solutions, including Enterprise Performance Management and SAP ERP Financials, and he played a key role in the expansion of SAP's portfolio of financial close solutions.

He joined SAP with its 2008 acquisition of Business Objects, where he lead EPM solution marketing, and he held solution marketing, global communications, and EMEA field marketing positions with Cartesis, a Paris-based EPM company subsequently acquired by Business Objects in 2007, which specialized in the consolidation and reporting market.

Previously, James held marketing and consulting positions with PwC, in its Enterprise Group Reporting Services team, where he supported a number of global fast-close projects, and at KPMG, where he was a tax consultant.

James has a business and finance degree from Kingston University in the UK and a Professional Qualification from the Chartered Institute of Marketing.

Elizabeth Milne has over 14 years of experience improving the software solutions for multi-national, multi-billion dollar organizations. Her finance career began working at Walt Disney then Warner Bros in the areas of consolidation, budgeting, and financial reporting. She subsequently moved to the software industry and has held positions including implementation consultant & manager, account executive, pre-sales consultant & working as part of the solution management team at SAP, Business

Objects and Cartesis. In 2008 she graduated with an Executive MBA from Northwestern University's Kellogg Graduate School of Management. She currently manages the accounting and financial close portfolio for SAP Solution Marketing.

Birgit Starmanns is Senior Director of Marketing for Finance solutions at SAP, and is currently responsible for the end-to-end positioning and messaging of Finance solutions across different SAP portfolios, including SAP ERP Financials, SAP solutions for enterprise performance management (EPM), and SAP solutions for governance, risk and compliance (GRC). She is also focused on launching new finance solutions leveraging innovative SAP technologies, including mobile, SAP HANA, and Cloud. Birgit has over 23 years of experience across solution marketing, solution management, strategic customer communities and consulting.

Prior to her current role, she was in solution management of SAP CRM (customer relationship management), and was responsible for the Partner Channel Management capabilities, and prior to that for the E-Commerce applications. Her functional experience in finance, including core SAP ERP and enterprise performance management, plus customer relationship management, has allowed her to focus on the integration of cross-functional business processes.

Prior to joining SAP in 1999, Birgit was a principal in management consulting organizations, including Price Waterhouse as well as smaller boutique firms, where she was responsible for managing project teams, redesigning business processes, and implementing SAP R/3 and SAP R/2 for numerous Fortune 500 and mid-size companies, with a focus on management accounting. Birgit holds a BA and an MBA from the College of William and Mary.

Index

R

S